NOW WRITE!
SCIENCE FICTION,
FANTASY, AND HORROR

NOW WRITE!

SCIENCE FICTION,

FANTASY, AND HORROR

Speculative Genre Exercises from Today's Best

Writers and Teachers

Edited by LAURIE LAMSON

JEREMY P. TARCHER/PENGUIN
a member of Penguin Group (USA)
New York

JEREMY P. TARCHER/PENGUIN
Published by the Penguin Group
Penguin Group (USA) LLC
375 Hudson Street
New York, New York 10014

USA · Canada · UK · Ireland · Australia
New Zealand · India · South Africa · China

penguin.com
A Penguin Random House Company

Pages 363–67 constitute an extension of this copyright page.

Most Tarcher/Penguin books are available at special quantity discounts for bulk purchase
for sales promotions, premiums, fund-raising, and educational needs. Special books or book
excerpts also can be created to fit specific needs. For details,
write: Special.Markets@us.penguingroup.com.

Library of Congress Cataloging-in-Publication Data

Lamson, Laurie.
Now write! science fiction, fantasy and horror : speculative genre exercises from today's best
writers and teachers / Laurie Lamson.
p.   cm.
ISBN 978-0-399-16555-9 (pbk.)
1. Science fiction—Authorship.   2. Fantasy fiction—Authorship.   3. Horror tales—Authorship.
4. English language—Rhetoric—Problems, exercises, etc.   Title.
PN3377.5.S3L35   2014   2013037258
808.3'8762—dc23

Printed in the United States of America
1   3   5   7   9   10   8   6   4   2

DEDICATED TO THE MEMORY OF SOME OF THE MOST
IMAGINATIVE, TERRIFYING, THRILLING, DELIGHTFUL,
THOUGHT-PROVOKING, AND INSPIRING WRITERS:

E. B. White, H. G. Wells, Jules Verne, P. L. Travers, J. R. R. Tolkien,
Bram Stoker, Mary Shelley, Dr. Seuss, Edgar Allan Poe, George Orwell,
C. S. Lewis, Ira Levin, Aldous Huxley, Frank Herbert, William Golding,
Philip K. Dick, Roald Dahl, Lewis Carroll, Octavia Butler,
Edgar Rice Burroughs, Anthony Burgess, Marion Zimmer Bradley,
Ray Bradbury, L. Frank Baum, Isaac Asimov

CONTENTS

IDEAS AND INSPIRATION

STORY DEVELOPMENT AND PLOTTING

HIGH STAKES AND TERROR

BUILDING WORLDS

THEME AND MEANING

MEMORABLE HEROES, VILLAINS, AND MONSTERS

COMMUNICATION AND RELATIONSHIPS

SCENE CONSTRUCTION AND STYLE

PRACTICING YOUR CRAFT

EDITOR'S NOTE

When I asked if I would carry on my aunt Sherry Ellis's legacy with another Now Write! title, I wasn't sure. Putting these books together is a labor of love and a rather daunting task, even as a team. I was hesitant and a little anxious about taking it on by myself.

I discussed it with our wonderful Tarcher editor, Gabrielle Moss. When she got excited about the topic I had in mind, I started warming up to the idea of "flying solo." A year later, I discovered she writes in these genres, so she also became a contributor.

I have very eclectic tastes in movies, music, and books. Before I began working on this anthology, it hadn't occurred to me that many of my favorite works were fantasy, science fiction, and psychological horror; even many of my own projects are magic realism. I started recognizing the stories that most captured my imagination, made me think the deepest, and stayed with me the longest often fell into the speculative genre category. I've dedicated this book to many of my favorite authors who are no longer with us on the earthly plane.

Being popular gives the speculative genres a sort of "lowbrow," easy-to-dismiss cultural reputation. I've come to see their importance, and value the fantastical approach to storytelling. At its best it can bypass our vigilant minds to explore deep, often unconscious fears and truths in a way that is manageable and supremely entertaining.

So I'm beyond pleased to share this array of insight and inspiration with all writers who dare take on the brave and meaningful work of pushing the limits of their own imaginations, and the world as we know it, to create something unique with their words.

Thanks so much to all the novelists and short story writers, movie and TV writers, poets and teachers who contributed to this anthology. A pleasure working with you.

UNDERSTAND YOUR SPECULATIVE GENRE

"The only way of discovering the limits of the possible is to venture a little way past them into the impossible."

—ARTHUR C. CLARKE

"Fantasy is a necessary ingredient in living. It's a way of looking at life through the wrong end of a telescope."

—DR. SEUSS

STEVEN SAUS

Where Does He Get Those Wonderful Ideas?
Making Speculative Fiction Speculative

STEVEN SAUS injects people with radioactivity as his day job, but only to serve the forces of good. His stories appear in anthologies such as *Westward Weird, Blue Kingdoms: Mages & Magic, Timeshares*, and *Hungry for Your Love*, and in several on- and off-line magazines, including *On Spec, Andromeda Spaceways Inflight Magazine, The Drabblecast*, and *Pseudopod*. He publishes books including the Crimson Pact series of dark fantasy anthologies (Alliteration Ink).

> *"All fantasy should have a solid base in reality."*
> —MAX BEERBOHM

> *"The hardest theme in science fiction is that of the alien. The simplest solution of all is in fact quite profound—that the real difficulty lies not in understanding what is alien, but in understanding what is self."*
> —GREG BEAR

Over the last decade the hard bright lines of genre have disappeared. You can lay the blame on the reduction in physical bookstores, literary cross-genre courageousness, or the alignment of planets—but the effect is real.

The labels sci-fi, horror, and fantasy have shifted and blurred so that it is difficult to tell where the lines are anymore. Margaret Atwood refuses to label *The Handmaid's Tale* as science fiction, but instead calls it speculative fiction. Is *PAN'S LABYRINTH* fantasy, horror, magical realism, or something else entirely? Hard science fiction, once the domain of two-dimensional characters, is now littered with fully realized personalities. You can find high fantasy written in clear journalistic prose, and horror concerns itself not just with fighting the zombies, but with offering a plausible explanation for how the zombies came to be. The need for the term *dark fantasy* to describe works such as the Dark Tower series and *Imajica* is itself a testament to the way these genre lines have bled into each other.

The blurring of genre creates readers who want something they've never seen before. Despite there only being two (or seven, or thirty-six) "fundamental" plots, we can still satisfy the reader's needs by having a new combination of ideas and creating an emotional core for all your characters.

It is important to have an emotional core to your story; that is, characters well formed enough that your readers empathize with their struggle. The days of a neat idea carrying a tale alone are long gone—but those skills are not specific to speculative fiction. Characterization is characterization, even if the character is a twelve-legged bug.

But those *ideas*. That's what makes speculative fiction, well . . . speculative. I don't mean "*Hamlet*, but with ray-guns!" No, the best stories make the genre aspects and ideas an integral part of the story, not mere window dressing.

Coming up with those ideas—especially ones that have never been seen before—is tricky. At the very least, you need a fresh take on an earlier idea. Once you've found that core idea, you can begin writing your story from there. I frequently write a first draft addressing the plot and then layer in more of the emotional core of the story with the second and subsequent drafts.

This exercise goes through what I do to generate that original, central idea and the world around it. It is especially effective for short stories; you can repeat the process to come up with more ideas for a longer work. Many thanks to Donald J. Bingle and Gary A. Braunbeck for teaching me parts of this technique.

EXERCISE

1. Get a starting topic. If you've been assigned one by an editor, great! If not, then we need to generate a "seed" to grow our story idea from. While random word generators—such as the one at creativitygames.net/random-word-generator/randomwords can be useful, I find that pictures really work a lot better.

   You can use a random picture generator on the Internet. Some examples are:

   beesbuzz.biz/crap/flrig.cgi

   bighugelabs.com/random.php

   secure.flickr.com/explore/interesting/7days/

   I had the best luck with large packs of postcards, such as "I Feel a Sin Coming On" by Anne Taintor or "100 Maverick Postcards" by Alan Fletcher.

   Two important notes:

   Use the first image you see; don't pick and choose.

   Avoid "topic" images—you don't want a picture of a starship for a sci-fi story, or elves for a fantasy story, and so on.

2. Pick only one element from that image or idea. For example, let's say the image is of a wedding. I might look at the woman's veil and focus on that aspect.

3. Repeat steps 1 and 2 for a cross-idea. So let's say my second image is of a field of butterflies on flowers; I might choose the butterfly wings.

4. Force the two ideas to come together. If you have a genre in mind, let that color the idea as well.

   a. Stick with the focused aspects you came up with. In this case, the butterfly wing and the veil.

   b. At this point, you have one of two things: a concept, or an image. One image could be a close-up woman with a veil made of butterflies. Or a concept could be that she has to wear a veil to protect against butterflies. (Or both, for that matter.)

c. Twist the concept, if desired. (Have the man wear the veil. If they're both the same gender, who wears the veil—or is that question the crux of the story?)

d. Ask your resulting concept or image, *"Why?"*—as if you were a two-year-old. Why does she (or he) need to protect herself (or himself) from butterflies? Are they real butterflies, or something that just looks like them? Where did the custom come from? Why?

5. Here's the key to making this technique something more than mere window dressing: How is the image or concept you came up with part of the central problems facing your characters? Is that concept or image the problem (or part of the problem)? Or is it part of the solution?

Perhaps we have new colonists on an Earth-like planet where these butterfly-looking animals are attracted to the pheromones when two humans are attracted to each other—because those pheromones smell like their food. The natives have a material they use to protect themselves, but for some reason (Why? That pesky question again . . .) no humans pay attention. The conflict could be that Sue and Bob want to be the first married couple, but not be eaten alive by faux butterflies.

Now you have your story idea and a good part of the world your characters will inhabit. More to the point, you have something that makes your speculative work *speculative*. But that idea won't publish itself in your head. Go forth and write, write, write.

JULE SELBO

Choosing Your Speculative Genre

JULE SELBO, PHD, is a screenwriter with produced work in feature film, network and cable TV, animated series, and daytime dramas. She has also written plays, graphic novels, and two books on screenwriting structure (Gardner Publishing), as well as articles on film genre and Pre-Code American cinema. She is working on her book *Film Genre*. She is a co-editor of the *Journal of Screenwriting* and head of the MFA in Screenwriting Program at California State University, Fullerton.

Most audiences choose the film they are going to view by its marketed genre. Most readers choose the book they are going to read by its marketed genre. It's obvious that a genre promises an experience that the film-viewer/reader wants to have. And if the story does not deliver—yes, it's true—the disappointed audience feels annoyance, regret, and sometimes downright anger. I would venture to say that in the genres of speculative fiction—sci-fi, fantasy, and horror—this is even more prevalent. Why?

Because these three genres attract specific audiences that tend to be knowledgeable and demanding and very, very picky—not to say prickly—if their expectations are not met. That's a lot of pressure for "genre"—a French-based word that was originally meant to simply denote "type" or "category," but one that has now taken on a much, more important place in the lexicon of narrative fiction.

I started as a playwright and short story writer and moved into creating stories for moving pictures; I have written film and/or television scripts in many different narrative genres* for Hollywood studios and networks. I have written fantasy for Disney, horror and sci-fi for George Romero, action/adventure for George Lucas, melodrama for Aaron Spelling, comedy for the Comedy Network, and more.

When I examined my early understanding of genre, I realized that my training ground was basically many decades as a film buff. Like many writers, I felt I understood the components of various genres by some sort of osmosis process, albeit steeped in thousands of hours of film viewing. I actually conducted a survey in 2009 of 100 working Hollywood screenwriters, and nearly 85 percent of them noted that they too relied on "sensing" the elements that made up a romantic comedy or a horror or a sci-fi film or (fill in genre) and had never actually put aside time to explore a certain genre's classic components, or examine the audience's reasons for enjoying a particular genre.

When I began to teach screenwriting seminars and noticed participants struggling with making their stories "pop"—or struggling to get to the base of the kind of story (themes, point of view) they wanted to write, I realized that sometimes there was no commitment to a genre. The writer was at sea and so was the reader. I began to see how helpful a deeper understanding of genre could be, and how genre could be used as a tool (along with story structure and character work) in the writer's toolbox. So I spent the last few years examining each film genre and its components, themes, and structures separately (Western, romantic comedy, disaster, war, buddy, etc.) and how to use them in the construction phase of my writing.

In using this new tool, I found there was more ease in my writing task when I embraced the right genre and right genre hybrid. Genre hybrid? As we know, most stories do not live and breathe in just one genre; thus most narratives are genre hybrids.† In all narratives, but especially speculative fiction genres, efficacious use of supporting genres is very important; they can do a lot of the heavy lifting of the story. However, it is important to solidify the overriding (main) genre

---

*The terms *narrative genre* or the more specific *film genre* are not to be confused with the sometimes-pejorative term *genre film*.
†The term was first coined perhaps by Steve Neale, film genre scholar.

of your narrative first; let it frame and lead. So let's do a quick overview of the basics of three genres in speculative fiction.

I suggest we think of science fiction, fantasy, and horror for a moment as "world" genres, for there are few inherent story components in these genres (genres that have stronger narrative dictates include mystery, romance, and crime). Their main feature is that they invite the audience into a specific world—and there are many fans enthralled with these worlds.

Science fiction genre stories have their roots in science. The writer's imagination can extrapolate and vamp on the chosen scientific nugget, and the fun of the sci-fi genre is its proximity to some scientific truth or hypothesis. (In other words, research can be your very good friend.) One of the first sci-fi films (as well as one of the first-ever story-based films) was 1902's *A TRIP TO THE MOON* written and directed by George Méliès, inspired by the novels of Jules Verne and H. G. Wells. It is the story of a group of scientists who build a rocket ship, fly to the moon, and confront moon creatures. Sci-fi has always caught movie audience interest.

STAR WARS: A NEW HOPE (1977) features science nuggets focused on space exploration and robotic science. The supporting genres of *STAR WARS: A NEW HOPE* are:

- adventure (a goal is set and the hero, against all odds, must strive to reach that goal for the betterment of community or all of mankind);

- action (lots of it);

- buddy (Luke Skywalker and Han Solo's arc toward bonding and trust); and a nod toward

- romance (Luke and Han are both interested in Princess Leia and that conflict has its own arc); and

- coming-of-age (Luke matures and learns to trust the Force).

These supporting genres help illuminate character and relationships while the adventure genre holds much of the plot line.

ETERNAL SUNSHINE OF THE SPOTLESS MIND was constructed around the scientific hypothesis of memory erasures; two lovers experience a painful break-up and both decide to expunge memories of each other. Its main supporting genre is romance: boy meets girl, boy wants girl, boy tries to get girl, boy gets girl, boy loses girl, boy realizes life is empty without girl, boy tries to get girl back, and boy gets girl (or doesn't). It is the romance genre line in this story that makes us care about the characters.

The fantasy genre allows the author to create an imaginary world, often using supernatural elements as primary inspirations for plot and characters. The world may be dreamlike, it may at times feel real, but it is always illusory. Think Harry Potter or Lord of the Rings novels and films.

Environments can be otherworldly but at the same time must be clearly drawn; rules of the society and mores and beliefs of the characters must be clear. Without boundaries such as societal expectations, rules of conduct, limitations on power, etc., it is very hard to create conflict. For example, Harry Potter's heritage of wizardry makes him an outcast in the "real" world; wizards have their own governmental system with factions that do not agree with one another; it has been foretold that Harry is the one to vanquish the megalomaniac Lord Voldemort; wands and invisibility cloaks are sources of limited power, and so on.

Supporting genres in fantasy help illuminate characters and help devise plot points. Note how the film adaptation of *THE WIZARD OF OZ* brings an ordinary farm girl, Dorothy, into an extraordinary world, Oz (the base of the drama genre is an ordinary protagonist who faces tasks/tests outside of the normal world), and puts her on a quest—first to get to Oz and second to get the Wicked Witch's broomstick (thus adding the adventure genre, for she has specific goals to accomplish) and brings her to understand there is "no place like home" (that understanding comes through maturation—an element of the coming-of-age genre).

TOY STORY lives in a fantastical world where toys have full lives outside of humans' interaction with them as objects of play. *TOY STORY* employs:

- comedy (based in incongruity);

- buddy (the arc of Woody and Buzz Lightyear as they go from adversaries to friends);

- adventure (Woody's goal of getting Buzz back into the fold before moving day is over); and

- action.

(The romance genre is introduced in *TOY STORY 2*.)

In all of these examples, the fantasy genre sets the world, while the adventure genre is the motor of the story.

The horror genre features plots where evil forces (events or characters) invade the everyday world and upset the social order. There *is* a narrative dictate in horror, which makes it different from the sci-fi and fantasy genres; the horror genre calls for a writer to create a space or situation for the evil entity to show itself and, in most cases, make life miserable for those who inhabit the story—by shaking up belief systems and/or running amuck with violent or subtle malfeasance.

There are various permutations that have unique expectations from the audience—such as slasher horror, psychological horror, sci-fi horror, monster horror, and thriller horror. Whichever permutation, a writer is challenged to raise the terror bar by sparking the viewer's imagination with original horrific situations—situations that are usually taken to the most excessive point the writer can imagine (excess blood, excess terror, excess body count, excess paranoia, etc.*). Horror villains are classically all "id": persons/entities that *want* what *they want* when *they want it* and don't let ego (what others may think of their actions) or super ego (sense of morality) get in their way. (I am totally paraphrasing/mangling Freud's definitions, but sometimes it's good just to keep it simple.)

Whether the villain is a monster (vampire, zombie, werewolf, etc.), or human, or extraterrestrial entity—the immoral, unreasonable,

---

*See Linda Williams, "Film Bodies: Gender, Genre, and Excess," *Film Quarterly*, volume 44, no. 4 (Summer 1991): 2–13.

self-centered evil of the force will move it from the thriller genre (suspense without the true and absolute evil component) to the horror genre.

Horror books and movies are hugely popular. My favorites are the ones in which I come to care about the characters. *ROSEMARY'S BABY* (novel and film) is classic horror; the pervasive evil is the devil himself; he is using devil worshipers to help identify the female human vessel who will give birth to his progeny. The supporting genres are:

- drama;

- tragic romance (boy doesn't get girl at the end, and lives and souls are destroyed); and

- mystery (plot points are structured so that a puzzle is slowly put together by figuring out the meaning of clues).

NIGHT OF THE LIVING DEAD features zombies intent on using the living as a food source. It leans on sci-fi (zombies rise from the dead due to radiation from a fallen satellite); it also uses the action genre. The lack of one of the "relationship" genres such as romance or buddy causes this film to be more of a carnival ride of terror than a personal/emotional connector—but there is a huge audience for slasher horror (the higher the body count the better).

What about combining sci-fi, fantasy, and horror? Would you put *ALIENS* in that category? What about *ABRAHAM LINCOLN: VAMPIRE SLAYER*?

Consider thinking of your narrative having an overriding genre and one or more supporting genres. Each of the genres will give you ideas for plot and character arcs. Understand the audience expectations of each of the genres, their desires for intellectual and visceral experiences. I would bet that identifying the basic components of the overriding speculative genre, and the particulars of its world, and then laying out what supporting genres will help you flesh out character and plot points will make the blank-page challenge of your next new project feel less daunting, more structurally sound, and more fun.

EXERCISE

1. Get very clear about your overriding speculative narrative genre; specificity will help you construct your story. Is it based in science (sci-fi) or solely your imagination (fantasy)? Does it have a truly evil component (horror)—or is it a "scary" story that builds anxiety without engaging a truly evil force (thriller)?

2. In choosing to write in one of the speculative genres, consider making it clear to your audience from the outset that they are going to "get what they paid for." Construct a scene or situation set in the overriding genre to open your narrative. Just keep in mind that the goal should be to create a scene or situation that makes the genre clear *as well as* includes a way to *get to know* one of your main characters so that the audience begins to understand/care for him/her. If you want to start your story with an event that does not feature your main character, best to keep it relatively short. Audience members are quick to understand a "setting the genre/world" scene and are waiting to engage in characters, so don't tax their patience.

3. List possible supporting genres. Decide which may lend a sense of originality to your piece. Which will illuminate characters and which will help raise conflicts between characters? Consider which supporting genres will help complicate/raise the stakes in your plot.

4. Frame your story in your overriding genre—build a scene/situation at the beginning, and build another one at the very end of your story. Also frame your supporting genre sequences within your story with scenes/situations featuring the overriding genre; this will keep your audience members connected to the genre they have chosen to experience.

GLENN M. BENEST

Writing Horror

GLENN M. BENEST is an award-winning writer/producer with seven produced film credits. He teaches professional-level screenwriting workshops, which have launched five films, including *SCREAM* and *EVENT HORIZON*.

After writing two horror films directed by Wes Craven (the writer/director of *A NIGHTMARE ON ELM STREET* and many others), I got to be an expert of sorts in the field of horror. What I learned about this particular and unique genre translates to fiction as well as film. Let me share some of those lessons with you.

In the first place, we must realize that the real star in the horror genre is not the hero but the source of the horror itself. Whether it's a haunted hotel in *THE SHINING* or the great white shark in *JAWS*, the crucial thing that makes a horror project really work is that which scares us.

Unlike other works of fiction or film, the protagonist in this genre does not need to go through a character arc. By a character arc, I mean someone who begins at one point emotionally and grows through conflict to be more vulnerable, more courageous, or more ethical.

In most genres, this is what a story is truly about. It's not about the plot; it's about the character growth of the protagonist. As a result, character is what the author is most concerned with—the plot is simply there to show step-by-step how much the character is changing during the course of the story. So plot comes from character, not character from plot. That's normally what makes truly great art.

In horror, whether we think of *THE EXORCIST* or *THE OMEN* or *PET SEMATARY*, what the protagonist simply needs to be is strongly motivated to confront what terrible evil is out there. Our central focus is not necessarily on character or how the character will grow during the course of the story.

Which doesn't mean we don't want strong characters; it simply means something is even more important in how we think as horror writers. Unlike other works of fiction or film, the story is not about character growth, but facing evil. Oftentimes, the hero is already courageous when the story begins or simply has no other choice but to face that which needs to be destroyed.

The audience that pays their money to read your horror novel or see your horror film is not there to appreciate the nuances of character—they are there to be scared silly. In some ways, this seems rather obvious, but I find in helping many of the writers in my screenwriting workshops with their horror projects, they seem to overlook this basic tenet. They spend way too much time on scenes that are dialogue-driven or expository, and way too little time creating memorable, scary moments.

It is a childish emotion, this love of being scared. That is not to say adults don't like to be scared as well. Clearly we do. But as adults, we are not responding to a horror novel or film with adult-like behavior. Rationally, if something scares us, we avoid it. But now, we are seeking it out. Why would we do this?

Because we are being transported back to a time when nameless fears held us in their sway. It simply means that as adults we have not outgrown our juvenile fascination with what goes bump in the night. Just like some of us still like the thrill of going on roller coasters at amusement parks. We like to be scared because it helps us face and overcome our most primal fears from childhood—the monster that lives under the bed or the creatures that haunt our nightmares.

We all come to your work of horror with certain expectations that you must deliver or we will be extremely disappointed. So think long and hard about your villains and the world in which they exist. Make sure you immediately thrust the reader or filmgoer into that world of dangerous creatures, crazed killers, or aliens who desire our demise.

Be very attentive to what makes your villains unique. Why do we need to see another story about vampires or zombies or rabid animals?

What made the ALIEN franchise so memorable was the originality of the monster—a creature that has acid as blood and could transform itself into whatever environment it was hunting in. How can we possibly kill such a creature? This monster is not of our world, it doesn't think like us, it has no compassion or conscience—and that makes it that much more frightening.

And when you write the scary scenes, milk them for all they're worth. This is the equivalent of writing the funny, touching scenes between lovers in a romantic comedy or the gross-out humor in a teen comedy. It is the very essence of what you're doing as a horror writer. It's what the audience members have paid their money for—so don't disappoint them.

This is why we came to your party. Make sure you give us what we came for. Use every trick in the book when you create your scares. Study from the best just as I did: whether it's Stephen King or Wes Craven or Edgar Allan Poe.

EXERCISE

1. Whatever villain you've picked to scare your audience, brainstorm with yourself and others to make the antagonist as unique as possible. Whether it's the largest anaconda in the Amazon with amazing abilities to kill, or a great white shark that can literally devour boats, make sure that your source of evil is something that has never been seen quite like that before.

2. Take a scene of horror you've written and find ways to make it scarier. For example, you can do this by cross-cutting scenes with another line of action to build the suspense. Or you can have false scares, where the audience thinks something terrifying is going to happen, but it's only the crazy next-door neighbor, dressed up in a monster mask to get a cheap laugh. Then, just as the characters feel some sense of relief—the real terror begins.

3. Find different ways to scare your audience. You can do this by slowly building the horror in a scene when the characters have

to enter a haunted house and creepier and creepier things occur—and then play this off with scares that are completely unexpected—like a hatchet coming out of nowhere and lopping off a head—horror that takes the characters and the audience completely by surprise. In other words, mix up the way you deliver the scares.

4. Find ways to bring humor into your horror project. Humor always plays well in the horror genre because it gives the audience a chance to laugh and dispel tension, before you ratchet up the suspense and horror even more. When you scare us, it makes every fiber in our being taut with tension—so occasionally we need a reprieve, and humor is how that reprieve is achieved. Find funny moments or comedic characters or humorous situations to achieve this goal. It will heighten your ability to scare your audience even more.

MARY WOLLSTONECRAFT SHELLEY

(edited with exercise by Laurie Lamson)

Introduction to the 1831 Edition of *Frankenstein*

MARY WOLLSTONECRAFT SHELLEY (1797-1851) was an English novelist, short story writer, dramatist, essayist, and biographer, best known as the author of the Gothic novel *Frankenstein: or, The Modern Prometheus*. She was married to the poet Percy Bysshe Shelley, who encouraged her work as a writer.

A key aspect of the Now Write! *series is the chance to learn from, and be inspired by, successful authors' writing journeys. Reading Mary Shelley's Introduction to the 1831 Edition of* Frankenstein, *I was struck by how much it reminded me of a* Now Write! *exercise introduction. She was giving future writers a gift by sharing the inside story of how this classic came to be. There were so many long-departed writers I wished could contribute to this book—and now I had found a way to include one! After all, who could be a more fitting contributor to this edition of* Now Write! *than the godmother of modern horror?*

In the summer of 1816, we visited Switzerland, and became the neighbors of Lord Byron. At first we spent our pleasant hours on the lake, or wandering on its shores; and Lord Byron, who was writing the third canto of Childe Harold, was the only one among us who put his thoughts upon paper. These, as he brought them successively to us, clothed in all the light and harmony of poetry, seemed to stamp as divine the glories of heaven and earth, whose influences we partook with him.

But it proved a wet, ungenial summer, and incessant rain often confined us for days to the house. Some volumes of ghost stories, translated from the German into French, fell into our hands. There was the *History of the Inconstant Lover*, who, when he thought to clasp the bride to whom he had pledged his vows, found himself in the arms of the pale ghost of her whom he had deserted. There was the tale of the sinful founder of his race, whose miserable doom it was to bestow the kiss of death on all the younger sons of his fated house, just when they reached the age of promise. I have not seen these stories since then; but their incidents are as fresh in my mind as if I had read them yesterday.

"We will each write a ghost story," said Lord Byron; and his proposition was acceded to. There were four of us. The noble author began a tale, a fragment of which he printed at the end of his poem of Mazeppa. Shelley, more apt to embody ideas and sentiments in the radiance of brilliant imagery, commenced one founded on the experiences of his early life. Poor Polidori* had some terrible idea about a skull-headed lady, who was so punished for peeping through a keyhole—what to see I forget—something very shocking and wrong of course; but when she was reduced to a worse condition than the renowned Tom of Coventry†, he did not know what to do with her, and was obliged to dispatch her to the tomb of the Capulets, the only place for which she was fitted. The illustrious poets also, annoyed by the platitude of prose, speedily relinquished the uncongenial task.

I busied myself *to think of a story*,—a story to rival those which had excited us to this task. One which would speak to the mysterious fears of our nature, and awaken thrilling horror—one to make the reader dread to look round, to curdle the blood, and quicken the beatings of the heart. If I did not accomplish these things, my ghost story would be unworthy of its name. I thought and pondered—vainly. I felt that blank incapability of invention which is the greatest misery of authorship, when dull Nothing replies to our anxious invocations. *Have you*

---

*John William Polidori—author of *The Vampyre*, the first vampire story.
†Peeping Tom of Coventry—made the mistake of watching Lady Godiva's naked ride, and according to some, her husband, the Lord of Coventry, removed his eyes.

thought of a story? I was asked each morning, and each morning I was forced to reply with a mortifying negative.

Every thing must have a beginning, and that beginning must be linked to something that went before. Invention, it must be humbly admitted, does not consist in creating out of void, but out of chaos; the materials must, in the first place, be afforded: it can give form to dark, shapeless substances, but cannot bring into being the substance itself. Invention consists in the capacity of seizing on the capabilities of a subject, and in the power of molding and fashioning ideas suggested to it.

Many and long were the conversations between Lord Byron and Shelley, to which I was a devout but nearly silent listener. During one of these, various philosophical doctrines were discussed, and among others the nature of the principle of life, and whether there was any probability of its ever being discovered and communicated. They talked of the experiments of Dr. Darwin, who preserved a piece of vermicelli in a glass case, till by some extraordinary means it began to move with voluntary motion. Not thus, after all, would life be given. Perhaps a corpse would be re-animated; galvanism had given token of such things: perhaps the component parts of a creature might be manufactured, brought together, and endued with vital warmth.

Night waned upon this talk, and even the witching hour had gone by, before we retired to rest. When I placed my head on my pillow, I did not sleep, nor could I be said to think. My imagination, unbidden, possessed and guided me, gifting the successive images that arose in my mind with a vividness far beyond the usual bounds of reverie. I saw—with shut eyes, but acute mental vision,—I saw the pale student of unhallowed arts kneeling beside the thing he had put together. I saw the hideous phantasm of a man stretched out, and then, on the working of some powerful engine, show signs of life, and stir with an uneasy, half vital motion. Frightful must it be; for supremely frightful would be the effect of any human endeavor to mock the stupendous mechanism of the Creator of the world. His success would terrify the artist; he would rush away from his odious handywork, horror-stricken. He would hope that, left to itself, the slight spark of life which he had communicated would fade; that this thing, which had received such imperfect animation, would subside into dead matter; and he might sleep in the belief that the silence of the grave would quench forever the transient existence of the hideous corpse which he had looked upon as the cradle of life. He sleeps; but he is awakened; he opens his eyes; behold the horrid thing stands at his bedside, opening his curtains, and looking on him with yellow, watery, but speculative eyes.

I opened mine in terror. The idea so possessed my mind, that a thrill of fear ran through me, and I wished to exchange the ghastly image of my fancy for the realities around. I see them still; the very room, the dark *parquet*, the closed shutters, with the moonlight struggling through, and the sense I had that the glassy lake and white high Alps were beyond. I could not so easily get rid of my hideous phantom; still it haunted me. I must try to think of something else. I recurred to my ghost story, my tiresome unlucky ghost story! O! if I could only contrive one which would frighten my reader as I myself had been frightened that night!

Swift as light and as cheering was the idea that broke in upon me. "I have found it! What terrified me will terrify others; and I need only describe the spectre which had haunted my midnight pillow." On the morrow I announced that I had *thought of a story*. I began that day with the words, *It was on a dreary night of November*, making only a transcript of the grim terrors of my waking dream.

At first I thought but of a few pages of a short tale; but Shelley urged me to develop the idea at greater length. I certainly did not owe the suggestion of one incident, nor scarcely of one train of feeling, to my husband, and yet but for his incitement, it would never have taken the form in which it was presented.

And now, once again, I bid my hideous progeny go forth and prosper. I have an affection for it, for it was the offspring of happy days, when death and grief were but words, which found no true echo in my heart.—*M.W.S. London, October 15, 1831*

EXERCISE

Let Mary Shelley inspire you:

1. Make friends with at least one other writer who is different enough in style or medium that you can encourage each other without becoming too competitive.

2. Read stories in your genre for inspiration.

3. Read and discuss scientific news for inspiration—does anything new in the scientific world suggest to your imagination an idea or story of horror, fantasy, or science fiction?

4. Give yourselves a writing challenge that includes an idea from your genre reading and one from your science reading—each writer contributes one idea to the challenge. Individually incorporate an image or idea from a dream or nightmare.

5. Give yourselves time to let the ideas marinate, but hold each other accountable to share the results.

KATE BERNHEIMER

The Grimm Art of Fairy Tales

KATE BERNHEIMER is the author of five books of fiction including her collection *Horse, Flower, Bird* (Coffee House Press, 2010) and *How a Mother Weaned Her Girl from Fairy Tales* (Coffee House Press, 2014). She has edited four anthologies including the World Fantasy Award-winning *My Mother She Killed Me, My Father He Ate Me: Forty New Fairy Tales* (Penguin, 2010), with *xo Orpheus: Fifty New Myths* (Penguin, 2013).

The first story I ever wrote was a fairy tale. It was serialized in a newsletter that my dearest childhood friend and I wrote and edited together, mimeographed at our elementary school, and distributed for a nominal subscription fee to family members. We had named the newsletter in a strange ritual. One muted suburban evening in the hush of one of our backyards, we whispered over and over again the initials of our two names: K B K B K B . . . D S D S D S D S . . . thus my name became Kubbe and hers became Deus (she got the better deal I am certain) and our newsletter was titled *Kubbedeus*.

Up in Deus's attic, we made paper dolls that were orphans. They lived in a cardboard box that had been sent via airmail from another country. It was stamped with words in a language we did not know. Most of the dolls had eye patches and had escaped from horrible circumstances we noted in pencil on their flat paper-doll backs: "No mother, no father. Sisters all died."

Deus and I both loved to read, and in *Kubbedeus* we published summaries of favorite books by Andrew Lang, Joan Aiken, Beatrix Potter, and so forth. Deus also published ardent editorials about our need for a woman president. Ploddingly (or shall we say with great dedication) I published fairy tale after fairy tale. The characters were borrowed from things I had read or had heard; the characters were utterly undeveloped; the plots were entirely unrealistic; and the stories all had blissed-out happy endings.

I began to send my stories to magazines and literary journals when I was around eighteen. I got some kind rejections and others that were not so kind. An editor told me that my story was "not logical." Another editor said that the "characters were flat." Another said that the ending of my story was *"happy"* and this seemed unrealistic. If the ending were changed to something more believable, he might publish it. Another editor commented that my stories were "Too imaginative— *There is not a beverage called a 'Pink Gorilla' that glows."* Also I was told that things "needed to be fleshed out." My writing was too unembellished. And where was the character motivation? What did the characters want? A girl couldn't just want to survive terrible beatings—she had to have more psychological motivation to leave that small town. Etcetera.

Also I learned that my stories were "not literary." Sadly, I learned fairy tale books are wolves leading us to stray off the "capital-L" literature path.

Over and over again for years I received rejections like this one, typed verbatim: "This is one of the most beautiful manuscripts I ever have read, but it is not a story." Over time, without even realizing it, I abandoned the source of my greatest childhood bliss—fairy tales. Is it any surprise that reading and writing began to lose pleasure for me? I didn't know why. I thought maybe I just wasn't very good at either, which was depressing, as books had pretty much saved my life earlier on.

It was not until many years later in a moment of fairy tale luck, that I stumbled across a shelf of fairy tale scholarship in the library. As I read through these studies (which took all sorts of different approaches: Marxist, feminist, Freudian, formalist, and so forth) I entered a state of amazing enchantment. I felt—once again—real.

And I recognized that every hurtful critique I ever had heard was true, except for one thing: the techniques editors called dung were my treasures. They were precisely the qualities I had to learn how to control, not abandon; I needed the discipline of fairy tale craft. I continue to seek to increase my dexterity in this diverse and supernatural form.

A brief tour of fairy tale techniques, as I at last understood them, and which I think can help any writer, if she or he gives them a chance:

Intuitive Logic. The fairy tale world does not conform to the rules of this world, outside of a book, but it does have rules. They will not be explained with insistence. A teapot will sing. A path will appear just when children need to escape terrible danger. A girl will outsmart a witch. Your chopped-off hands will turn into silver and save your life later. In my early fiction, my characters often argued with those around them that they were misunderstood; when I removed all efforts to justify logic (try removing transitions like "therefore" and "because"), my readers stopped arguing the stories were illogical.

Flatness. In many old fairy tales, characters are not very deep, psychologically speaking. Snow White, the target of murderous impulses by relatives (sisters or mother) does not suffer depression as a result. She does have responses however: fear, sadness, etc. They are logical and not lingered on deeply. There is nothing wrong with stories that explore ideas about psychological depth; I like many of these stories. Yet flat characters leave room for the reader. In the space left behind, one can think in new ways—imagine new planes of existence. By flattening characters out, fairy tales exceed the limitations of individuality, uniqueness, and self.

Happy Endings. Happy endings are underrated and misunderstood. In lots of old fairy tales, terrible things precede the beautiful images that begin and end most fairy tales; besides, what's wrong with a little consolation in a world teeming with senseless violence, poverty, grief? J. R. R. Tolkien once defended happy endings as a vital technique in literature—reflecting, "Joy beyond the walls of the world, poignant as grief." If I want to end a story about death with an image of a white horse running down a beach, as men in tuxedos and women in evening gowns wander drunkenly into the sea, leaving a pretty girl on the beach, counting pennies in the moonlight—if I can create poetic joy in the words—this is okay. (That's an ending from my early story rejected for its happy ending, and requesting that I revise it accordingly—I was twenty-four and the letter came from *The New Yorker* in a full-page hand-written letter. Perhaps it wasn't a very dexterous story, but I remain uncertain the happy ending holds all the blame.)

Fairy tales are storybook worlds. You can cast the spell.

EXERCISE

Find a very short, very old fairy tale or myth and look for instances of intuitive logic, flatness, and happy endings in it.

Then look at one of your own new stories and look for examples of explained logic, character depth, and tragedy. Remove efforts to explain the logic; eliminate character depth; but don't erase the tragedy—just quickly and without transition, add a strange, strangely blissful image afterward—*beyond the walls of the world*—your own Grimm gesture, artful, sublime.

VINCENT M. WALES

Credibility

VINCENT M. WALES is the award-winning YA speculative fiction author of *Wish You Were Here* and *One Nation Under God* (both DGC Press). When not writing, he is active with volunteer work and has long been an activist for free thought, alternative lifestyle, and mental health issues. He currently lives in Sacramento, California, and is generally considered to be more fun than diphtheria.

One of the most important aspects of a story (and of an author) is credibility. This is an important trait that's not hard to gain, but easy to lose. And few things can ruin credibility like factual inaccuracy. No matter how obscure an area of knowledge is, someone out there will know if you're wrong and won't hesitate to let you know where you screwed up.

Take James Cameron's film *TITANIC*. After the film was released, none other than renowned astrophysicist Neil deGrasse Tyson called Cameron on the carpet for a glaring (to Tyson and other stargazers) mistake: The star field shown during the scene in which Rose is looking at the sky after the shipwreck was wrong for that time and place. When Cameron re-released the film in 3-D, he made the field correct.

Writers of speculative fiction often find themselves writing about science, which is an especially easy area in which to make mistakes, since most fiction writers don't have scientific backgrounds. We write what sounds good and hope the reader's suspension of disbelief will carry over and deem it plausible. Sometimes it will, but not always.

The first time I saw *JURASSIC PARK* I was so annoyed by a scientific foul that I literally couldn't enjoy the rest of the movie. In the film,

Dr. Alan Grant "knows" that the visual acuity of the *T. rex* is based on movement (i.e., if you stand perfectly still, it can't see you). Dr. Grant might be a great paleontologist, but this is simply not something anyone can possibly know, or even suspect, by studying fossils. It just isn't possible. This "fact," however, was of critical importance in the film, as the knowledge prevented Dr. Grant and Lex Murphy from becoming the *T. rex*'s next meal.

The significance of this sort of error checking was brought home to me when I was writing my first novel, *Wish You Were Here*. My artist friend was reading a draft of the book in order to begin working on the cover art. In one chapter, I described a scene where a rabbit is (evidently incorrectly) prepared for cooking over a fire. In an email, my artist friend explained to me how one would properly field dress a rabbit. Thus began my dedication to researching such things.

My second novel, *One Nation Under God*, is a dystopian future story. Since specific dates are significant in the story, I made sure that when I mentioned a full moon on May 1, 2026, it really will be a full moon on that day. Because, hey . . . you never know what's on Neil deGrasse Tyson's nightstand.

EXERCISE

In order to develop good researching habits, I recommend starting with the material of other writers, since you're not likely to be as forgiving with their work as you would with your own. For this exercise, choose any book from your bookshelf and select any chapter or story in it. Go through each paragraph carefully, making note of any statement of fact that would apply just as much to the real world and not just the world of the story. Then check everything.

The hero in a fantasy novel rides a horse for sixty miles in four hours. Possible or not?

A rancher in 1850 buys barbed wire for his fences. Possible or not?

A cop shoots out the tires of a moving vehicle, bringing it to a quick stop. Possible or not? For that matter, *permissible* or not?

In short, leave no assertion unchallenged. Your readers won't.

LISA RENÉE JONES

How Do Sub-genres Impact Your Creation of a Hero?

LISA RENÉE JONES is an award-winning author who sold her multi-state staffing agency in 2003 and has since published more than thirty novels and novellas across several genres, including her Harlequin Blaze trilogy and Zodius sci-fi series (published with Sourcebooks).

Creating a hero is one of the most important things we do as authors. Our hero has to do more than "look" like a hero. He has to act like one. His actions have to back up his character in a way that leads readers to define our hero and make him worthy of his title. How the writer takes the internal and external events that occur in the story to make this happen is critical to having readers relate, and/or empathize, with the character. The way this connection is executed is critical and it's important to understand how the genre impacts that execution.

The paranormal hero and the conflicts in the story: Usually the hero is saving the world from some horrible apocalyptic terror. That makes him pretty darn likable right there. He can shoot anything between the eyes and not miss. He's a hero so, of course, he would only actually shoot the bad guys. He has some destiny that, no matter his present state of mind, says he's special. His journey to accept/become that destiny is critical to who he is as a character.

There will be a lot of external conflict in most paranormal stories. Stories might include demons, monsters, or just bad people/beings who are after something that will be horrific for the world. There's a ticking clock, and the good guys need to beat the clock to keep the bad guys from winning. Another common thread is that the heroine is forbidden to the hero, monsters are trying to kill her, and he must save her.

In the "save the world and woman" scenarios, there is a lot of fighting, running, searching, and so on. This is where the hero can get lost. However, his mighty weapons, his yummy body, or even his bedroom skills cannot be all that makes him a hero. When there is a lot of external conflict, it's easy to forget the emotional conflict. Who is he? Who was he as a child? Who does he want to be? How do these things impact everything he says, does, desires, despises, and loves? In a romance, how do these things make the story and the love that is created between the two main characters stronger?

For instance, if the hero is suddenly a vampire, then he needs blood. He must find a way to get that blood. Why does this impact him emotionally or why does it not? How does it impact his ability to love and trust, as well as his choices in life and this story? Does the hero hate blood? Did he witness a horrible wreck and lose someone and the blood brings back those memories? He needs to have baggage because we all have baggage. That baggage doesn't define us, but how we handle it does.

Don't let the paranormal world building and action make you forget the character of the hero. The story is a romance or a horror story or a suspense. Think about the internal motivations of the character. If those motivations are clear, then the hero can even tread on territory that isn't always considered hero-like and we will forgive him, because we see where he is coming from and what drives him.

In a romance, there are two primary characters. Think about their internal conflicts, not just the external ones, that bring them together or tear them apart. External conflict matters, but internal conflict and growth have to occur along with external actions.

How does the external conflict in a scene develop/change the internal conflict?

External should move internal forward.

The suspense hero and conflicts in story: Now you have a hero who is often a soldier, in law enforcement, or some kind of macho character. Not always, but often. Again, we have this larger-than-life hero. He's doing something by choice to save a tiny part of the world he wants to impact. That's big. That gives him the assumption of being a hero, but it doesn't mean he is. Just because someone is a judge, a doctor, or a police officer doesn't mean he does it with honor and pride.

Your hero is likely to have a killer chasing him and the heroine, or to be chasing one himself. The running, the fighting, the searching for the bad guys, becomes a conflict that can take over. Remember: *External should move internal forward.*

Why does the hero do what he does? What has messed with his head in the process and changed or molded his viewpoints? How does the life he's created, the choices he's made, or not made, impact the story and his relationships? Is he a reluctant hero or a willing one, and why? Does he have a deep need for vengeance that secretly drives him and is slowly destroying him?

The contemporary hero and conflict in story: In most cases, a contemporary story has removed demons, the guns, and the nasty stuff we all hope never really touches our lives. Only . . . wait. Does it? There are intense things in life that impact us that have nothing to do with guns, vampires, running for your life, or killers. The real-life demons. Losing a job, losing a dream, losing a child or spouse, or just your confidence because of something horrible.

These are real stories that could really happen without much suspension of reality. They are driven by internal conflict, but you must find creative ways to deliver the story without it becoming boring. You must reach out to the reader with emotions and relatable life events that are not the boring parts we all use books to escape from. You can take a mundane scene and use your craft to make it emotional. To do this, the main character/s must really pop from the page and feel real.

The trick to these stories is creating a platform that allows the hero to be a hero and not allowing that platform to be too limited and/or contrived. If it's a romance, he needs a way that he becomes his heroine's emotional hero. If this is not a romance, then maybe he just needs to be his own hero, but he doesn't know if he has it in him. If you don't dig deep enough and build a large enough story, with the ins and outs of life that stretch deeper than the fluffy surface, then you will have readers frustrated. For example, there can't be something easily resolved by talking and the hero and another person don't just talk. You don't want the reader to throw the book against the wall and scream, "Just tell him!"

This kind of story building also doesn't allow your hero that platform he needs to do things that make him a real hero. To come off as a true hero, you have to give him a way to shine by way of your storytelling.

EXERCISE

Now that we've looked inside the genres:

1. Outline your story with a beginning, a middle, and an end. Each should have an emotional arc for the characters. I'm not talking about a synopsis of what happens, but more of what do they (the key characters) *feel* when it's happening.

    This doesn't mean that you have to know everything that is going to happen, but you need an arc. Point A leads to point B to point C. A storyline that lets you do that is important. One thing people forget to do when they outline is define emotional growth, and therefore they forget that the story must include the emotional arc.

2. Character outlines. Who is the hero? Who is the heroine? Why does she fit your hero and help him be a better hero? Or vice versa. In contemporary drama it is often the hero that helps the heroine find her way to the other side of a battle. Thus, he becomes a hero for her. Knowing your characters helps shape their responses and the external conflict.

    An example of an outline follows.

The Character Sheet:
- Basics—name, hair, eyes, age.
- Siblings—ages, names, and how their relationships are with the character you are outlining.

- Parents—Who are they? What do they do? What were they to the hero in the past and present, and how have experiences with them molded the hero's life? Are they alive? Are they dead? Rich? Poor? Alcoholic? Was the father a famous athlete the hero had to learn to be like, or never thought he could be like? Did this impact his relationships with siblings?

- Home life—growing up and how that impacted the hero's future.

- Favorite stuff—foods, sports, clothes, and little things that make us all who we are/unique. This could be a love of old cars, a history buff, a comic geek, like some people I know who can't get enough comic books, and so on. For example, my hero in *The Storm That Is Sterling* loves Dr Pepper and M&M'S.

- The events that formed any torment inside the hero.

- Past loves—how and why they ended and how they impact the person's life.

- Jobs—past and present. How did he get where he is now?

- Education—Did he go to college? Did he want to but couldn't afford to? Was he caring for a sick family member and could not? Or . . . ?

- Tragic events in life, if any. Having only happy times can be just as important as having many bad times. Past experiences equal present reactions.

This is my basic list, and as I write I often tweak this and I always add to it. I also keep this list for ongoing reference because I need to ensure my character doesn't change in future books. Repeat this character outline for the heroine and villain characters you are starting to develop who will have their own books later, or show up again in other books. You don't want a character to be developed one way, draw the readers to him/her and be unintentionally altered when he or she shows up later.

I hope I've offered at least a few tidbits of helpful information.

PIERS ANTHONY

Wood Knot Dew

PIERS ANTHONY is a longtime speculative fiction writer who got a BA in creative writing, made his first story sale in 1962 after eight years of trying, then went on to publish more than 150 books, twenty-one of which were *New York Times* paperback bestsellers. Currently he lives on his tree farm in backwoods Florida with Carol, his wife of fifty-five years.

My spot definition for the science fiction genre is the literature of the possible. You make one assumption that may be contrary to fact, then build a story around what could be if that non-fact were true. The reader's willing suspension of disbelief leads you into a thrilling adventure. Thus it is true speculative fiction, and I have written a lot of it in the course of close to fifty years since my first sale.

My definition for fantasy is the literature of the impossible. Virtually all of it is contrary to fact, and also, to common sense. You know it never was, is not now, and never will be, but if it is done well, you enjoy it anyway. It is perhaps the purest form of escapism, because you know it lacks all credibility. I have written a lot of that too, and made my fame on it.

The particular fantasy series I am best known for is Xanth. That is so far out that sensible rules of fiction hardly apply. They say you can have an ordinary character in an extraordinary situation, or an extraordinary character in an ordinary situation. Well, I like to have unbelievable characters in an unbelievable situation, and ludicrous puns abound, in violation of any serious rule of writing. For example in *Night Mare* the protagonist is Mare Imbrium, after whom a section of the moon is named: a female horse who carries bad dreams to deserv-ing sleepers. When she communicates, it is in the form of a spot dreamlet that appears over her head, showing a human woman who can speak human. Once when an evil man caught her and put a bit in her mouth so he could ride her, her dreamlet speech was muffled by the gag. So are my readers revolted? Hardly. In three quarters of a moment, readers can send me half a slew of puns. So when asked where I get my ideas, I can say from my readers.

What, then, could I possibly have to teach anyone about effective writing? Well, let me make a grunting effort. A cardinal rule is to make it believable. You might think that for me that's like stepping on a stinkhorn: it makes a foul-smelling noise and a pink polka-dot stench that keeps folk away in droves. Yet it can be done with the right ap-proach. You need to get the reader on your side, not only willing but eager to suspend disbelief. If you can make the reader laugh early on, you're probably home free. If you laughed when reading this, I've got you. Now I can get serious.

One key is to be consistent in your framework, to the extent fea-sible, so that it hangs together. I suspect that the person who said, "A foolish consistency is the hobgoblin of little minds" was thinking primarily of copy editors, but there is a place for a sensible consis-tency. Another is to have little human details in your inhuman fantasy, such as your monstrous ogre having a sore toe, or your fire-breathing dragon suffering an itchy wing. That humanizes them, because you remember when that clumsy elephantine oaf stepped on your toe in the dance, and when you were jammed on the plane and got that in-tolerable itch right in the middle of your back where you couldn't reach it, and folk stared as you contorted. You identify, and then you can accept the ways in which these characters differ from you and still root for them.

And difference is important. You don't want your main character to be just like every other main character in fiction. You know, strong, handsome, beautiful, smart, talented yet intriguingly vulnerable. These qualities are fine, but they don't suffice. You want a significant difference that will distinguish your character from all others in the universe without making him/her too different to be appealing. There is the challenge, and the success of your piece may depend on how you handle it.

So how have I handled it? Consider my recent Xanth fantasy novel *Knot Gneiss*. That's a different sort of title. The main character is Wenda Woodwife, who speaks with the forest dialect, saying things like, "I wood knot dew that to yew." In Xanth you can clearly hear the spelling, so you immediately know her origin. Today she is a perfectly ordinary garden-variety fantasy princess who loves children, but her accent makes her immediately distinct. You just know that when she married Prince Charming she said, "I dew." So there is her difference, constantly apparent without interfering with the clarity of her situation in the story.

EXERCISE

Find some minor but nice way to distinguish your main character from all others in the past or present, or who may in some alternate future come into being. Maybe even make notes of prospective traits you can draw on at need. I maintain a huge "ideas file" of notions for that purpose, because the best ideas are apt to come at odd and often inconvenient moments rather than when you need them. I scribble them down in pencil, then transcribe to the file when I'm at the computer. They can come from anywhere when you're working, playing, eating, romancing, or reading. No, don't copy mine; that wood knot dew.

IDEAS AND INSPIRATION

"I have never had a dry spell in my life, mainly because I feed myself well, to the point of bursting. I wake early and hear my morning voices leaping around in my head like jumping beans. I get out of bed quickly, to trap them before they escape."

—RAY BRADBURY

AIMEE BENDER

The Secret Room

AIMEE BENDER is the author of four books, including *The Girl in the Flammable Skirt* and *The Particular Sadness of Lemon Cake* (both Knopf Doubleday Publishing Group). Her short fiction has been published in *Granta*, *The Paris Review*, *Harper's*, *McSweeney's*, and many more, as well as translated into sixteen languages. She lives in Los Angeles and teaches creative writing at USC.

This writing exercise came out of teaching Angela Carter's wonderful book *The Bloody Chamber*. Her language is so rich it is like eating piles of maple fudge in a hot bath during a thunderstorm. But she also courts a certain darkness, and that's how the depth floods in.

This exercise works best with a group of at least four. A writer could do it on her own, but it's best to get images from outside oneself, I find. I'll explain it with a group, and then offer a modified version for the solo writer.

I use exercises like these all the time—for myself, and in my classes. Who really knows where the good work lives? We grope, and the groping is incredibly important. There can be stifling pressure on the ideas we hold too sacred, and there can be freedom and invention in stories that come from unexpected places. All the exercises I give are just trying to tap into those less-traveled territories.

EXERCISE

Items needed: four people, paper, timer.

With the group of four, rip off three small pieces of paper each.

On one, write down a type of room in a house. Could be a big fancy house or a very ordinary house. (Kitchen, laundry room, etc.)

Fold it in half, and write 1 on the outside.

On the next, write down a luxurious material—could be a fabric, a gem, a type of glass, a beautiful metal, anything. Something sumptuous.

Fold it in half, and write 2 on the outside.

On the third, write down something organic, something that can decay. Something that would transform if left in a room over time. It can be alive at that moment or dead.

Fold in half, and write 3.

Now, pass these around so that everyone gets three slips from three different people. Don't open them yet.

I'm a big believer in the element of surprise here, as a way to trick the mind into going to new places. There's a formality to this set-up but it only helps.

Set the timer for ten minutes. The wonderful and inspiring Lynda Barry is big on timers, so I'm taking a cue from her here. They do add an element of intensity that can be helpful.

Open up 1. And then open up 2.

The room in this house (1) is made almost entirely out of 2.

How unusual! Please describe. How did it come to be? What does it look like? How did the architects figure out how to make such a room out of such an unusual material? Why? What about the standard items of this room, made out of this very non-standard medium? (A ruby sink—how does that work?)

At ten minutes, the timer will ding. Somewhere inside this gorgeous room is 3. Perhaps starting to rot. Open up 3. It's not at all clear how 3 got there in the first place.

Set the timer for ten more minutes, and write about the new presence of 3 in 1 and 2. How did it get there? Why? Is there a person there with it? Or a history? Allow the tone to darken here.

Read and share.

If alone, a writer can do this in a few ways. He can write the slips of paper himself and make a few piles so that the combo is a surprise. Or, she can go online to find words that are a little out of her usual wordpile. It just helps to get jogged out of our standard choices. The new word opens up much more than just a word—it releases a whole new set of imagery and with that, feelings and ideas.

Or the solo writer could ask friends to write down five materials, five rooms, and five organic materials on little slips of paper and then, without looking, bring these home and do the exercise five times.

KIM DOWER

Steal from Your Dreams with a Twist
of Fevered Writing

KIM DOWER is a poet with two collections: *Air Kissing on Mars* (Red Hen Press, 2010) and *Slice of Moon* (Red Hen Press, 2014). Her poems have appeared in journals including *Ploughshares*, *Eclipse*, *Rattle*, and *Barrow Street*. She has taught creative writing at Emerson College and teaches Come Dressed as Your Favorite Poem, at Antioch University Los Angeles.

One of our great poets, John Berryman (*The Dreams Songs*), says that poems "are only meant to terrify and comfort."

I often think about that when I write. This is why, perhaps, so many wonderful poems have a bit of the otherworldly, fantastical, or horrific lurking in them. Writers may be advised to "write what we know," to write from our own experience, but as a poet I've found it can be more surprising and revealing to write about what I don't know—to lie and pretend; to imagine the worst (or the best), the "what ifs." When I write about what I've experienced, I flip it on its side: twist, add, embellish; try to create as unique an experience as I possibly can. I want my poems to be authentic and ring true, yet I'm always asking myself, *Is this as surprising as it can be? Is this as fantastic?*

One of the best ways I've found to jump-start my imagination and create imagery, yet still feel emotionally connected to the material, is to tap into my dreams. Certainly dreams come from our own experiences, and they come ready-made—filtered through our hearts, minds, and obsessions, already twisted and flipped—our daily rituals, random memories, deepest fears turned inside out, perverted, obscured, coming back to us in another vision, another version of the day. Our subconscious offers each of us incredible material from which to work.

The trick is to grab those luscious details while they're hot and write them down fast. My exercise involves merging two practices—recording our dreams and automatic writing (also known as fevered writing). Automatic writing—writing without stopping or editing in one continuous flow—while recording our dreams is guaranteed to awaken our imaginations and create surprising ideas, because our mind can sift through our sleep memory while darting in and out of our awake thoughts and we're able to drill right into the rich imagery found in both our sleeping and awakened subconscious.

This exercise requires nothing but a pad and pen, a clock or stopwatch, and most importantly, you having just awakened, coming right out of a dream state (pre-coffee, still in bed if possible). The least you will get out of this practice are a brand-new word coupling or two that will delight and inspire, and a few images and ideas you've never thought of before that may even terrify you (and eventually your readers!).

You will see just how otherworldly you are inside your own head. Keep your pad and pen by your bed and repeat this exercise each morning for as long as you can. The fantastical may happen!

EXERCISE

Wake up. Do not think.

Grab your pad and pen or pencil—whichever glides best and quickest for you.

Do not think.

Put your timer on for 12 minutes, or look at your clock and give yourself 12 minutes.

Your task will be to write for 12 minutes without stopping, without editing, without lifting your pen from the paper. One continuous flow of thought.

Record your dream, if you remember it, and if you don't, just start writing about what you think you may have dreamed. Be as visual as you can. Write about the cross-eyed lions chasing you, the icy mountain you jumped from, the giant bird fluttering in your face, the clouds that devoured you. Write about the animals you were riding through the park, the ones you brought home to live with you. Write about breathing as you fell through the sky or the car you raced through an undiscovered planet. What did it feel like? Where did it take you?

Write and don't stop until your timer goes off or until you notice it's been 12 minutes. Read what you've written.

Do this exercise anytime! Even after coffee. After dinner! Fill pads and more pads. Pretend you are someone else while you write—different sex, age, nationality. What did this person dream?

Again, never lift your pen. Do not edit. Write. Record fragments from dreams.

At the end of each week, read all the words you've filled your pads with. You will find a poem or story waiting for you.

BRIAN JAMES FREEMAN

Writing About Your Childhood

BRIAN JAMES FREEMAN's novels, novellas, short stories, essays, and interviews have been published by Warner Books, Borderlands Press, Book-of-the-Month Club, Leisure, and many others. He is the managing editor of *Cemetery Dance* magazine. He is also the publisher of Lonely Road Books where he has worked with Stephen King, Guillermo del Toro, and other acclaimed authors.

Writing about your childhood might seem like a strange topic for a book that will help you write speculative fiction, but many short stories and novels have scenes featuring an incident from a character's childhood for a good reason: Showing where the character has come from can quickly answer questions about why they are the way they are.

Several of my books, such as *The Painted Darkness* and *Black Fire*, feature a back-and-forth structure where chapters alternate on a continuing basis between a character's past ("then") and his present ("now"), showing how events from earlier in his life affect and even foreshadow events in the future.

For *Black Fire,* I actually wrote the "then" chapters first and then I wrote the "now" chapters so the events could mirror and echo off one another. If something dramatic happened to a character in a "then" chapter, the long-term effect might be revealed in a "now" chapter. Nothing too heavy-handed, just subtle touches to show the reader where this character came from, while building the mystery behind the strange events in the peculiar story.

Now this doesn't mean you should do what I do and write all of your books in the "now" and "then" style. In fact, if you want to write popular fiction, I'd recommend *against* this structure, because it isn't very commercial.

How can you use this technique to make your speculative fiction stronger? Flashbacks are generally considered bad form, but you could certainly reference events or incidents from the character's past and then show, in subtle ways, how the character has grown or changed over time due to those events.

You can also use the reader's knowledge of these past events to make what's happening in the story more intense or thrilling. For example, if you reference a character's terrifying childhood incident involving snakes, it'll be even more powerful for the reader when you throw that character into a room full of snakes later in the story.

Including key information about a character's past is an effective technique for any kind of fiction, not just speculative fiction, so it's a strong skill to develop for all of your writing. Good luck!

EXERCISE

1. Close your eyes and think of your earliest childhood memory. Picture as much as you can about the event: where you were, who was there, etc. Now open your eyes and write what you've remembered as a scene in a story and try to make it as real as you can by describing the sights, sounds, smells, and emotions as best as you can recall. What you can't recall, make up! This is fiction after all.

2. Think about something that happened early in life that you now realize affected decisions/choices you made later on. Write that event as a scene in a story, and then write a scene showing the long-term effects of the event on the character.

3. If you're already writing a story, is there an opportunity to give a character (hero or villain) more depth by showing a scene from earlier in life that helps the reader understand how the character ended up where he or she is today? Don't just say the character "had a bad childhood." Show the reader.

BRITTANY WINNER

How to Channel Your Imagination

BRITTANY WINNER and her identical twin sister Brianna are America's youngest multiple-award-winning authors and writing teachers. Their first novel *The Strand Prophecy* became a national best seller on their thirteenth birthday. They have now written four novels, a graphic novel, and a writing book. They were recognized as prodigies by The World Council for Gifted and Talented Children.

There is nothing like coming up with the first idea for a new story. It's thrilling; I can see from the first vision that a new world is waiting for me. I want to dig deeper; I want to know what happens next. It's this passion that drives me, and the reason I became an author.

I had a love for storytelling for as long as I can remember. I am addicted to the idea that nothing is impossible and that incredible things can happen. The stories I read when I was young were mysteries and adventures that took me to places I had never been before. When I read about how the underdog would win, I was inspired. I knew that when I closed my eyes there were an infinite number of worlds to be discovered, and I couldn't wait to open the doors in my mind and walk through them.

Though you cannot tell while reading this essay (thanks to spell check), I am dyslexic. That's right, I am a dyslexic author, a living oxymoron. It doesn't affect me much now. I have learned ways to overcome it with time and determination, but I wasn't always like this.

When I was younger, my parents always told me I should write a book, and I always responded the same way. "Writing is boring and hard! I HATE it." The truth was I didn't hate it. I was afraid of it. Frightened of failure and being judged, terrified I would never finish or it wouldn't be good.

But at night I would close my eyes and dream of imaginary worlds. During the day, my sister and I would create stories and draw pictures. But neither of us intended to write our stories down; we are identical twins after all, and both of us had dyslexia. We may have always stayed this way, making up excuses and never starting out of fear, but our father had no intention of letting that happen. He told us to begin writing a novel. He told us that he believed in us, that it would be fun and that we would enjoy it. We were always open to new ideas and loved adventures. So out of curiosity, we started to create a new story. We both closed our eyes for one minute and imagined a new world.

That story became our first novel. We began writing in fourth grade and ultimately our novel became a national best seller on our thirteenth birthday. Now, four novels later, we have never stopped closing our eyes and dreaming. In every person's life, there are good times and bad times. It is easier to create new story ideas when life is good. But when you are stressed-out with everyday problems and your source of energy is coffee, writer's block is common. That bolt of lightning or vision doesn't come. You can get caught in a swirl of negativity.

We have refined a way to channel that lightning and create your vision whenever you want. It is a method that is inspired by what we have done our entire lives.

Here is an example. My summary is: "The woman shot the gun." The genre I want to write in is science fiction.

I set my timer for one minute and visualize this scene in as much detail as I can, thinking about my summary.

Then I write it down.

A tall woman wearing a black armored police uniform pointed the laser rifle. The gun was a sleek sliver and the trigger was cold against her finger. Her mind raced. *Will I be able to live with myself?* she thought. *What kind of person will this make me? I never thought I would have to do this.* The seconds felt like minutes as she stood pointing the weapon at the doorway. She knew she had to make a decision. A moment later she closed her eyes and pulled the trigger. The laser blasted the door's control panel. Its parts slammed violently onto the ground through the sparks and black smoke. She stared at the door for a moment. The control panel sealed the door and cut off the oxygen supply for those behind the door. She took out her small black communicator and pressed the top button. "I trapped the escaped criminals in the west wing; they will be dead in a few minutes."

This was the job she signed up for, a hard choice to do what was right, even if that meant she could never sleep soundly again.

EXERCISE

THE IMAGINE METHOD

1. Get a timer and set it for one minute.

2. Pick a genre.

3. Create an eight-word summary for your scene.

4. Start the timer.

For one minute close your eyes and think about your summary and genre you choose. Grab the first image that comes to your mind and don't let it go.

Ask yourself these questions while you are visualizing your scene.

Where is your character?

What is going on around him/her?

What does your character look like and what is he or she wearing?

After the timer goes off, write it all down. Keep continuing to create and experiment until you can see the scene in your mind, or create the scene that comes next in your story. If you just close your eyes and imagine, the possibilities are endless.

VONDA N. MCINTYRE

An Exercise in Dreamsnake

VONDA N. MCINTYRE is a science fiction writer and founding member of Book View Café, a publishing co-op. Her book *Dreamsnake* (Spectra, 1994) won the Nebula, Hugo, Locus, and Pacific Northwest Booksellers Awards.

W riters all dread the question, "Where do you get your ideas?" Not because it's a stupid question. It's a rather profound question. It's usually difficult, or impossible, to answer. The question inspires such apprehension that various cynical, sarcastic, or amusing answers have evolved, such as, "I subscribe to the Plot-of-the-Month Club."

But *Dreamsnake* is unusual. I know where I got the idea: Avram Davidson's exercise at the 1972 Clarion Writers' Workshop. Avram made up two lists of words, one pastoral, one technological. Each of us drew a word from each list. We were to write a story using both words. We went off to lunch, moaning piteously about the ridiculous assignment. How could you write a story based on *Alpha Centauri* and *laughter*, or *psychoanalysis* and *lizard*, or *snake* and *cow*?

How did I end up with *snake* and *cow*? Maybe the slips got mixed up. Maybe Avram didn't consider snakes pastoral. Maybe it was a joke. In any event, I thought life was hard.

"Why don't you name your main character Snake?" said one of the other students. Then laughed. She was one of the few people in the class who thought her two words were promising. (I don't remember what words she drew, but I do remember that she wrote a good story.)

"All right, I will!" I said, provoked.

That evening, the dorm hallway was deserted. Nobody stood

around talking; nobody climbed the walls. Only one class member actually did climb the walls—and hide behind the ceiling beam to drop down on unwary passersby—though another liked to climb the roofs looking for ways to steal the gargoyles. Everybody was typing.

Almost everybody. I was stymied. What was I to do with the wretched cow?

Somewhere around midnight the secondary meaning of cow, the verb form, wandered in out of left field (or possibly the back forty), and I wrote, "The little boy was frightened . . ."

I got twelve pages into the story before I bogged down again. I had the main character, the healer Snake; her patient, the little boy Stavin; and three serpents genetically engineered to produce medicinal venom: Mist, the albino boa constrictor, Sand, the rattlesnake, and Grass, species and purpose unknown, as yet, to me.

It's tempting to claim I was bogged down because I was tired, but in truth I couldn't figure out what a serpent named Grass would do.

I turned in my twelve pages the next day. As I remember it, almost everybody else turned in a completed story (good ones too—at least half a dozen were published), but I had excuses. I wasn't a student. I was the workshop organizer. I had a lot of organizing to do. I had to sulk because one of the local students threw a party and didn't invite me. I had to track down some chicken feet so Avram could make soup.

My story languished for several weeks, very badly stuck on page twelve. People asked me about it. I glared.

Finally, during Terry Carr's week as writer-in-residence, I realized that a serpent named Grass should have hallucinogenic venom. The idea came from out in the ozone (or maybe the back forty again), and my only excuse for not realizing it sooner is that during the 1960s I was a science geek. I'm one of the few people around who understood Bill Clinton when he said he couldn't inhale. My response to the question, "Did you smoke dope in the sixties?" is the minority reply: I admit I was too chicken. (The majority answer is, "Of course—didn't everybody?")

I stayed up all night writing the story of Snake and her serpents, including the dreamsnake Grass. In the morning I staggered to class and turned in my story and struggled to stay awake. That day's story photocopies came back. We all picked up our copies. I staggered back to my room (guarded by a poster from Ursula K. Le Guin: two buzzards on DayGlo pink, with the caption, "Patience, my ass! I'm going to kill something!"). I fell asleep.

The door of my room burst open and slammed against the wall. Someone stormed in. I sat up, half asleep, completely disoriented.

She flung down the manuscript. She was the student who suggested the name Snake. "How dare you," she cried, "write a story that makes me feel *sorry* for *snakes!*" And stormed out again, slamming the door behind her.

"Huh," I said, and went back to sleep.

The next day the story got a pretty good reception, though the class snake expert and boa constrictor owner said that even genetic engineering would not excuse a venomous constrictor. Never mind, I said, it's too heavy to carry—I'll make it a cobra. Terry Carr asked to look at the polished story for Universe, his extremely prestigious anthology series. I was pretty puffed up by the end of class.

A week later, as I polished the story, Terry wrote to tell me not to bother submitting it; he didn't want to see it after all. I never did sell Terry Carr an original story.

Instead, I sent "Of Mist, and Grass, and Sand" to *Analog*. It isn't what you'd normally think of as an *Analog* story, but *Analog* was the magazine I grew up reading. I always sent my stories first to *Analog*, even though John W. Campbell always rejected them without comment. (He was renowned for his lengthy comments on stories he rejected. Other people's stories.) Ben Bova had recently become editor. To my astonishment and pleasure, he bought the story.

"Of Mist, and Grass, and Sand" was nominated for the Hugo and won the Nebula (despite a review that said it was a bad story because it wasn't a proper *Analog* story). Astronaut Edgar Mitchell, one of the guest speakers, handed me the award—a thrill equal to winning.

And Terry Carr reprinted it in his Best of the Year anthology.

I hadn't planned to expand the story, but the characters didn't like being left, figuratively, hanging by their thumbs. They protested.

That's another thing many writers will tell you, besides that they have no clue where they get their ideas: a writer's characters will walk into the writer's mind and start talking.

When this happens, any smart writer won't ask where the ideas came from—she'll shut up and take dictation from her characters about their lives.

EXERCISE

Avram's Exercise:

1. Choose a dozen or so words of a pastoral nature.

2. Choose a dozen or so words of a technical nature.

3. Randomly pick one word from each list.

4. Write a story based on the two words.

5. Variations: Change up the subjects of the lists. Politics. Medicine. Religion. Archaeology. Comedy. Law. Your favorite subject here.

6. If you write an app for the exercise, let me know, K?

KEALAN PATRICK BURKE

Walking the Dog

KEALAN PATRICK BURKE is the Bram Stoker Award-winning author of The Timmy Quinn series, *Currency of Souls, Master of the Moors*, and *Kin*.

Argue the legitimacy of writer's block all you like—and people do—the fact remains that there are few things worse for a writer than sitting down at the keyboard with a head full of ideas only to find that the words won't come. We've all been there at one time or another. Perhaps there's a deadline looming so close you've lost the luxury of the time needed to organize your thoughts. Maybe the pressure is so great it's hampering your muse. Or maybe you just have too many other things on your mind for the words to find a straight path to your fingers: bills, repairs, what's on TV right now . . .

Whatever the case, it's stressful, and it's happened to me more times than I can count.

But, rather by accident, I found a way around it.

My problem was one of intimidation. There were days when I would sit at the computer knowing what I wanted to write but unable, or unwilling, to write it. It seemed like a task that was greater than my capacity to deal with it. How do I sit here and essentially create a world from nothing when I feel as if I'm missing half the tools? Gods of literature do not approve of ill-fashioned worlds. My situations seemed convoluted, my action stilted, my characters forced . . .

In the end, I looked out the window and saw a man walking his dog, and that became the solution. Did I start my story: "A man walked his dog"? No. Did I create the world in which this man and his dog belonged? Not at first. I reduced it almost entirely to dialogue and imagined the conversation this man might have with his dog, but not just an ABC run-of-the-mill conversation. After all, if you're going to have the dog as one of your key players in this little tableau, you might as well make it interesting:

"Every day," Patch said.

The old man raised his eyebrows. "What's that?"

"Every day the same old walk."

"You don't approve?"

"I don't not *approve, exactly. But it wouldn't kill you to change direction once in a while."*

"I suppose we could do that."

"How about swinging down by the school? The children love me."

"Yes, they love you. The older ones can be cruel."

"You let me worry about that."

"If I let you worry about that, we're both in trouble."

"How about the beach, then?"

"The sand is filthy."

"That's part of why I like it."

"Plus, there's that homeless guy."

"I like him too."

"I don't."

"Why not? He's never interfered with you."

"Maybe, but there's something I don't like about him."

"Maybe it's the fact that he stole your fashion sense."

"Very funny."

"And yet you didn't even crack a smile."

More often than not, I have no idea where this dialogue is leading me, but it spins out into a story of some sort by the time I get to the end. It creates itself *based* on the exchange. The characters let me know their thoughts, their characteristics, their dilemmas, and the conflict at the core of their tale. They work it out for themselves and for me, on the page. And even if I run out of steam and never complete the piece, I have overcome the block that kept me from writing anything at all. And that's what I always do when the words are not coming with their usual aplomb. I start with dialogue.

EXERCISE

Try it yourself. Have a look around you. Snippets of conversations caught in a crowd at the mall, or in the park, are usually enough to engage my imagination. A woman is on the phone and says: "Yes, but if it had been the blue one, nobody would have been angry." Imagination kicks in. A blue what? Who was angry and why? It's creative eavesdropping designed to engage the muse.

Even if you're at home and looking out the window, you don't even need the auditory cues to get your creativity in gear. That woman sitting in her car singing along to some song you can't hear. Is she always this carefree and happy? Does that joy flee her heart by the time she gets home when she realizes that yet again she has to face . . . what? Or was she listening to a tape of her old band playing their biggest tune? Mixed in with that joy is nostalgia and regret that she left the band back when they were on the verge of superstardom. Perhaps she's wondering where she'd be now if things had worked out differently.

And that's where you come in. You're a writer. You can time travel, teleport, read minds . . . it's what we do. So when the words aren't coming, rather than sitting there in frustration glaring at a white screen, *find* the words. Sometimes it's like *Where's Waldo?* but they're there, hidden in the mundane, the ordinary, waiting like a lit match to touch the fuse of your creativity.

You just need to remember how and where to look.

And sometimes it's nothing more complicated than a man walking his dog.

"I used to want to be a writer, you know."

Patch looked up at his master. "I didn't know that. Why didn't you pursue it?"

"I didn't know where to start."

"At the beginning?"

"It's not always that easy to find it."

"Isn't that where we are right now?"

SABRINA BENULIS

Magical Inspiration

SABRINA BENULIS has a master's degree in writing popular fiction from Seton Hill University. Her debut novel, *Archon*, was released by Harper Voyager (the science fiction and fantasy imprint of HarperCollins) and is the first installment of the Books of Raziel trilogy. She's learned to follow her dreams, both literally and figuratively.

I think every author or serious writer hears the question at one point in their career: "Where do you get your ideas from?" And as someone who writes speculative fiction (fantasy, horror, and science fiction), I often reply, "Well, I just use my imagination." But both I and the reader know that there's much more to it than that. The problem is explaining the magic.

How do writers—especially speculative fiction writers—get inspired?

Is it images? Songs that we love? Fleeting moments that we'd like to capture in text forever? Memories? Worse yet, it can be so hard to admit that sometimes, the magic is more like a slow evolution—and sometimes that evolution stagnates, writer's block sets in, and we wonder if we'll ever have the energy to dazzle our readers that final time.

Because inspiration is so important—both for new and seasoned writers—that means it's just as important to share personal methods of sparking it. Here are a few of my own in no particular order, and I hope they can ignite your creativity as much as they've ignited mine. On those days when you just don't have the energy to work, having a little fun can sometimes make all the difference.

EXERCISE

1. Peruse art and photography books.

    Have you ever looked at a fantastic painting and noticed your mind working, grinding its gears to weave a story around the image? If so, you are a visual writer like me, and many more times than I can count, I've found that a great way to jump-start some flagging creativity is by picking up an art or photography book and flipping through the pages. The best way to do this is to select a subject that interests you and consequently pick up a beautiful book illustrating that subject in a way that speaks to you on a creative level. And it doesn't have to strictly be a book of van Gogh sketches or Ansel Adams landscapes. I'm talking about things as diverse as architecture photos that you like, *Vogue* magazine, or even a cookbook. Those are pictures too, and you'd be surprised by what can nudge you into story writing.

2. Listen to the soundtrack of your favorite movie.

    Yes, any music can be inspiring. But you've associated the music of a favorite movie with particular scenes, with particular emotions in the scene, and also a specific atmosphere and pace. In other words, let's say you are eager to write an action scene, but you can't quite nail the rhythm of the action and find it lacking somehow. When this happens to me, I take a few minutes to listen to a soundtrack from some television show or movie I admire, one that matches the type of scene I am trying to write or atmosphere I am trying to convey. More often than not, I find it much easier to write that scene afterward. This is because you, the story writer, are making a movie with words. So why can't those words have their own catchy soundtrack? Maybe even one that you already love.

3. Weave together spontaneous images and ideas.

    While this is certainly related to #1, it's not quite the same. In this instance, we're looking for inspiration not in the images themselves, but in the end result when we weave them together. For instance, perhaps you love the fantastical imagery of jeweled insects used as money, the idea of a world smothered in golden sand, and a war between two races over access to the last lake on earth. Now, these are all separate ideas and images I happen to like that I also simply dropped on this page. There is no real story yet to be found. But perhaps you are already forming a story around them in your mind, getting inspired. The point here is that sometimes a great way to get our creative juices flowing is to force them to make connections we otherwise would not. Try it yourself with three random ideas and images you like. You'll probably be pleasantly surprised by what you can think up.

4. Take a few random lines of dialogue and see what you can do with them.

For example, what does your mind conjure up in this instance:

"No," she whispered, clutching the cup to her chest. "I'll never let you have it."

What story are you creating right now? Is our newly developing character carrying a Holy Grail no one else can touch? Is she just holding a cup of tea and talking about something else entirely? Does she sound afraid, angry, or determined? Are her intentions good or evil, and if she is trying to hide something, what might that be?

Your possibilities here are endless, as is the realm of your imagination.

Perhaps the problem lies not so much in explaining the magic as it does in finding where we might have stashed it away in the little kingdom of our dreams.

ELLIOT LAURENCE

Unlimited Ideas

ELLIOT LAURENCE has a multifaceted background as an architect, designer, inventor, musician, writer, actor, director, and teacher. In 1991 he received an Educator of the Year award for his teaching methods at the Academy of Art University in San Francisco. He is the author of two books: *Why Anything Anyway* (unified theory of conscious enlightenment) and *The Creative Quotient* (unlimited creative power).

When it comes to writing anything, it is about coming up with a good, believable premise and then giving it a good twist or two or three. At the same time, it has to have plausible solutions within the context you are writing. This is true for comedy, drama, mystery, as well as sci-fi.

The first part is about coming up with a good premise or idea. Sometimes we are just simply inspired and that is always great, but inspiration is like money you find on the street: It's great when you find it, but you can't depend on it. It is better to develop a dependable method that can work whether you feel inspired or not. I have some exercises that can help create an endless amount of ideas that work every time, that not only build bridges between bouts of inspiration, but also increase their frequency.

The first concept to start with is to create whimsically and not seriously. "The road to great ideas is paved with idiotic ones." Why is this phenomenon true? Because when you are serious about your idea, you tend to be single-minded, stubborn, and limited to that idea alone and will eventually have a creative block and/or not be able to see what you are doing in any objective sense or take any kind of criticism constructively. However, if you come up with ideas whimsically, you can envision several ideas to a certain point, let go of them, develop more, and then sit back and look at all your ideas more objectively, refine and combine them, or develop even more.

A lot of people think that if you don't work on your ideas seriously, your ideas won't have depth. The fact of the matter is that whatever depth you bring to the table, it will naturally, at some point, be infused into the story you are writing. You cannot manufacture depth beyond your own level of being, and you cannot stop your depth from being interjected into whatever you are writing, even if it is comedy.

Think about this: It is estimated that there are approximately 500 billion stars in our galaxy, the Milky Way, and there is an estimate that there are at least 100 billion galaxies that we can possibly know at this time; on top of that our universe is expanding at an accelerated rate, not to mention other dimensions and dark matter. So with this in mind, do you think that anything you could possibly imagine is possible somewhere? It is even possible that whatever we can possibly imagine could truly come into being somewhere, simply *because* we imagine it.

EXERCISE

The exercise involves taking two or more things that you wouldn't think would go together and making them work. You can even ask other people for things that don't go together and really challenge yourself. In fact, to a reasonable point, the more difficult the mix of ideas, the more interesting the story becomes, because the audience will wonder how in the world will these ideas all come together.

For example: *tuna fish*, *trombone*, *sofa*, and *tar pit*. (That's pretty disconnected, right?) And in keeping true to what I'm writing about right now, I will make up some things on the spot.

So the story will be about a mysterious disease that when you contract it, causes you to have the taste of tuna fish in your mouth and get severe headaches that first strike with the sound of an unbearable trombone tone sliding up and down the musical notes and ringing in your ears, while your blood slowly turns into tar. Investigators eventually trace the source back to a factory that is producing sofas filled with a deadly foam that when you come into contact with it, gives you this disease. The owners and workers in this factory are aliens that use this factory as a cover for a hidden agenda of taking over Earth. Their planet mainly consists of certain tar that accumulates in huge pits on their planet and is more plentiful than water and is made from a highly concentrated tuna fish-like oil. The reason they use sofas is because they know that people are getting lazier and this is an effective way to get to everyone.

I could make it comical if I said their planet was called Trombonia-X.

You see—it is not that hard. Now I could create ten or more ideas like this on 3 x 5 cards and organize them on the table or wall and weave them together or eliminate whichever ones I feel are too much for the story's continuity.

I will ask you a few questions and all you have to do is answer them with the first thing that comes to your mind, no matter how ridiculous.

You are standing in some imaginary place—where is it?

You are wearing something unusual—what is it?

Someone suddenly is standing in front of you—who is it? And they say . . . ?

You tell them . . . ?

You see a piece of paper on the ground and pick it up. It has a magic word on it—what is it?

Okay, stop! The fact of the matter is that as long as I ask you questions, your mind will manufacture answers. So keeping that in mind, the thing that keeps us from coming up with ideas and solutions is not a matter of not having enough answers, but not having enough questions.

So going back to the "tuna fish, trombone, sofa, and tar pit" story, I allowed my uncensored, whimsical, nonjudgmental mind to use each unrelated image to evoke responses and, in turn, my mind automatically connected the dots as well as answers. As you go back to the story or stories you just made up and read and reread them, additional images and plots will emerge.

The important thing is to not *force* ideas, just let them associate ridiculously all they want. Later you can rein them in and develop continuity.

The third element is to reincorporate your ideas:

So like when I said that the victims had a tuna fish taste in their mouth and their blood turned to tar, I later reincorporated the fact that the alien planet was mainly made up of this tar-like substance that was made up of a tuna fish-like oil substance.

If you follow this process, it will never fail you. This can also be used to develop the main characters and their motivations and goals. The only problem now is you will have too many choices and won't know which story to develop first!

STEVEN BARNES

Creativity on Demand

STEVEN BARNES is a *New York Times* best-selling author who has written twenty-five novels of science fiction, mystery, and suspense. He has also written for television's *The Twilight Zone*, *The Outer Limits*, and *Stargate SG-1* among others.

In the course of a career spanning twenty-five novels and thirty years, I've found that I have to bounce back and forth between structured and unstructured thought processes to keep the train moving. The ability to create new text every day, and then edit and polish it, is the most critical element in what I call the Machine, my engine of creation. As a result, I thought I'd offer a few thoughts on feeding the nonlinear part of the process.

At every turn in your writing, you will be faced with choices, decisions about the direction you should go, what someone should say, what a character might do. And when you back yourself into a corner, it will be your flexible creative mind that gets you out of it. More than one writer has enjoyed and excelled in the game of "How do I get out of this?"

If you've never entertained yourself with this one, the basic rule is that you get your characters into a jam, and then see if you can write them back out of it. Keeps you alert, that's for sure!

At any rate, as long as you have the twin qualities of focus and flow (both of which can be developed with meditation), the more creativity you have and the better off you are.

The understanding of creative problem solving, the ability to design and predict aha moments, moments of unusual clarity, is an incredible boon to those in the arts as well as the sciences. Basically, the brainstorming process works as follows:

1. Clarify the problem. Define as clearly as possible exactly what the difficulty is.

2. Do massive research. Swamp yourself in every possible piece of information that could possibly contribute to an answer. This is done both to give you raw material to chew over and to keep your conscious mind occupied.

3. Brainstorm every answer you can come up with.

4. When you have reached the absolute limit to what you can come up with, *take a complete break*. Exercise, take a nap, make love, go see a movie, etc. It is when your conscious mind is totally preoccupied with another task that the aha moment will occur.

The key to brainstorming is that you *must* give yourself specific permission to come up with absurd answers. Otherwise you will think only in a direct, linear path, and miss the chance of a high-level breakthrough.

For instance, you're writing a scene in which a character faces certain death—surrounded in the kitchen by vicious escaped bank robbers with a dozen guns. How do we get out of this? You start brainstorming.

Could your character be a karate expert? No. She's sixty-seven years old, with one leg, and you don't want to change that. Can she appeal to their humanity? No, you've already established that one of them killed his own mother for a piece of Juicy Fruit. Well, then . . . could God reach down and take her out of this freakin' situation? Well, no, but . . . (the image of the roof being lifted up, and God reaching down suddenly strikes a nerve). What if something *else* lifted the roof up? A *T. rex*? No, Spielberg's cornered the market on Jurassic carnivores. How about . . . a tornado? Or a hurricane? What exactly *is* the weather in this scene? Could it be that you never considered that?

Even a bad rainstorm could wash out roads, trap criminals in the house, kill the power . . .

Hmmm. Kill the electrical power? If this were built up properly, would the audience go for that?

Maybe not—but what if the power outage created the crisis in the first place . . . and it's the power coming back on that changes the situation? Eyes adjusted to darkness don't like light . . . So maybe there aren't a dozen guns. Make it two guns. And the light comes on, and they shield their eyes, and she wrenches herself away and hops out into the storm, where the fractured electric lines flap about in the yard, sparking . . .

Hmmm.

This is the way brainstorming works. Give yourself permission to think of the absurd, and go from the impossible to the improbable to the possible to the *Yes! That works!* moment that we all love.

This is another instance where the practice of keeping a dream diary can come in useful. It is quite valuable to specifically exercise your creative muscles.

If the image of an object comes to you: Is it a goal? (Does someone want it?) Is it a disaster? Does it pose a dilemma? If so, to whom? Why? How might they want to resolve it, and what kind of goal might result?

If it's the image of a person—who are they? What might they want? What might their inner demons be?

What about if it's a place? Or an action?

Practice playing with these pieces, specifically stretching and twisting your mind. Such mental gymnastics are the tools you will need to build a career.

EXERCISE

Newspaper clipping exercise: A brainstorming exercise I recommend heartily is to open the newspaper and give yourself one minute to find an article upon which to base a story idea. You don't have to write the story, but *do* block it out briefly.

This kind of practice gives you invaluable skills. It is important that you have confidence in your ability to think yourself out of any corner you might back yourself into, that you can generate a hundred ideas an hour for days at a time.

And the only way you can do that is to practice generating creativity on demand. These exercises work. I would suggest that you try them, and devise others of your own. They've served me well over the course of a career verging on four decades. They'll serve you as well.

STORY DEVELOPMENT
AND PLOTTING

"There is no route out of the maze.
The maze shifts as you move through it, because it is alive."
—PHILIP K. DICK

"If you don't know where you are going, any road will get you there."
—LEWIS CARROLL

DIEGO VALENZUELA

The Constant Writer: How to Plot an Entire Story in Minutes and *Never* Run Out of Ideas

DIEGO VALENZUELA is a young sci-fi and fantasy writer born and raised in Mexico City. He's worked under the tutelage of best-selling author Piers Anthony and has co-written science fiction screenplays with best-selling writer and friend María Amparo Escandón. He's in the process of preparing his debut novel "Reverie of Gods" for publication.

Writers are liars—this has been said many times by many different people, and for good reason. However there's one thing no writer, no matter his or her success or talent, can lie about: writer's block. Writer's block is a monster, no doubt, but like all monsters, it can be defeated—easily, if one comes properly prepared.

I'm certain there have been many brilliant wordsmiths who can weave continuous paragraphs of beautiful, complex, and vivid sentences without breaking a sweat, but have nonetheless found themselves staring at a blank page, unable to write a word. Why? Many times, we discover that, even if we have something we want to write about or to express artistically, we're short of ideas.

And I'm sorry to say, but good and original ideas are an absolute necessity—especially in genres like science fiction or fantasy, where creatures, artifacts, and stories not easily found in this green world are mandatory. It may seem daunting, but the truth is good ideas are easy to come by—writing them proficiently is the hard part.

I hope with the following to aid you with the easy part by sharing a technique I've found extremely helpful in times where creative ideas are scarce. This way, there may be a million things keeping you from writing (because your dog sometimes needs to be walked, and that treadmill is gathering dust), but a lack of ideas will never be one.

I'm a firm believer that there's no such thing as pure inspiration; all ideas come from somewhere—be it other books, movies, personal experiences, or something you overheard in the gym. There's always an endless source of inspiration around you, and here's a method to tap into that.

EXERCISE

If you're a writer, chances are you have a very rich and hopefully varied library of music. In the best of cases, this library can be found in your computer perfectly ordered within iTunes or similar software. Here's what I want you to do with that:

1. Open a blank page of whatever word processor you're most comfortable with.

2. Imagine you're about to outline the table of contents of your new fantasy/sci-fi novel. Write the numbers 1–30 down the side of the page. We'll fill in the actual chapter titles soon.

3. Put your entire music library in "Shuffle" mode and write the title of the first song that randomly appears, thus naming chapter 1. Say you're a classic rock fan, so chapter 1 is now called "The Great Gig in the Sky." Great start!

4. Hit the "Next" button in your music library and see what song is randomly playing now. Put that song's title as chapter 2. So maybe you're a progressive metal fan, and chapter 2 becomes "The Night and the Silent Water." Now we're getting somewhere.

5. Keep going until you've filled the list of chapter titles in the table of contents of your imaginary new novel. Now, my friend, after just a few minutes of listening to music, you have a story.

Sure, it may look like an undecipherable thread of unconnected titles at this point, but that's when your imagination comes into play. Start thinking up ideas based purely on these song titles, and make connections. Maybe "The Great Gig in the Sky" describes an opening scene where two gods fight in the clouds—one kills the other, and it dissolves into a great lake of magic power-granting water in chapter 2: "The Night and the Silent Water." Keep this going and you've got yourself a plot.

Be smart, don't be too strict, be creative, and let the ideas flow organically. The list you first create obviously doesn't have to be the final index of your novel. Use each title as a creative starting point, craft ideas, move them around, disregard the useless ones (because there's not much you can do with "9th Symphony"), and keep the ones you like. If, like many successful authors such as George R. R. Martin or Terry Goodkind, you prefer not to have chapter titles at all, no problem! Get rid of the titles in the end, once you've outlined your story.

The beautiful thing about this is that the possibilities are truly endless because you'll never run out of songs (and there are always movie titles, TV episode titles, etc). You'll be exercising your creativity and you'll hopefully map an entire plot in just minutes. Do it a million times if you need to—trust me, you'll never be bored. There are no excuses now, go write!

DANIKA DINSMORE

Put It in Space

DANIKA DINSMORE is an award-winning spoken-word artist and screenwriter. The first book in her middle-grade fantasy adventure series is *Brigitta of the White Forest* (2011) and the second is *The Ruins of Noe* (2012). The third is *Ondelle of Grioth* due out fall 2013.

In my travels as a teacher and writer, I have come across many people (almost always adults) who are intimidated by the idea of writing speculative fiction. In awe of world building, of making up language and culture, they wonder where on earth (or in the galaxy) it all comes from. In my writing classes, it begins with the exploration of ideas.

One of my favorite idea-generating writing exercises started as an inside joke. A student in my story class at Vancouver Film School commented that his screenplay sounded too much like the movie THE BOURNE IDENTITY. I jokingly responded, "Well then, put it in space." We all paused as the idea sunk in. What *would* this story look like in space? It was worth exploring.

"Put it in space" became the default punch line for the remainder of the term. Students would pitch ideas to me like, "It's *To Kill a Mockingbird* . . . in space!"

Then, a few years ago, I was attending a writers' conference, listening to a panel of agents and editors, dutifully taking notes, when one of the agents said, "I want to find the Lady Gaga of literature." Without even thinking, I wrote in my notes, *"It's Lady Gaga . . . in space!"*

And something inside me clicked.

Characters tend to inspire me first, then the situations around them. The idea of Lady Gaga on an interplanetary tour was too tempting for me to pass up. The story would be funny, irreverent, campy, unapologetic. Completely inspired, I dug my heels in and my latest project was born: "Intergalactic: A Pop Space Opera."

After this brainwave, I started using similar idea-generating exercises in my workshops, experimenting with other phrases like ". . . with dragons," or ". . . with time travel," and ". . . in an alternate universe." Every class always has a good laugh while sharing these ideas, but inevitably, there will be one that causes us to pause and ponder, swirling the idea around like tasting wine.

One time a workshop attendee used a favorite lawyer movie for the exercise (I'm not at liberty to say which one). When it was his turn to share, he said, "It's [lawyer movie] with time travel." There was a pause in the room, an audible *click*, and he sat up straighter. We all thought the idea was brilliant. I told him, "You should write that."

He's in the middle of writing that story right now.

But wait, you ask, won't people recognize the story? Isn't this plagiarism?

I have several answers to that. First, we never write anything in a vacuum. Our ideas are a collection of observation and experience, tales that have come before us, and common threads that connect us as human beings. There are only so many core stories; the characters and settings are what keep changing. And, if you like, you can always begin this exercise with a core story archetype (rags to riches, grail quest, rebirth) rather than a specific story (it's a rags-to-riches story . . . on the moon).

Second, it is your job, as the writer, to make the story your own. If you breathe life into your original characters, use your own personal language and style, allow the plot to organically reveal itself rather than to force it into someone else's structure, it will most likely not even resemble the story that inspired you in the first place. This is what happens to stories when we own them (or they own us, as is often the case with me).

This is not about writing the next *Pride and Prejudice and Zombies* (although that's fine too). This exercise is about inspiration and exploration, for those who are intimidated by writing speculative fiction, or not.

And, really, if I asked everyone in one of my workshops to write *Eat, Pray, Love* in space, we would get a workshop full of variations on that story. Wait a second . . . *Eat, Pray, Love* . . . in space . . . *click!*

EXERCISE

Make a list of three things:

- a personal story of your own, a relative's, or a friend's;

- an historical figure or moment in history;

- a book or movie or TV show set in the real world (*To Kill a Mockingbird*, WHEN HARRY MET SALLY, CSI).

Now take the phrases "in space," "with dragons," and "with time travel" (or use your own: zombies, wizards, elves, aliens, in a future dystopia, in an enchanted forest, etc.) and tack a phrase on the end of each item on your list (i.e., *CSI* with dragons).

Next, write each story's one sentence logline (logline = somebody must do something before something bad happens). For example: A team of crime scene investigators must prove a young dragon did not kill the king before the beast is hunted down and destroyed.

Take your favorite of the three and set your timer for 15–20 minutes. Start with the line, "This is a story about . . ." and write without stopping until the timer goes off. *Do not cross out or edit*, just let yourself brainstorm on the page. Rinse and repeat as many times as you like!

XAQUE GRUBER

Call of the Wylleen

XAQUE GRUBER is a writer for television (*Dynasty Reunion: Catfights & Caviar*), film (*BROKEN ROADS*), and online (The Huffington Post). He is from New England and lives in Los Angeles with his two pet mice.

A few years ago, I was working in a Los Angeles television production office where I kept two mice in a terrarium. They became the office pets. I became attached to Nugget and Hopscotch (both female) watching them play and sleep and eat and clean each other just the same as much larger mammals.

One of my coworkers was Taryn, a young mother with three children. While the office conversation with Taryn would often turn toward the subject of raising children, motherhood, giving birth, my eyes would glance over at the two tiny pet mice in their glass terrarium. I found the mice to be much more evolved than most realized, displaying sensitivities like any mammal, even emotion.

Watching our office pets, talking about motherhood, seeing the small (almost fetal) "hands" of the mouse grab a seed and nibble away on it . . . I must have made a subconscious connection and blurted out to Taryn, "If you could give birth to any animal (other than a human), what would it be?"

She looked at me and said, "That is the strangest question I have ever been asked."

I took that as a great compliment. The strangest question ever? Wow! She was about thirty. So in her thirty years of being asked questions, mine topped the list as the strangest. I knew I was onto something.

My mind went immediately to a character that I wanted to create. A woman who gives birth to animals. But why was she giving birth to animals? And how? And who would she be?

In the news was a story about menopause, and how a woman can experience a spike in fertility toward the end of menopause. Hmmm ... my character could be an older woman, almost to the age where no one would expect a pregnancy could even occur.

A script was taking shape in my mind. A woman nearing age sixty is pregnant with an animal. I toyed with the idea of making this a dark futuristic drama in the vein of CHILDREN OF MEN or THE HAND-MAID'S TALE where technology has made it possible for human women to birth animals in order to keep species alive, but I was having a hard time developing this. The tone was feeling very serious and the story was growing more epic, like a full screenplay or a novel, and the thought of that was exhausting.

I like humor. I love bizarre, absurdist, strangely fantastical situations—like Lewis Carroll's books or Monty Python films. This story had a premise I liked (woman giving birth to an animal), but the dark, serious direction I was heading was taking all the fun out of it.

At the time, I was newly obsessed with the BBC series *Downton Abbey*. I was so in love with the writing and the characters and the dialogue that I imagined myself as a footman in a manor like Downton, just for a day, in 1914. Wouldn't that be incredible? I must have watched it three times in a month. Did I mention I was obsessed?

And then—EUREKA! If you're going to steal, steal from the best. And *Downton Abbey* was the best thing I'd seen on TV outside of *Mad Men*—also a period piece and another obsession. For years, I had been told that period settings would turn off a reader, but the success of *Mad Men* and *Downton Abbey* proved to me exactly otherwise. My central character would be a maid in a Downton Abbey–like estate in the 1950s—just after World War II, at the dawn of television. And much to her dismay, and her boss's dismay, she'd be birthing animals in the mansion. Imagine Dame Maggie Smith's character in *Downton Abbey* watching a maid lay a large wild goose egg on the Oriental carpets—the whole script was rethought using my same, original, basic premise. I also consulted with a British-ism dictionary of the 1950s and peppered the dialogue with all sorts of fun English slang.

Suddenly my exhaustion with the script turned into elation and I wanted to do nothing but write! I felt such a wacky premise would be best suited for a short feature (for now). Shorts are such a fabulous and underrated format, and I highly advise any frustrated feature or TV writer to take a stab at a short. It's like a brisk swim in a freshwater lake. You emerge feeling alive again. In less than twenty pages, you have a beginning, middle, and end—and lots of juicy stuff in between. Don't worry about if it is ever shot. It is written.

The character was named Wylleen Thornby (I was fascinated with Damien Thorn from *THE OMEN* as a teen), and the script became a nineteen-page short called *Call of the Wylleen.* Jack London's classic tale of the wilderness seemed to be a solid reference point for a humorous title. Most who have read *Call of the Wylleen* have laughed and enjoyed its bizarre story. A successful sitcom writer said, "Until I read this, I never knew bestiality could be made funny and charming."

So how does Wylleen's menopause cause such a spike in fertility that wild beasts and birds want to mate with her? Well, it just did. And you can get away with that in a short, because it's not about the why—it's about the characters, their emotions, and their journey. I wove dark elements—almost horror-esque moments—in there, as well as heartfelt scenes. The script has gone on to open many doors for me as a writer.

And it all happened because I connected a random conversation about motherhood with watching my surprisingly civilized pet mice frolic. By the way, Taryn's reply to my most bizarre question: She'd want to give birth to a mouse because you wouldn't feel it as much.

EXERCISE

Take a random conversation in your home, office, the train, etc. Write down the dialogue as people are speaking.

Using that conversation as a theme, combine it with something unrelated that you're witnessing.

Turn that into a short story or short film (less than twenty pages) with a beginning, middle, and end.

Use current news stories or inspiration from a favorite TV show or film to help shape the tone. Feel free to adventure into a different time period.

Now write!

SEQUOIA HAMILTON

The Joy of Six

SEQUOIA HAMILTON is the founder of Ojai Writers Conference and co-founder of Ojai WordFest, an eight-day literary festival in Southern California. She is the owner of Global Writing Adventures, including her Paris Writers Retreat. She is an author of "Perfume on My Passport" and publisher of "Paris Stories–An Anthology."

We live in a golden age of concise storytelling. We text, we tweet, we post, we IM, and we emoticate.

What if we lived in a world restricted by an economy of words—where each person was allowed to utter only six words in response to every question?

Legend has it that the first six-word challenge was posed to Ernest Hemingway to settle a bar bet. Could he write a novel in ten words or less? Clocking in at six words, he offered: "For sale: baby shoes, never worn."

A story of six words can speak volumes.

In 2006, *Smith Magazine* posed a writing contest inspired by Hemingway's classic storytelling challenge with a focus on personal narrative: "One life. Six words. What's yours?" Their passion for non-fiction confessionals was dubbed Six-Word Memoirs.

When 200,000 insightful slivers of life, brilliant in their brevity, rolled in, Smith had birthed an overnight online community of nano-memoirists hungry for more. Within four years, the fledging zine's contest—a game changer they call "their happy accident"—spawned a multi-million-dollar franchise replete with an interactive website, series of books, board game, calendar, and T-shirts.

Favorite micro-minis from the Smith website include:

Paranoia: My potato is watching me.

He proposed on the Scrabble board.

Full moon, wife dances, I howl.

Life is better in soft pajamas.

And a few on the craft of writing:

A writer not writing; certain death.

Talent. Please stop hiding from me.

Teaching creative writing; starting with this.

Though Smith founders created the user-generated website to showcase biographical content, soon other writers and wordsmiths of various genres wanted in on the fun. A half-dozen word challenges popped up all over the Internet, Chicken Soup-y like:

Craft a poem in six words.

Pen lyrics to a rap battle in six words.

Write a prayer in six words.

Construct an obituary in six words.

Tell a horror story in six words.

Describe an imaginary world in six words.

Even a blog about RVs got fifty-one submissions for a call for "Six Words About Your RV Life."

The undisputed king of the "what ifs," speculative fiction, fits perfectly with this challenge. Can you weave a fictional tale in six words with irreverence, humor, or suspense? This was a question posed from *Wired* magazine to legends of sci-fi, fantasy, and horror.

Concise masterpieces emerged:

Computer, did we bring batteries? Computer?—Eileen Gunn

His penis snapped off; he's pregnant!—Rudy Rucker

With bloody hands, I say good-bye.—Frank Miller

In a recent writing workshop, I posed this challenge to writers with a twist: Spin a tale in six words and then allow your six-word creation to inspire a one-paragraph story.

A young teen, not yet sure of a story to write but wanting merely, profoundly, to find a way to cope with her father's passing through the therapy of writing, submits:

NO MORE CIGARETTES, JUST CHERRY LOLLIPOPS
by Sandra Perkins

I'm ten years old, it's past my bedtime, and I pretend to just be up for a glass of water. And he wakes up to get a lollipop, because he shouldn't smoke anymore. And he smiles, and ruffles my hair, and tells me he loves me and to get some sleep because the Hospice nurse is coming in the morning. I tell him I love him too, and go to bed. And two weeks later, he is dead.

Her story moves me. I can relate. I was only twenty-four years-young when my fifty-four years-young mother died suddenly from complications with a rare form of arthritis, triggering cardiac arrest. The doctor walked into the ICU waiting room and uttered these six words, "I'm sorry, she didn't make it."

Life's short; so is six words.

EXERCISE

Deceptively simple and surprisingly addictive, six-word challenges can be powerful writing exercises that can lead to deeper, richer stories. Here are a few prompts I use in my writing classes:

1. Describe your novel, story, or concept in six words. Think of it as a six-second elevator pitch.

2. On index cards write six-word descriptions of: your protagonist, what your protagonist wants, the challenge standing in the way of the protagonist's goal, the theme, the world of your story, the rules of that world, etc. Use the back of the cards to list additional notes.

3. Write six-word nano-memoirs for the main characters in your story.

4. To create a new story, write a six-word headline, followed by a short paragraph (like the teen writing student example above). Write three to six new headlines and paragraphs and arrange their order to ensure you have a beginning, middle, and end, with story and character arcs.

5. As a remedy for writer's block, try these six-word fill-in-the-blanks. Complete the following adding only one word, possibly having characters in your story talk to one another.

   "Didn't recognize you without your _____."

   "My, what happened to your _____?"

   "Please don't tell anyone about _____."

JAMES WANLESS,
AKA "CAPTAIN PICK-A-CARD"

Tarot for Writers

JAMES WANLESS, PHD, is a futurist and pioneer of new thinking. He is the creator of the Voyager Tarot, the author of *Way of the Great Oracle*, *Strategic Intuition for the 21st Century*, *New Age Tarot*, *Wheel of Tarot*, and *Intuition@Work*. A natural Green Man, he is also the author of *Little Stone: Your Friend for Life*, *Sustainable Life: The New Success*, and Sustain Yourself cards.

When Laurie first asked me to contribute to this book, I didn't understand why, until she explained that the tarot could be a useful tool for writers, even more so for writers working in these speculative genres, since you guys tend to make more overt use of mythology and symbolism.

My writing experience is with nonfiction consciousness type books, so I wouldn't dare tell you how to write fiction. I enjoy it, but I don't know how to write it. What I can tell you about is the tarot; especially my version—the Voyager Tarot.

Some tarot readers and designers of tarot cards adhere strictly to traditional interpretations while others (like me) have their own style and approach. Getting tarot people to agree on how to use and interpret the cards is a lot like trying to herd cats. They are a highly individualistic breed, often eccentric, with their own way of looking at things—I suppose they're a lot like writers.

Traditional tarot uses the cards to read the future. Assumed is the idea the future is pre-destined and we are "victims of fate." The cards show if you're doomed or lucky.

The Voyager Tarot reinterprets the tradition for our modern

consciousness as we become more aware we have a say in our fate. In addition to genetics and the "luck of the draw" of upbringing, free will plays a part in our lives, especially if we're consciously aware of it and take responsibility for our own development.

To me the tarot is a map to wholeness, the "GPS of the soul," a tool and ally on the universal, archetypal hero's journey. Each card of the major arcana from 0 to 20 represents an archetypal energy, a tradition of mythological figures or deities, a constellation of qualities or characteristics. As a whole these cards represent a pathway from the zero point of infinite possibility (the "0" card, traditionally known as The Fool, I call it Fool-Child) through all types of internal experience to wholeness and completion (the "20" card, traditionally called The World, I renamed it the Universe).

The minor arcana resemble the playing cards we know today, with each suit representing different aspects of our being—mind (Crystals cards, traditional name: Swords), emotion (Cups cards), body and the material realm (Worlds cards, traditional name: Pentacles), and spirit (Wands cards, traditional name: Pipes).

In my teaching and practice I am always figuring out new ways to use the cards to explore where we are in or out of harmony, what we might need to focus on and develop more of, what we might need to watch out for, what could be the result if we go on the hero's journey the cards are pointing toward.

Plus they're fun to look at and contemplate. Tarot cards are visually rich and packed full of symbolism. In the Voyager deck I completely re-imagined the iconography of the tarot as complex collages designed to help users connect with their own unconscious and develop their intuition.

If you're intrigued by the tarot, why not visit a mystical or new age shop and explore the multitude of decks available? Select the one that speaks to you. You can also find them online. Each deck generally comes with its own booklet with the designer/creator's interpretations of the cards, but don't let those limit you. They're just a starting point for your own intuition and imagination.

Once you get familiar with your deck, here are several ideas for how you could use the tarot as a tool for creative writing. For this exercise I'm going to reference Voyager cards, but it could probably work with any tarot deck.

EXERCISE

1. Have fun exploring the deeper meaning of a card, both its positive and negative aspects, by seeking out as many associations as you can find about a particular symbol or archetype in the cards, such as the Fool, the Emperor, the Priestess, the Moon, etc.

2. Start a new story, or do a card reading for a story you already have in progress: Separate out the major arcana cards and randomly pull five of these cards. Could they become the major characters, themes, or plot points in a story?

    For example, you pull Magician, Lovers, Strength, Death, and Sun. Explore what these cards represent, their positive and negative attributes, and how they could be combined or interact to form a story. A conflict between a magician and a pair of lovers. Or is the magician one of the lovers? Is he (or she) seeking to harvest some form of strength from the sun to cheat death?

3. Character reading: Perform a reading for a character to gain deeper insight. From the whole deck pull three cards: the first represents the character's past, the second represents the present, and the third represents the future. What insight or ideas does this reading give you about where your character is coming from and where he or she is headed?

4. Character conflict reading: in my deck, among the minor arcana there are twelve "watch out" cards. These are Anger, Disappointment, Sorrow, Fear, Stagnation, Negativity, Confusion, Dullness, Narrowness, Delusion, Oppression, and Setback. Rather than a doomed fate, I see these as what to watch out for in yourself or life, yet they each have a positive side too. The Delusion card (10 of

Crystals, a quality of mind) could be about innovative thinking, the ability to see what others can't. But "delusions of grandeur" could get you into a lot of trouble.

Pull one of these cards to discover a character's fatal flaw. Or your hero could represent the positive side of the card, while your monster or villain who menaces your hero could be the extreme embodiment of the negative quality of the card.

5. In the traditional minor arcana are the royalty cards—Prince, Princess, King, Queen. I'm not into monarchy stuff so I created an alternative: Child, Man, Woman, Sage. Each has their own characteristics, and remember, each suit represents an aspect of being. So you could use these cards to create characters and put them in conflict with each other. How does a Crystal card (mental) man interact with his Wand card (spiritual) daughter, materialistic (World card) wife, or Grandfather who's really more of an emotional (Cup card) child?

I could go on, but now I will leave it to you to explore the tarot for yourself and discover what a wonderful tool it can be for personal development and creative writing.

MICHAEL REAVES

Freelancing Sci-Fi TV

MICHAEL REAVES has been a freelance writer for more than thirty years. He's written and produced nearly 400 episodes of TV, as well as books, movies, graphic novels, and short stories. He's won an Emmy, and a Howie Award for Lifetime Achievement at the 2012 H. P. Lovecraft Film Festival. Also, having turned sixty, he's now an official curmudgeon—so stay out of his yard.

In the last twenty years or so, things have changed dramatically in virtually every aspect of TV production. (Dude: I spent the first five years of my career on a typewriter. That's all you need to know.) When I was coming up, there were three networks. That was it: ABC, NBC, CBS. Those were the markets. If you couldn't sell to a show on one of those three, you were pretty much reduced to puppet theater in your garage.

It started to change in the seventies with first-run syndication shows like *Star Trek: The Next Generation*. The numbers people began paying a lot more attention to demographics. They still made their choices by the Neilsen families, but the Neilsens weren't Ozzie and Harriet anymore.

Then along came cable, and things really got confused. What with Nickelodeon, the Disney Channel, TBS, AMC, BET, and plenty more diving into programming every day, it really was starting to look like hog heaven for couch potatoes.

The merciless proliferation continued. The Learning Channel, the Discovery Channel, the History Channel, Animal Planet, the Oprah Winfrey Network, for God's sake. We were dazed and buffeted, certain that if we had to endure one more *Gilligan's Island* marathon on Boomerang, our brains would pop like an octogenarian's kidneys.

And, eventually, along came the miscegenation of the Web and TV. Web TV is definitely not your father's TV. This is more like your crazy old uncle's (the one with the spiked puce hair and the ermine neck collar). However, even though much has changed over the decades, there's also much that hasn't, and never will. Storytelling is storytelling, and hasn't changed since the days when the venue was shadow play on cave walls.

With this in mind, herewith some nuts and bolts advice:

Lots of aspiring writers ask me what qualities I look for in a freelancer when I'm wearing my producer or editor hat. The answer is very simple: I look for someone I can use more than once. By that I mean someone who's reliable, who'll turn in something producible, and turn it in on time. In short, someone who'll make me look good. That's it. That's all there is. There's no handshake or code word, no Illuminati-style secret club. I just want someone who'll make my job easier. I made a living for more than thirty years by being very good at my craft, but that was only half of it: I also had several go-to writers I knew I could count on. You'd be surprised how rare such a person is. When someone comes along who can write good comedy and good horror in the same script, grab him! 'Cause there're maybe five writers that good on the planet at any one time.

Unfortunately, you can't count on being discovered without making some effort. So go thou and mingle; attend Writers Guild events, sci-fi conventions, parties, etc. Meet people. Talk to them; you'll be surprised at how much most folks love to give advice. And, if there's a specific show that you love and want to write for above all others, watch that show until you know it by heart, liver, and spleen. Then sit down and write a script that hasn't been seen before, that feels fresh and new while staying true to whatever tropes it conjures. This is as true for sci-fi and fantasy as it is for straight drama or comedy; no matter the genre, if it's an episode of series TV, it's about one thing: family.

With that in mind, write something that has a sense of inevitability in the way it unfolds, yet still manages to surprise and thrill while unfolding. You want to bring people to your story's end with them feeling that it couldn't have been resolved any other way, an ending the inevitability of which is supremely satisfying, and yet staged so elegantly that they don't see it coming. If you can do that, you've created gold.

Want an example? How about the ending of *ROBOCOP*, in which corporate yuppie bad guy Dick Jones is fired by the director of OCP, thus negating the protection guaranteed by Directive 4 and leaving Robo free to shoot him a whole lot. An ending that's inevitable in hindsight, yet leaves the audience laughing in delighted surprise every time. I remember complimenting one of the two screenwriters on its ease of execution; its simplicity and inevitability. He replied, "Yeah—it was so simple it only took me three weeks to think of it." I'm not surprised. That's another truism about inevitable endings: The more effortless they seem, the harder they are to dream up.

It may sound overwhelming; in which case, consider another line of work. But remember: I did it, which means just about anyone can. It isn't easy, and it takes knowing the series inside out. And don't just research the series; learn as much as you can about the show runners as well. Why? Pop quiz: Let's say I'm a producer on a weekly series. I've got one slot open and two scripts from two different writers. Everything about them is pretty much equal: They're both producible, well written, and original in ways that illuminate the characters without costing half the season's budget. The only difference between the two writers is that one of them is someone I don't know, while the other is someone I met at a convention, at the gym, in rehab, or whatever. Which one will I buy? (The answer counts for half your grade.)

That's the way it's done. If you can do it, you'll never do anything else remotely as satisfying. Making stuff up and getting paid for it is the big time, no question. It's also the most fun you can have with your pants on. Trust me; I've been doing it for more than thirty years, and it still beats working for a living.

EXERCISE

1. So, keeping in mind that TV is family, let's say you've decided to set your show on an interstellar spaceship. Work out the interrelationships between your characters. Exploit such concepts as the generation gap, always seeking a new twist.

2. Remember that aliens are successful only if their reactions are human. Theodore Sturgeon, one of the greatest science fiction writers, wrote one of the best episodes of *Star Trek* ever by asking, *"What if Spock were compelled to return to his home world every few years to mate—or die?"* (It's called "Amok Time," and if you haven't seen it, rent it or stream it right now before proceeding further. Go ahead; I'll wait.)

3. Come up with several storylines featuring each character. Now pick the last person you would think could carry one of the stories, and try it from his/her/its POV.

4. Depending on the parameters of your scenario, use the tropes of sci-fi to examine the characters' humanity in ways straight drama won't allow. These can be biological differences, cultural differences . . . whatever. Remember the three basic conflicts: *Man Against Man*, *Man Against Nature*, and *Man Against Himself*. Using those I co-wrote an episode of the web series *Star Trek: New Voyages*, which made the final nominations for the Hugo and Nebula Awards.

5. Don't be afraid to draw from archetypes, as long as they aren't stereotypes. (The difference? Well, a lazy way to write sci-fi was to take a Western plot and set it on Mars, for example. Guns became blasters, Indians became Martians, etc. It was looked upon with contempt because it dealt only in stereotypes. Then Joss Whedon came along with *Firefly*. And if you don't get the difference, there's nothing more I can tell you.)

When the World Turns to Shit, Why Should I Care?
Character Arc in Dystopian Stories

RAYMOND OBSTFELD is the author of more than forty books of fiction, non-fiction, and poetry as well as more than a dozen screenplays, most of which have been optioned. He recently collaborated with Kareem Abdul-Jabbar on a *New York Times* best-selling children's book *What Color Is My World?* (Candlewick) and a middle-school novel *Sasquatch in the Paint* (Hyperion-Disney). He recently completed a YA novel "The Time-Reaper's Tattoo," and Hallmark has bought his script *A Little Christmas Con*.

Dystopian fiction is all the rage. *The Hunger Games, Battle Royale* (wait, are they the same story?), *The Walking Dead, WORLD WAR Z, The Stand,* and all the others that seem to tap into our giddy fear about (and secret desire for) the End of the World. These works are especially popular in the young adult market because tweens and teens don't have an emotional stake in the world as it is. After all, this is the world that tells them what to do, what to think, and who to be. Why would they champion a society that "oppresses" them? No wonder they crave a world gone topsy-turvy in which one will be judged not by the color of one's letterman jacket but by the quality of one's crossbow skills.

I created such a world in my Warlord novel series (written as Jason Frost, the hunkiest name I could come up with). In the series, an earthquake separates California from the mainland, a radioactive dome from the destroyed nuclear plants keeps people from escaping or entering the island of California, and all civilization has broken down to the point of people just scrambling for survival any way they can. Plus, the protagonist carries a cool crossbow.

Better writers than I will tell you how to create those worlds. What I'm going to deal with is how to make us care about the people in those worlds. I'm going to do this by providing a worksheet that will help you understand how the dystopian world and the adventures they face affect them. Knowing this keeps a novel from just becoming a series of familiar action scenes that are ripped off from other similar stories. When that happens, the story becomes tepid, a pale photocopy of a photocopy of a photocopy.

The danger of dystopian stories is that the writer becomes so enamored with the details of creating this world that she ignores the characters that inhabit it. Remember that the world is only the setting to highlight the protagonist's arc, not the purpose of the novel.

Most stories are about the protagonist changing as a result of the plot of the story (also known as the Character Arc). What elevates a pure action story into a more memorable story is our emotional commitment to the protagonist. This commitment is increased by making the protagonist's goal more than just survival, but about becoming a better, happier person.

EXERCISE

BUILDING THE CHARACTER ARC

First, we have to figure out what kind of protagonist we're dealing with. Is she likeable or unlikeable? Is he skilled and knowledgeable, and will he use those skills immediately to distinguish himself as a leader? Or is he weak and unknowledgeable and therefore the story is about him learning how to become stronger and smarter? The Character Arc depends on answering the following questions:

1. *Who is the protagonist outside the circumstances of the dystopian world?* The big mistake that many beginning writers make is defining a protagonist's emotional state by a major flaw. That means that they

select one characteristic and beat us over the head with it in every scene. Maybe she's sad because her father died or abandoned the family. Maybe she's painfully shy because of some childhood trauma. Whatever this characteristic is, it is used to elicit sympathy (making her likeable) and to give her an obstacle to overcome. So far so good.

But characters are more complex than that. If you're writing a YA novel, you can usually get away with more superficial characterization. If you're writing for sophisticated teens and for adult readers, you will need to create more nuanced characters. How? By imagining who the character was before the dystopia. What did she do in her daily life? What did she read, eat, listen to, watch on TV? What did she do right before going to bed? Eat ice cream, read poetry, text her friends? By telling us some of this, you will be creating a contrast between what she had and what she now has. This loss creates stakes and makes us care more about her.

If the dystopian event (the disaster that caused society to go bad) has already happened, you can suggest the way the world used to be through objects, memories, flashbacks, etc. If it hasn't happened yet, and is a part of your novel, the scenes that come before the event will show us who she was and what she will need to become.

2. *What is the protagonist's main character strength?*
Character strength is about character qualities they possess (not physical attributes). In this case, pick the main one: compassion, intellect, leadership, etc. This strength will be the key to making plot choices because you will need to construct scenes in which the character strength is challenged and the character will have to dig deep to use it to overcome obstacles.

3. *What is the protagonist's main character weakness?*
Select the main weakness of character. This does not mean superficial things such as he talks too much or his jokes aren't funny. This is about a character flaw that prevents him from achieving

fulfillment and happiness: lack of discipline, inability to judge people for who they really are, a need to be liked by everyone, etc. This weakness will also guide plot choices because you will need dynamic scenes in which this weakness causes the protagonist to occasionally fail. These failures increase suspense because the reader then isn't sure whether the protagonist's strength or weakness will triumph in the climax.

4. *What is the protagonist's main practical skill?*
   Usually, the protagonist should have something he is good at. There are several reasons for this:

   a. It shows he has a passion for something. Characters that are passionate about something are more likeable.

   b. It adds depth to the character because it allows you to provide a back story about how he got caught up in this passion. This story is an excuse to tell us about other relationships, traumas, struggles, and so forth in an interesting way. This provides a more active scene to give us information and therefore avoids the ominous "info dump" (in which the writer stops the momentum of the novel to dump background information).

   c. It creates suspense because we know that whatever this passion is, it will play a key role later in the novel. The more seemingly useless the object of the passion, the more interesting and clever its use can be.

   It doesn't really matter what it is, as long as you make it seem interesting. Comic book collecting? Guitar playing? Toad racing? They're all equal in this world. The first TV Movie of the Week was called *How I Spent My Summer Vacation*, starring a young Robert Wagner. In this story, Wagner played a spoiled, talentless, jobless playboy who had one skill: He could hold his breath for a long time. It's a joke in the film because it's used to amuse his partying friends around the swimming pool. But later, when his life is threatened and he's being gassed in an elevator, this ability saves his life.

5. *What is the protagonist's main practical weakness?*

Sometimes a major physical weakness hampers the protagonist's ability to successfully complete the adventure: out of shape, bad knee, weak eyesight, etc. This physical weakness sometimes reflects the character's psychological weaknesses. For example, does he use the physical weakness as an excuse not to try harder? In the film *Young Adult*, Charlize Theron plays a once-popular girl who's grown up to have a terribly depressing life. When she goes back to her small hometown, she encounters a dumpy guy she ignored in school. He'd been beaten by a group of kids that thought he was gay (though he wasn't) and the beating had left him with permanent leg injuries. Since high school, he's worked crappy jobs, brews whiskey in a still in his garage, and glues different parts of action figures together to make hybrid figures. He's used this injury—and the injustice of it—as an excuse to turn his back on such an unjust universe and justify his alienation.

6. *Is the protagonist likeable? If not, what is her "redemptive quality"?*

Sometimes a Character Arc starts with a character who is demonstrably unlikeable. The suspense then is whether or not the character will ever change to become a likeable character. The problem the writer faces is making readers care enough about an unlikeable character that they want to stick around to find out what happens.

This dilemma is resolved by giving the unlikeable protagonist a redemptive quality. The quality implies that there is something good inside the person that, given the right circumstances, can emerge to save the protagonist from a life of being a jerk.

In the novel and film *A Clockwork Orange*, protagonist Alex is a violent, remorseless thief, rapist, and murderer. Why should any of us want to stay in this character's company? First, because he's a compelling and unpredictable character with a strong narrative voice. Second, because he has a redemptive quality: his love of Beethoven's music. The reader believes that this quality reveals a spark of human goodness that if fanned into flame, will consume the deplorable Alex to leave the good Alex to rise up out of the ashes.

BUILDING THE CHARACTER INTO THE STORY

Now that you have defined the protagonist, you need to construct scenes that show these qualities and flaws in dynamic ways. Avoid just telling us about them. Instead, reveal them in an active way, showing the characteristics in action rather than in passive talking heads or monologue scenes.

LOIS GRESH

Story Endings: Where Monsters Lurk

LOIS GRESH is a six-time *New York Times* best-selling author, *Publishers Weekly* best-selling paperback author, and *Publishers Weekly* best-selling paperback children's author of twenty-seven books and forty-five short stories. Her books have been published in approximately twenty languages. Lois has received Bram Stoker Award, Nebula Award, Theodore Sturgeon Memorial Award, and International Horror Guild Award nominations for her work.

You know what it's like. You're reading a fantastic story, but about halfway into it, you guess what's going to happen. Sure, you like the protagonist, and oh yes, you love the setting and the fine-tuned prose. But none of these factors matter if you guess how the story's going to end.

To keep the attention of your reader, you must keep him guessing. Something must pull him through the story to the very end.

Let's look at what I think of as typical monster stories. I recently edited an anthology called *Dark Fusions: Where Monsters Lurk* (PS Publishing, 2013). Two-thirds of the submissions were typical monster stories, in which a kind protagonist—often a child with a single parent—confronts a lurking evil he can't see or identify. But something's wrong: The pool water's too murky in bright sun, the grass is dark from an unseen shadow, the wind suddenly picks up for no reason on an otherwise calm day. As the story progresses toward the middle, perhaps a friend disappears or the protagonist finds a beloved family member dead by the murky pool (or in the dark grass or tossed by an inexplicable wind).

Quite often, the monsters take human form. For example, thriller novels feature human killers, as do space operas, military science fiction, and many other genres.

We keep reading a story because we care about the protagonist and how he's going to survive and save the day. We're hoping the author packs a punch at the end of the story and surprises us. Otherwise, if we can guess the ending (oh, the monster comes out of the murky pool and kills somebody), what's the point of reading the story at all?

One thing you must do in a good story is make sure the protagonist changes in a meaningful way from the time the reader meets him to the time he encounters the monster. His actions at the end must reflect how he's changed, and they must occur at great cost to himself or his beliefs. If you choose a final action that evokes great emotion in your protagonist, then your readers will be moved, as well.

Most typical monster stories end in one of three ways:

1. The protagonist finally sees the monster and fights it. Either the protagonist wins and kills the monster, or he loses and almost dies—or he does die.

2. The protagonist joins forces with the monster and also becomes evil.

3. The protagonist learns that there really is no monster.

No matter which of the three endings you write, the reader will be disappointed. So how do you get around this problem?

One solution is to change the monster in a meaningful way. Suppose the monster evolves and is no longer a threat. In this case, does your protagonist become the more evil of the two entities?

Or suppose the monster is not actually the creature or entity that the protagonist encounters at the end. Instead, the real monster still waits, ready to spring out and attack just when the protagonist thought he'd saved the day.

Or suppose the protagonist makes the monster suffer endlessly rather than supply a more humane method of death.

Or suppose the protagonist discovers that we're all monsters, that this supposed force of evil is actually no big deal.

There are countless options, so there's no need to opt for one of the three standard endings.

In my dark fairy tale, "Wee Sweet Girlies" (in my collection *Eldritch Evolutions*), a young girl must battle a terrible monster from the beginning of the story until the end. Does she kill the monster? Does she join forces with the monster? Does she learn the monster isn't real? None of the above. Does she change in a meaningful way and do her actions reflect these changes? Yes. Read the story and you'll see what I mean.

In *Terror By Numbers: A Wall Street Thriller* (Book View Café, 2012), a girl battles true evil in the form of a monster she doesn't know exists until deep into the novel. Remember, in most thriller and horror novels, people die, and this requires a monster, often a human one. I'm not going to give away the ending of my thriller, but I guarantee it doesn't use any of the standard three options. Hopefully, the ending will surprise you.

EXERCISE

1. Choose a short story or novel that you haven't read yet. Halfway into the story, jot down how you think it might end. List all plausible endings that come to mind. Now finish reading the story. Did you guess the ending? If so, were you disappointed? If not, think about why the ending satisfied you. Did the solution surprise you yet remain plausible? Did the protagonist change over time? Did the ending affect you emotionally in any way?

2. Write 2,000 words of a new story of science fiction, fantasy, or horror. Make sure your story includes one monster, human or otherwise, that threatens the protagonist, her family, and/or her way of life. Make sure your protagonist will learn something about herself and grow as a human being over the course of the story. Now list all plausible endings that come to mind. Cross out the standard three endings. Choose one of the remaining endings from your list and write the rest of the story.

MICHAEL DILLON SCOTT

Begin at the End . . .

MICHAEL DILLON SCOTT is one of Ireland's most successful and prolific authors, with one hundred titles spanning fantasy, science fiction, and folklore. His collections, *Irish Folk & Fairy Tales*, *Irish Myths & Legends*, and *Irish Ghosts & Hauntings* have remained in print for the past twenty years and are the definitive and most-quoted works on Celtic folklore.

Over the years I have met many writers, and I think I can divide them into two broad categories: those who plan their work, and those who do not. I am in awe of the latter—I simply do not know how they do it. They sit at their machines or before the blank sheet of paper and the story flows out of them.

However, in my experience, even those who do not plan their stories have an ending in mind and will work toward that particular conclusion. (And even as you are reading this, somewhere a writer is contradicting me and saying that he or she never knows how the story is going to end, that he or she is as surprised by the ending as the reader. Which just goes to show that there are as many ways to write as there are writers. There is no right way.)

There are more series in our genre than in any other. It began with the penny dreadfuls in the nineteenth century, where *Varney the Vampire* ran for two years and more than a hundred parts in magazine format before it was published in novel form in 1847.

Dickens issued most of his great works in monthly parts before releasing the hardbound novel. Readers quickly developed an appetite for revisiting their favorite characters.

Tarzan began as a series of short stories in *All-Story Magazine* in 1912 and the novel did not appear for another two years.

The great science fiction magazines, *Amazing* and *Astounding*, published short stories featuring the same characters, continuing the tradition of episodic stories featuring recurring characters. And this is a tradition that is kept alive in the cinema, on television, and in novels today.

Readers love series. Publishers are thrilled with series. And writers (mostly) love to write them.

But a writer beginning a multi-book series needs to be aware that they are looking at several years of writing. When I started writing back in the 1980s, trilogies were common, now it is quartets, quintets, sextets, and more multi-book series. These are big books too—the slender science fiction or fantasy novel is a rarity!

Recently, I finished the sixth book in a YA fantasy series. I started writing the first book in that series in 2005. It was published in 2007 and the last book in 2012. The Flamel series is now more than half a million words in print (and there is at least three times that amount in edits, rewrites, and pieces I've pulled out of the story).

The Secrets of the Immortal Nicholas Flamel was conceived and plotted as a six-book series, and there is no way I could begin that journey without knowing the books in detail, knowing the climax of each book, and especially, knowing the ending of the series. I needed that destination before I began.

Before I started the first of the Flamel books, I wrote the ultimate ending—the final paragraph. It took me almost seven years to get there, but when I reached it, that ending slotted in complete and unedited.

So here is my suggestion (especially if you are thinking of a big multi-book series): Start with your ending.

All writing is a journey toward a destination, that final page in the story. Like any journey, it makes perfect sense to begin with a destination in mind. The entire story becomes a lot easier if the ending is written. Once you have your ending, you have your story, because you can then start working backward and asking yourself the great writing questions: "How did that happen?" and "What happened before that?" Eventually you will work back to the beginning of the story. And the process of questioning yourself and the story will expose the weaknesses in the tale and also allow you to discover its strengths.

The same process—beginning at the end—also works for characters.

Begin with the characters as they are at the climax of the story, then start working backward. By establishing how they are at the end of the story, this will allow you to determine how they should be at the beginning. If you discover that they are the same character at the end as they were at the beginning, then I am going to suggest that something is amiss. Every story changes your characters.

Beginning with the end has one other huge psychological advantage. You will never end up in that situation where you don't know what happens next . . . because now you do!

EXERCISE

1. Take a piece of work you have already completed, and start with the finale. Summarize the last chapter/section in a few sentences on a piece of card—yes, an old-fashioned file card. Now, go back and do the same for the chapter before that. Work backward toward the beginning. Looking at your file cards: Does the ending fall naturally? Is it the natural consequence of all that has gone before?

2. Take a news headline as the final sentence in a story. By asking yourself, "*And what happened just before that?*" work backward to where the story began.

3. Create the same character in two different ways. First begin with a standard character biography, list the likes and dislikes, background, family, and so on. Now, begin with the same character, but fully formed and begin to work backward. What story elements have contributed to the character's development?

HIGH STAKES AND TERROR

"It does not do to leave a live dragon out of your calculations,
if you live near him."
—GANDALF, IN *THE HOBBIT*, BY J. R. R. TOLKIEN

"What terrified me will terrify others; and I need only describe the spectre
which had haunted my midnight pillow."
—MARY WOLLSTONECRAFT SHELLEY

WILLIAM F. NOLAN

Of Heroes and Villains

WILLIAM F. NOLAN is the best-selling author of nearly one hundred books. He has won top awards in three genres (mystery, sci-fi, and horror) and his works have appeared in some 350 anthologies and textbooks. He has taught college-level creative writing, and his books include *Logan's Run* and the award-winning nonfiction volume *Let's Get Creative: Writing Fiction That Sells!*

To achieve true heroism, a protagonist must perform heroic deeds. What constitutes heroism? Perhaps saving a squalling infant from a burning building? Maybe helping a crippled old lady survive an air crash? Or pulling a trapped child from the ruins of an earthquake? Saving the life of a drowning man? Yes, all these are genuine acts of heroism—but how much more dramatic, more exciting and satisfying to witness the defeat of a villain as strong (or stronger) than the hero?

Chester Bent, in Max Brand's most famous Western, *Destry Rides Again*, out-fights and out-shoots our hero, but Destry prevails at the climax. An axiom of fiction writing could well be, "Strong villains make strong heroes, and, conversely, weak villains equal weak heroes."

Seems antithetical, doesn't it? Allow me to elaborate . . .

One example that comes to mind is Superman: Here we have an archetypal character of seeming ultimate goodness. Pure, righteous, upstanding; he has defeated a host of bad guys, but the chief villain pitted against him is Lex Luthor (an antihero if there ever was one) who seems not only malevolent, but indestructible as well. A strong villain indeed! Their ongoing battles are monumental, and the conflict they generate never fails to deliver.

Another example, this time from the cinematic world of director George Lucas's Star Wars saga, is Darth Vader—a towering threat to young Luke Skywalker. In the original series, Vader is a figuratively (and literally) larger-than-life menace, determined to crush the Rebel Alliance, and subjugate everyone in the galaxy to the dark impulses of the Emperor.

From literature, we can examine Ian Fleming's James Bond books, which are full of despicable characters who long to thwart the iconic British super spy: Goldfinger proved to be a worthy enemy, as did Dr. No.

Sometimes a villain is so much larger than life that it actually overshadows the hero, earning a special fame of its own. Bram Stoker's Count Dracula is one such character, as is the sadistically evil Dr. Hannibal Lecter from *Red Dragon* by Thomas Harris.

As these examples amply demonstrate, as a writer, if you set out to create a work of compelling suspense, you must develop a villain that is truly *real*. Your scoundrel must be plausible; a cardboard menace is not going to elicit fear and belief in your reader. You need to make sure that he (or she) is a fully developed, three-dimensional character. Moreover, keep in mind that the battle between villain and hero must have its dark moment—a climactic point when all seems lost, and your hero finds himself on the knife edge of defeat. If your reader does not believe that the hero just *might* lose, then the element of suspense will be missing. In other words, don't be afraid to give your hero a really bad time: Put him through the fire. The tougher you make the job of defeating the villain, the more the reader will identify with the hero, and therefore empathize with his epic struggle.

The task of defeating the heavy must always directly involve your protagonist, male or female. No falling rockslides or lightning bolts from the sky to get the job done (the ancients referred to this gimmick as a *deus ex machina*, or "god from the machine," who would swoop in to save everyone if the writer couldn't figure out how to; it's a cheat, and an insult to your audience). Ideally, good should triumph over evil in your climax; in reality, however, not all stories end that way, so don't be afraid to let the reader speculate. Neat resolutions can make for boring tales, especially for today's jaded audience.

On another note, your evil creation need not always be human. H. G. Wells created wicked Martians in *The War of the Worlds,* and Arnold Schwarzenegger's character in *The Terminator* was a killer android. In my short story "Lonely Train A' Comin'," the menace is a living train that literally devours its passengers. My hero blows it to pieces, nearly dying in this act of destruction. Again, I had to make the train real; I had to convince my readers that such a train *could* exist. Otherwise, the story would have failed.

Finally, let me reiterate: Strong villain, strong hero; weak villain, weak hero. It's all up to you, the writer.

EXERCISE

1. Create your own villain, in-depth. Make him or her (or it) truly frightening. Allow him to commit an evil act (or acts) to prove how bad he is. Give him a fully realized background. Where is he from? What is he capable of? Make him real.

2. When your hero first confronts the rogue, allow the hero to lose the first encounter. Maybe the hero loses twice. This sets up the final battle at your climax in which the hero prevails.

3. How does your hero win the day? Perhaps your menace has an Achilles' heel that your hero can manipulate. If not, create one.

4. Try writing from the villain's viewpoint: What nasty deed does he want to accomplish? What dark goal does she have in mind? How does it justify its behavior? Take us into your villain's mind.

5. At your climax (a payoff to your previous suspense), have the final battle keep the reader guessing as to who will win and how, until, at the last moment, after nearly losing, the hero triumphs.

CHRISTINE CONRADT

The Eleven Tenets of Fear

CHRISTINE CONRADT has written more than forty indie films and made-for-TV movies in the horror, thriller, and crime drama genre. Her films have aired on networks like FOX, Lifetime, Lifetime Movie Network, and USA. She is the writer of *SUMMER'S MOON*, *CHRISTIE'S REVENGE*, *MATERNAL OBSESSION*, and *HOTEL CALIFORNIA*. She holds a BFA in film from USC and a master's degree in criminal justice from Boston University.

I've been an avid lover of all things macabre since I was very young. My favorite holiday was Halloween; it was a time when I could unleash one of my creepy alter egos—an evil witch, Vampira, Bride of Frankenstein. One year, I wanted to go as a dead cheerleader. I was going to be deathly pale with bluish postmortem lividity and bleed profusely from a gash on my neck, but my mother nixed it, saying it was too morbid for the younger children. Ah, well.

Not much has changed. I love the horrific, the gruesome, the eerily aberrant, the supernatural. I try to tap into that childhood fascination when I'm writing a horror scene, but coming up with something truly terrifying isn't always easy. I've found that going back to the nature of horror, what really scares us, can help me connect to the place where paralyzing fear is born.

I believe there are eleven things people across the board are scared of. I call them the Eleven Tenets of Fear. They are:

1. *Pain*. Enduring emotional or physical pain elicits fear. This is the premise behind torture. Militaries have been known to play audiotapes of someone screaming in pain before interrogating POWs.

The POWs believe the screams are coming from real prisoners and begin to imagine the pain the person must be experiencing. The fear created in their own minds leads to compliance. The film *SAW* used pain as its primary tenet, asking the audience, "Could you saw off your own foot to save your life?"

2. *Death/mortality.* Most people are afraid of death and many are fascinated with it. Every religion includes beliefs about what happens after one dies. The notion of eternal life or reincarnation is often a comforting thought for people who face imminent death or have lost a loved one. The FINAL DESTINATION franchise is built around the inability to escape death.

3. *Disfigurement.* Ugliness and disfigurement are associated with evil and social exclusion. Witches, monsters, and demons are often portrayed as ugly creatures. Sometimes they are naturally disfigured (think Freddy Krueger) and sometimes they hide behind ugly masks (like Michael Meyers in *HALLOWEEN*).

4. *Retribution for perceived or real wrongs.* People are inherently retributive (an eye for an eye), and acts of retribution are often seen as justified (consider the father who walks in on a man molesting his child and beats him to death). The notion that our transgressions could unleash retributive acts of horrific proportions is scary.

5. *Evil forces.* Forces beyond our control are often the basis for horror films. *ROSEMARY'S BABY, POLTERGEIST,* and *THE AMITYVILLE HORROR* all use the insuperability of evil forces to scare audiences.

6. *Loss of a loved one.* Fictional characters are often motivated to act because a loved one has been killed or kidnapped. Human beings form strong ties to others, and the stronger the connection, the greater the fear of losing it.

7. *Abandonment/being alone.* Finding yourself having to face something awful alone is even more horrifying than facing it with someone else (remember when the divers resurface to find the boat has left them in *OPEN WATER*?). Humans inherently seek out

others to connect with; we don't like to be alone. That's also why in books and films, evildoers often live off by themselves. We perceive the desire to be alone as deviant and creepy.

8. *The unknown.* We often feel that what we can't see or don't understand poses danger. This is why masks and costumes are scary (they obscure the person wearing them) and darkness is disturbing (something terrible could be close to us and we wouldn't know).

9. *Hell.* Hell represents all things painful. It's the home of Satan, which is supremely powerful and evil. It has no temporality or spatiality. For Christians, it is an eternal place of punishment. The belief in the existence of hell, and the fear of it, has been an enforcer of moral conduct for thousands of years.

10. *Our limitations as human beings.* We are fascinated by our own limitations, and horror films and books play on this. Nearly all horror figures have the ability to exceed human limitations. Vampires are immortal; ghosts are invisible; witches can cast spells; werewolves have super-human strength, etc.

11. *The depth of our own depravity.* "If it bleeds, it leads" is true for a reason. We are fascinated by humans who are not bound to the same moral codes we abide by. Serial killers, who torture, murder, cannibalize, and do things the rest of us would never consider, show us that those abilities are, disturbingly, buried somewhere in human nature—a potential we all share.

These tenets appear in almost every successful horror film and horror story. Let's look at three popular examples that were listed in *Time* magazine's "Top 25 Horror Movies" and assess which tenets were included.

THE EXORCIST. Little Regan is inhabited by a demon, and an exorcism is her mother's only hope for getting her daughter back. Fear tenets: disfigurement (Regan gets boils on her face, and her body contorts); loss of a loved one (mother losing daughter to the demon); evil forces (demonic possession); limitations as humans (can a mortal Catholic priest beat the all-powerful demon?); death (the demon can and does kill); and the unknown (why did it choose an innocent little girl?).

CARRIE. After being picked on for years, a teen girl discovers she has telekinetic powers that she can use to destroy her prom. Fear tenets: death (Carrie kills her tormentors); retribution (Carrie's act is one of retribution against those who mistreated her); evil forces (Carrie has supernatural powers); the unknown (no one was aware of Carrie's powers until it was too late); our limitations (there is no defense against Carrie); and the depth of human depravity (what is Carrie willing to do to her tormentors and what were they willing to do to humiliate her?).

JAWS. A seaside community is plagued by a huge, predatory shark. Fear tenets: pain (shark bites hurt); death/mortality (the shark can and does kill); disfigurement (loss of limbs due to shark bites); evil forces (according to Quint, sharks have "lifeless, black eyes" suggesting a lack of a soul); loss of a loved one (people and pets are being eaten by the shark); abandonment/being alone (what if I'm the only one left alive?); the unknown (ocean swimmers can't see what's below the surface of the water); and our limitations (how can we out-swim the world's largest shark?).

When assessing ideas for a horror film, I often go back and create a checklist of these eleven tenets and explain how my story/screenplay has (or will) address them.

EXERCISE

Think about your favorite horror film/story (or an original idea you'd like to write). How many of the eleven tenets can you identify? For those that are missing, write down a few ideas on how they could be incorporated. The more you have, chances are, the scarier your story will be.

DERRICK D. PETE

Anatomy of Choice

DERRICK D. PETE is a screenwriter whose latest fantasy adventure is being developed by Pierce Brosnan's production company. He has an MFA in screenwriting from UCLA. His undergraduate degree is in chemical engineering, and he has two international patents related to the purification of methyl tertiary butyl ether over a zeolite-Y catalyst.

A s a writer of fantasy and sci-fi films, I find that getting lost in the worlds we create can be very easy to do. After all, effectively communicating the science in our story must be as important as spinning a complicated web of fiction. Otherwise, it would just be fiction, not science fiction. As a proud, card-carrying member of the sci-fi/fantasy screenwriting club, I understand the lure of the unknown world or the magical wonderland. Therefore, I make the bold assumption that creating new worlds is what you do best—that's what led you to this genre. So, I want to focus our attention on a topic that gets far less attention, but is equally as important.

Memorable characters are the foundation of any screenplay, for any genre, from fantasy to film noir. I knew I wanted to share an exercise related to character development, but what angle or unique perspective can I offer? I thought through various alternatives. What about: "Memorable characters transcend time; memorable personas define the time?" While the statement is true, I was hard pressed to make this truth practical to screenwriters developing memorable characters for their individual projects. Another statement came to mind: "Men identify with heroes; women identify with teams." Again, this statement would make for an interesting intellectual discourse, but the needle on the practicality meter barely moved (this principle deals more with the audience as character rather than characters within our own films). So, after much soul searching, I made a choice and a cosmic principle was born. I'll name it Universal Cosmic Principle 1108a: Memorable characters make memorable choices. In order to create multi-dimensional characters who will live in the memory of the audience, you must master the *anatomy of choice*: crisis, cause, crucible, and (con)sequence. It is important to note that every choice made by a character will have these four elements. Effective manipulation of these elements will increase dimensionality and CVM (clear, vivid, memorable) characters.

Crisis. It is critically important that we place our characters in situations that demand an urgent choice. For most films, binary choices work the best (do or don't, yes or no, live or die, etc.). The crisis must be of such a magnitude that it insists on a decision . . . NOW. Additional opportunities for crisis generate additional opportunities for urgent choices. Does Ed Exley snitch or not (*L.A. CONFIDENTIAL*)? Does Celie leave Mister's house or not (*THE COLOR PURPLE*)? Does the Fourth Wife fake pregnancy or not (*RAISE THE RED LANTERN*)? Does Vincent Vega sleep with Mia or not (*PULP FICTION*)? Characters make choices all the time; however, it's the choices they make in the midst of crisis that maximizes our understanding of them. If a character chooses to brush his teeth in the morning, that doesn't mean much; however, if a character chooses to brush his teeth even though the building is on fire, that choice reveals something unique about that character.

Cause. Every choice a character makes is motivated by a set of conditions provided within the terrain of the story. We must understand the reasons behind a character's choice. We do not, however, have to agree with the choice a character makes. I've identified *six causes* that appear to be sufficient *filmic reasons* for a character's choice during crisis:

1. obsession for a given quest/passion/goal

2. moral/ethical essence

3. primal emotions (i.e., fear, love, envy, anger)

4. duty

5. psychological scar (i.e., abandonment, abuse) and

6. revenge (specifically for the murder or mistreatment of a child, spouse, lover, parent, or sibling)

These causes each carry a different weight or value with the audience, and it's important to be aware of that. The causes for the choices a character makes in a film must be provided within the terrain of the story. When David Helfgott chooses to attend the prestigious musical conservatory against his father's wishes, we understand that choice because we understand the passion he has for music *(SHINE)*. When Nicole chooses to lie about the bus accident, we understand that choice because we see the psychological damage caused by incest within her family *(SWEET HEREAFTER)*. When Jack dies for Rose, we understand that choice because we have seen the love between the two of them *(TITANIC)*.

Crucible. The combination of *crisis* and *cause* can produce an inescapable crucible for our characters. If the choice our character makes is to achieve maximum effectiveness, the boundaries that constrain the choice must be clearly defined. What are the parameters or the circumstances that encapsulate the choice? As we constrict the boundaries, close the walls in on our characters, and limit the possibilities for escape, we heighten the tension and reveal character on multiple levels. For example, being chased by the cops for murder is surely a crisis for a character. Combining that with a cause such as an obsessive pseudo-neurotic passion may not carry much weight with the audience. However, if the cause of the murder was revenge for the death of a child, then the crucible begins to form in the mind of the audience. For example, the choice to drive off a cliff rather than face the police *(THELMA & LOUISE)*; George's choice to stay in Bedford Falls *(IT'S A WONDERFUL LIFE)*; David's choice to kill John Doe *(SEVEN)*.

(Con)sequence. Every choice a character makes has consequences.

A sequence of events without a spark (crisis, cause, crucible) becomes confusing and hard to follow. However, if events in a film are in direct relation to the consequence of the choices made by our characters, then our film has a natural undercurrent that demands resolution. If you think of plot as a sequence of events, then it becomes obvious that a character's choice produces a series of consequences, which then lead to another sequence of events. What if McMurphy chose to leave the psychiatric hospital while he had the chance *(ONE FLEW OVER THE CUCKOO'S NEST)*? What if Gaz chose not to bare it all on stage *(THE FULL MONTY)*? What if the underdog fighter chose not to go the distance against Apollo Creed *(ROCKY)*? Those would be entirely different films with characters we would have long forgotten. It's clear, in great movies, memorable characters make memorable choices.

EXERCISE

If you are rewriting a previous screenplay or in the process of developing a new one, make sure you can answer each of the following questions:

1. What are the choices being made by the lead characters? Are those choices "filmic"? Can any or all of those choices be heightened by examining the "anatomy of choice"—crisis, cause, crucible, and (con)sequence?

2. The choice a character ultimately makes is often rooted in the flaws of that character. What is your character's most human quality (i.e., flaw)? For example, is your character absentminded, abusive, alcoholic, aimless, anxious, arrogant (and that's just the As)? Identify the flaw(s) in your character. It will directly impact the choices he or she makes.

3. Are the choices being made by your character resulting in the appropriate "filmic" (con)sequences? Diagram the series of events

based on your character's choices. Do the events follow a logical flow with ever-increasing stakes?

4. What is the first choice your character makes? Does it reveal character? Your first character introduction not only sells the character; it sells the movie (or it doesn't). Make your character choices memorable. Make every choice count.

TODD KLICK

How Spielberg and Shakespeare Grab 'Em in Five

TODD KLICK is the best-selling author of *Something Startling Happens: The 120 Story Beats Every Writer Needs to Know* (Michael Wiese Productions) and *The Screenwriter's Fairy Tale: The Universal Story Within All Movie Stories.* He has won the Nicholls Fellowship, optioned three scripts and sold five, and he has deals to develop stories for the London and Broadway stages.

So I'm at this industry mixer in Century City five years ago, and I chat with a movie studio script reader. I ask her to sum up her workday. "Well," she said to me, "I read the opening pages of screenplays, and if they don't grab me in five pages, I toss 'em into the garbage and move onto the next."

Her blunt confession horrified me. For a writer who works hard on scripts for months, sometimes years, the thought of having my words tossed so flippantly into the trash seemed outrageously unjust. Swallowing this bitter pill, I started a deep study of what master storytellers do to grab audiences. While on this story quest, I learned timeless techniques used since Shakespeare and still applied by great writers and directors today. And once I applied their tricks of the trade to my own scripts, my stories suddenly avoided trash bins and attracted options and sales instead.

Before I share those ancient writing secrets and exercises with you, here's some history to explain why these techniques work.

The Globe Theatre, which hosted Shakespeare's plays, attracted a tough audience. The Groundlings, as they were called, would crowd the stage and jeer if an actor or play dared to be boring. Shakespeare quickly developed writing devices to fend off the fickle spectators and keep their attentions riveted to the story instead.

It was all about rhythm for the English playwrights: rhythm that created a mood or feeling, like the beats of a beautiful ballad. In the early 1900s, screenwriters, most of whom were weaned on stage plays, adopted these same rhythms in their early screen stories. In the crucial opening minutes of successful plays and movies, there were specific story beats the playwrights and screenwriters would consciously or subconsciously hit. The five beginning beats, which I've gone ahead and named, occur each minute in this order: *At-tension, The Build, The Ratchet, Another Notch,* and *The Jaw Dropper.* Take for example, Shakespeare's *Hamlet* and Spielberg's *RAIDERS OF THE LOST ARK:*

Minute 1: At-tension

During minute 1 of *RAIDERS OF THE LOST ARK,* Indiana Jones and his crew head deep into a dangerous jungle. During minute 1 of *Hamlet,* Bernardo wonders who lurks nearby in the dark.

Whether it's a drama, thriller, comedy, horror, sci-fi, rom-com, or Western, successful movies and plays start with tension. The best writers choose one of five ways to hook you with tension: danger, anxiety, hostility, unease, or sex. Spielberg and Shakespeare chose unease with a hint of danger to start their stories.

Minute 2: The Build

Audience anticipation is built by "building upon" already existing tension. Professional writers know that opening a story with tension will grab the audience, but if they don't escalate the tension, audiences will lose interest fast. A good way to prompt an escalating tension is by using the phrase, "Not only does." *Not only does* Indiana Jones head deep into a dangerous jungle (minute 1), but now Indy finds a deadly arrow (minute 2).

Not only does Bernardo wonder who lurks in the dark (minute 1 in *Hamlet*), but now Marcellus claims to have seen a dreaded apparition (minute 2).

Minute 3: The Ratchet

Next is what I call the Ratchet. My dad taught me how to use a ratchet wrench when I was a teenager. The ratchet was perfect for tightening bolts inside my old Chevy's engine block. As the ratchet screwed the bolt closer to the metal plate, I could feel the tension escalate in my wrist. Great writers use this same ratchet principle during minutes 3 and 4. A phrase to help you build the tension even more from the previous minute is: "Not only that, but now." *Not only that, but now:* "The poison is still fresh," Satipo says in *RAIDERS OF THE LOST ARK. Not only that, but now* a scary ghost enters the stage in *Hamlet.*

Minute 4: Another Notch

A phrase to help you ratchet the tension another notch in minute 4 is: "If you thought that was bad . . ." *If you thought that was bad,* now Indiana Jones's ally pulls a gun on him. *If you thought that was bad,* now Horatio turns pale and trembles with great fear in *Hamlet.*

Minute 5: The Jaw Dropper

You've ratcheted the tension the first four minutes, but now you need a twist to keep the audience off guard. The masters make the audience's jaw drop during this minute. They do this by showing the characters something extraordinary or astonishing—something they've never seen before. It's a subtle nuance that's distinct from the previous four minutes. For example, in *Hamlet,* Horatio says the ghost looks just like the deceased King of Denmark—the dead father of his friend Hamlet! Truly a jaw-dropping experience for him.

In *RAIDERS OF THE LOST ARK,* a jaw-dropping number of black poisonous spiders crawl onto Indy and his friend's backs! Spielberg uses the minute 5 Jaw Dropper again and again, like in *JAWS* when the shark yanks the naked female swimmer underneath the water and devours her—a jaw-dropping event in her life, to say the least.

Whether you're a playwright, screenwriter, novelist, or graphic novelist, learn the rhythms of theater and film and apply them to your own stories. The beats have worked for 400 years, and will continue to work for centuries to come.

EXERCISE

1. Write a minute 1 "At-tension grabber" using each of the five methods mentioned above. Which one works best for your story?

2. Once you've decided which At-tension grabber to use during minute 1, build upon it by using the phrase "Not only does . . ."

3. Ratchet up your tension from the previous minute by using the phrase "Not only that, but now . . ."

4. Once you've ratcheted up your tension in minute 3, ratchet it another notch during this minute by using the phrase, "If you thought that was bad, now . . ."

Now that you've properly built the tension in the first four minutes, throw in a jaw-dropping twist to really keep your audience on its toes. What is something extraordinary or astonishing you can show your main character in minute 5? What is something they, or the audience, have never seen before?

SARA B. COOPER

Bump in the Night

SARA B. COOPER is an acupuncturist who turned TV writer when a client gave her spec script to the series producers of *Star Trek: The Next Generation*. In addition to creating the Cardassian race for the series, Cooper has written for shows such as *The X-Files*, *Chicago Hope*, *Homicide*, *House*, and *Sanctuary*.

In 2007, Eduardo B. Andrade and Joel B. Cohen published a paper called "On the Consumption of Negative Feelings." The premise was that when individuals who choose to avoid fearful things were ". . . embedded in a protective frame of mind, such that there was sufficient psychological disengagement or detachment, they experienced positive feelings while still experiencing fearfulness." In other words, while snug in our homes or in groups at a movie theater, most people love a good scary story. And what is scarier than a good monster?

I was seven years old when I read my first monster story. In it, a vacuum machine was turned into a mechanical sound eater. If anything made noise, the machine would "suck out the sound," rendering the noisemaker inert. Unfortunately, its inventor soon realized that when the sound vacuum encountered a living thing, it would suck the noise right out of it, leaving it dead. The last line of the story describes the protagonist, trapped in the house with her invention, hiding from it and suddenly being aware of the sound of her heart as she hears the vacuum's wheels moving toward her. I didn't sleep for months.

Why did this scare me? It was about a person who did something without thinking about the consequences and thereby created a situation she couldn't control that was deadly. That fear rules my whole life: that I will do something without thinking it out, and it will have dire consequences. Anyone else have something like that? Yeah, I thought so.

There's another fear I have—that something that I had *nothing* to do with comes in and takes control over my life. Again, I feel I'm not alone in this. Thankfully, I put my neuroses to work, as any writer does.

A good monster has to engender fear. The writer has to be aware of what scares them. Not just spiders or women with too much plastic surgery (although I suspect there's a monster story there . . .), but those quiet fears that we may not even be aware of.

Jung wrote in "On the Psychology of the Unconscious," "*It is a frightening thought that man also has a shadow side to him, consisting not just of little weaknesses and foibles, but of a positively demonic dynamism. . . . Let these harmless creatures form a mass, and there emerges a raging monster.*"

"It is a frightening thought"—there is our drama. Our normal, rational self's fear of our inner demon. A cold, honest look at our darker selves takes courage and a willingness to let go of self-judgment. We must look for the demon within in order to create the monster without. Take a splash of whatever inner rage, anger, or just murderous impulses you can find inside; take an equal part of the fear that your inner demon will take control. Split them up between your monster and your protagonist. Then you have a story.

Secondly, we have to look at the manifestation of the monster— what is its form? I remember that first scary story. Many monsters and many more years later, I'm still struck by how the scariest things are often the most simple, familiar objects. It falls into my "What is scary?" list. Here are just some of my items:

The unfamiliar: This includes things that look and act differently than we do. Take the movie *ALIEN*, for example. The monster there looks, breeds, and communicates differently than we do. The irrational, the unexpected.

The unseen: For people who are sighted, most of their sense of reality comes from visual cues. To hear something without seeing it creates a profound sense of fear.

TOMA, M E

6402

Tuesday, September 27, 2022

31268116954674

Being out of control: This includes having control taken from us because our monsters are stronger or have super powers, as well as being manipulated or tricked by someone or something.

Making a mistake that will cost lives: Building a creature that will kill others as in Frankenstein's monster, getting a gremlin wet, or allowing cloned dinosaurs to get out of the compound.

The familiar gone wrong: Anything that defies the rules of our reality. A child's toy that can suddenly talk and walk and has a murderous streak; a car that has a mind of its own; shadows that move on their own accord and can cause you to spontaneously combust if you touch them.

Lastly there has to be stakes. What's in jeopardy? Death and loss are always good motivators. There are all forms of death and loss. You could lose your sanity. Your identity. It could be the loss of every other living soul. The loss of a loved one. Pick one or come up with your own form of living death.

To drive home the stakes, you've got to have a Redshirt. You *Star Trek* fans know what I'm talking about. For all you others, Wikipedia defines Redshirt as: "A stock character in fiction who dies soon after being introduced. The term originates with fans of *Star Trek* television series (1966–1969), from the red shirts worn by Starfleet security officers who frequently die during episodes. Redshirt deaths are often used to dramatize the potential peril that the main characters face."

Also, don't be afraid to "bleed your lead." This really drives home the stakes.

EXERCISE

1. Take time to make a list of things that make you feel scared, anxious, unsettled. Find your fear.

2. Manifest it in some form.

   a. Pick a familiar "safe" object or living thing in your home—a blender, your printer, a plant or animal, or a loved one. The more innocuous and seemingly safe, the better. We all know a knife is dangerous . . . but a hamster?

OR

b. Create something that falls outside of the rules of our normal reality. Avoid the well-used tropes of vampires, werewolves, zombies . . .

3. Pick the stakes/jeopardy.

4. Write a short story of how your protagonist first begins to realize something is wrong, tries to fight/escape, throw in a Redshirt or two, and let it finish so that the reader is left unsettled (i.e., the protagonist doesn't win).

BEN THOMPSON

Diabolical Evil for Beginners

BEN THOMPSON is the author of the books *Badass*, *Badass: The Birth of a Legend*, and *Badass: Ultimate Deathmatch* (both published by HarperCollins). He has also written articles for *Cracked*, *Fangoria*, and *Penthouse* and was once selected "Seattle's Sexiest Dungeon Master" by a local newspaper.

It's no secret that we all have a soft spot for villains. From the most hardcore, cigar-chomping, Harley-riding gang enforcer to the puffy-cheeked Boy Scout leader who helps old ladies cross the street while earning their archery merit badges and tying slipknots, all of us have an inexplicable fascination with planet-destroying evil super-geniuses, chainsaw-wielding cannibal psychopaths, time-traveling alien Fascist space tanks, and whatever other soulless, diabolically malicious bastards seem to find their way into our fiction on a regular basis.

It's not that we're bad people. Sure, we might struggle with the occasional bout of crippling megalomania or an uncontrollable death rage against all humanity after a particularly gnarly day at the cubicle farm, but most of us simply aren't going to react to a stack of annoying TPS reports by building an army of mutants and trying to conquer Mars. Call it apathy, call it a lack of ambition, or call it a marginally rational brain that possesses the ability to remind us that revenge probably isn't worth having James Bond drop in through a skylight and shoot you in the head with a Walther PPK when you least expect it, but we just aren't hardwired that way.

Villains, however . . . villains aren't confined to our pitifully narrow definitions of morality and sanity. These hellacious bastards don't have a problem taking everything just a single step too far, making sure the punishment is fifty times worse than the crime, and reacting to adverse living conditions by acquiring a couple dozen weapons of mass destruction and wreaking vengeance on everyone who ever wronged them. And, while you and I probably aren't going to set off a dirty bomb in our boss's office just because he asked us to come in on a Saturday, deep down we can kind of respect the fact that these villains would rather be stabbed in the eye with a samurai sword than let anyone push them around. We can almost get on board with it. Sure, we know this dude is a bad guy, and we still want our hero to punch his face in, but the good villains—the *really* good villains—are so cool you're almost sorry to see them go. It's what makes them some of the best characters in fiction. Here's a method for making one memorable.

EXERCISE

1. *Take a Guy.* Villains aren't born at the controls of solar system–devouring spaceships with legions of loyal followers ready to lay down their lives according to their leader's whims. They all come from somewhere. Sure, maybe they're smarter or stronger or more handsome than your typical citizen, but even the mighty Sauron started out as your average run-of-the-mill Elf before he was changed into a gigantic glowing eye that radiates pure unadulterated hatred. If you want your villains to be even a little bit relatable, the reader has to at least superficially understand where the dude is coming from. And that means starting at the bottom. Who is this guy? Where did he come from? What was his childhood like? His mother? What are his hopes and dreams? His fears? What sort of music does he listen to? What did he study in college? The reader shouldn't be hearing stories about your diabolical villain eating apple pie in the kitchen of his idyllic boyhood home, but dropping subtle little hints about his backstory will humanize him and give a third dimension to his character.

2. *Ruin His Life.* Villains rarely grew up aspiring to evil. Victor von Doom didn't wake up one morning and say, "Hey, I'm going to conquer the Eastern European country of Latveria, install myself as dictator, build an army of robotic clones, and then encase my body in a bulletproof metal suit that shoots lasers and lets me walk on the ocean floor." Something terrible happened to force him to such desperate measures. Rather than give up and lay down, he responded by unleashing his insanity and turning himself into Doctor Doom.

You need to take your regular guy and push him too far. Maybe the scientific establishment doesn't appreciate his ability to fabricate artificial human life out of orange goo and recycled animal parts. Maybe some jackass murdered his family and he's a little sore about it. Maybe the hero surpassed him in a test of physical strength and rode off into the sunset with the girl, so now our guy is dealing with inadequacy issues because he knows he could intellectually run circles around that meathead. You can't be too brutal—something made this guy strive for world domination, and whatever drives a guy to something like that probably has to be really, really bad. Cut his arms and legs off. Burn him with acid. Put him in a wheelchair. Have kids be really mean to him in school, slap the lunch tray out of his hands, then not pick him for kickball. Whatever it takes. Be ruthless . . . your villain sure will be.

3. *Plot Vengeance.* Now that you've got a desperate man or woman with a chip on his or her shoulder and nothing left to lose, it's time for a sweet, delicious, organic, free-range dish of vengeance served cold (naturally) with toasted almonds and a fat scoop of guacamole. Whom does he hate? Why? How is he going to ruin them? What's his ultimate goal in life, the end result of his evil machinations? Why is he doing this? What are the potential obstacles to his scheme, and how is he going to prepare for them? How far is he willing to go with this? Does he realize he's the bad guy and just not care, or does he feel completely vindicated by the righteousness of his cause?

4. *Pump Him Up.* Once you've settled on your motive, it's time to find the means. Usually this takes the form of a sizeable stack of cash money acquired through illicit means, but this isn't always the case—sometimes it's just a big machete and a hockey mask, or an ancient curse that allows him to absorb more physical punishment than the Terminator. Hannibal Lecter had his super intellect. Vader could choke people from across the room and carried a weapon that could cut steel like it was styrofoam. Godzilla had radioactive fallout mutate him into a city-stomping reptilian monstrosity. The Shredder used dark magic and a lifetime of martial arts training to fight the Teenage Mutant Ninja Turtles. Your guy needs a weapon, be it a wallet, a brain, or an assault rifle, and the opportunity to use it. What are your villain's powers? How did he get them? What are their limits, and what are their shortcomings? Does he show them off or keep them hidden? When it's time for combat, what does he fight with?

5. *Give Him Some Henchmen.* No matter how smooth and intelligent he is, Hans Gruber isn't going to take over the Nakatomi Tower by himself—he needs an army of well-equipped East German terrorists to do his dirty work while he kicks back and looks menacing. Evil geniuses don't make their own PB&J; they surround themselves with associates who make up for their own shortcomings while simultaneously providing our hero an endless stream of faceless jobbers to cleave through on his way to rescuing the girl. Dr. Frankenstein is smart, but he needs an Igor to fetch him brains. Sauron is omnipotent, but he's just a floating eye and isn't going to get much done without breeding some Orcs. Skeletor has magical powers and the body of a beefy-armed bodybuilder, but he's got monster men who run around to do his dirty work for him so he doesn't have to. Find out where your villain is weak; then give him henchmen to fill in the cracks. Does he ride a talking bear or just drive a car like a normal human being? Does he have an army of Cyborg minions, a fleet of mercenary employees, or just one single guy with a broadsword who shows up at really inopportune times?

Why do these people follow him, and where do they come from? How does he provide for them? How does he inspire their loyalty? How far are they willing to go for him? How much of a threat do they pose to the hero? Does he even need henchmen at all, or is your villain a one-man wrecking crew? If he's a lone wolf, how does he swing that?

6. *Make Him Good Arch-Nemesis Material.* You want to make as many parallels between your hero and your villain as you possibly can. These guys are in the same boat—the hero just did the right thing, and the villain went completely out of his gourd and plummeted off the deep end of sanity. Luke Skywalker could have easily been Darth Vader if he'd just made a couple of terrible life decisions. Moriarty is just Sherlock Holmes if he used his powers for evil. Even Ahab and Moby-Dick have something in common—a ruthless desire to kill each other. Draw parallels where you can, shoehorn them in where it fits, and do it without making it too cheesy and contrived. Every little detail matters.

7. *Give Him a Fatal Flaw.* So now you've got a bad mother with a single-minded need to avenge himself on the world, the means to do it, and the opportunity to exact his cruel justice on all who wronged him. How is he going to be stopped? Is he a little too powerful?

Luckily for human existence, most villains have one fatal flaw that eventually causes their downfall. Usually it's hubris, which is a fancy term for extreme overconfidence. These guys know they've got the upper hand, and the moment they snatch it, they start talking all crazy and giving up their evil plans and letting the hero get out from underneath their heels rather than simply crushing their throat. They lose at the moment of their greatest victory.

Your villain doesn't need to give in to hubris, but if you want your good guys to emerge victorious, you'll need there to be some weakness they can exploit. It could be a henchman of questionable loyalty. It could be a piece of crucial information the hero has that the villain doesn't know about. It could be a crippling jealousy you can play on to get the bad guy to drop his guard. There needs to be something for the hero to take advantage of, and you need to lay it out there early and often.

Congrats! You're off and running with a delightfully evil character. Good luck on the world domination thing. Just remember that you can never make your villain too evil, too ruthless, or too cunning. Don't pull any punches, because to be perfectly honest, if your story sucks, nine times out of ten it's because your villain sucks.

EDWARD DeGEORGE

Seeking the Darkness

EDWARD DeGEORGE is the producer/lead writer for the Web series *Sombras*. His horror fiction has appeared in anthologies such as *Hell in the Heartland*, *Día de los Muertos*, and *Spooks!*

Writing horror is about bringing fear and dread to the reader as though you were Prometheus. It is your gift to the world. A terrible, terrible gift.

Fear can be found in many places. The most primal of these is in darkness. Picture man at his earliest, huddling in caves, building fires to hold back the night. Could he be certain the sun would rise to banish the dark? Where light symbolizes good, darkness is synonymous with evil. The things of darkness seek to harm you and can make you afraid.

Because we depend so on our sight, we fear being unable to use our eyes. What we cannot see, we cannot identify. It is the unknown. It is every worst monster our imaginations can conjure, forces against which we are helpless.

I remember many dark-night walks home from a friend's house. The short path took me off suburban sidewalks and through an innocent field, but a deserted place. The light at night, from the moon, from the stars, it lends everything an unnatural pallor. Is the field shunned? Does something lurk in the tall grasses? Is something about to reach out and touch me with icy hands?

As Grandma would say, "Nothing good ever happens after midnight." Children understand. They fear things that hide under the bed, where your only protection is to pull the covers up to your chin. I remember that chilling scene in THE GRUDGE where the young

135

woman found out that even the last refuge of her bed was no longer a safe haven.

Closing your eyes won't approximate the feeling. You need to immerse yourself in utter darkness, your eyes wide open, but making not a whit of difference.

I recommend not a writing exercise per se that involves paper and pencil, but experiences to write about later. Commit these experiences to memory. Use your imagination to stoke your fear. If you can frighten yourself, it may help you to frighten your reader.

EXERCISE

1. Take a walk in the dark. No, I don't mean at nine-thirty. Venture into the true dark after midnight, when the streets are deserted and the neighboring houses unlit. In the dead of night you can even find fear in your own backyard. How many steps away from the safety of your home is one step too many? Summon fear. Remember the sensations: your breath, your heartbeat, your body temperature.

2. Crawl under the bed. Imagine being buried alive. The sound of the dirt as it hits the coffin lid. The entire weight of the earth presses down on you. Every breath diminishes your supply of life-giving oxygen. Paralysis grips you. And something is in there with you, crawling at your feet.

3. Hide in the closet. Imagine your hunter stalking you. Feel the tension of being someone or something's prey. It's only a matter of time. Something draws closer. And you are trapped.

Scare yourself. Feel fear, nurture it, then write something that will terrify your readers.

LISA MORTON

The Setting in Horror

LISA MORTON is a screenwriter, Halloween expert, and the author of dozens of short horror stories published in books and magazines like *Dark Delicacies*, *Cemetery Dance*, and *Zombie Apocalypse!* She won the Bram Stoker Award for First Novel with *The Castle of Los Angeles* and her first fiction collection, *Monsters of L.A.*, was published by Bad Moon Books.

Think about your favorite horror stories in literature, and I'm betting that a place will figure prominently somehow. Bram Stoker's *Dracula*? It made Transylvania an iconic horror locale. Stephen King's *Salem's Lot*? Heck, the setting is so important that King chose it for the title. How about all the haunted house novels, short stories set in graveyards, or the books in which a middle-aged narrator must return to battle evil in the small town where he was born?

Horror is successful when it disturbs or frightens the reader, when it creates both an overall atmosphere and provides quick shocks, and choosing a setting is one of the best ways to provide a mood underlying the whole piece. It would be difficult, for example, to create a prolonged, sinister feeling for a story set in a sunny meadow . . . but move that same tale to an isolated, moonlit street with only one empty house at the end, and your eerie quotient has just been turned way up.

A great horror setting can serve to make your reader instantly uncomfortable, before you've even mentioned a monster or a murder. Look, for example, at David Morrell's award-winning *Creepers*, about a group of urban explorers who decide to tackle the Paragon Hotel, a once-great art deco structure now falling to ruin. Morrell has taken the typical haunted house and removed the ghosts; even without the supernatural inhabitants, old buildings carry their own unnerving charge. But Morrell isn't content to just let his setting sustain a low-key mood; throughout the novel, he also uses the location to surprise, as when part of it suddenly gives way or creates another danger for the group. In this case, the setting *is* the monster.

Sometimes a horror location can carry an entire series of stories. H. P. Lovecraft's fictitious town Arkham, Massachusetts, appeared in a number of his classic works, including "The Colour Out of Space" and "The Shadow Over Innsmouth." Lovecraft not only created a history for the town, but used it as the home for other recurring elements from his mythos, including Miskatonic University (and Lovecraft's creation of Arkham was so skilled that it was used by other authors after Lovecraft's death, and even provided the name for a publishing company, Arkham House). More recently, Gary Braunbeck's Cedar Hill, a non-existent town in Ohio, has been home to dozens of short stories and novels; Braunbeck has so carefully mapped every detail of the town's history and layout that it's hard to believe it doesn't exist. (But given how much terror has happened in that burg, I think you'll agree that it's a good thing it isn't real!)

Sometimes a setting is designed to serve as a sort of stand-in for a typical American location. Green Town, Illinois, for example, doesn't exist anywhere but in Ray Bradbury's *Something Wicked This Way Comes* (and several of his other works), but Bradbury plainly intended the town to serve as a classic American small town, instantly recognizable to anyone who has even driven through one. Because Green Town is an "everytown," when it is invaded by horrifying elements (Mr. Dark's carnival in *Something Wicked*), we almost feel as if our own hometown is in immediate danger.

Even a small setting can be used to generate suspense and discomfort. Charlotte Perkins Gilman's classic story "The Yellow Wallpaper" is about a woman going mad in a single room, one where the walls are covered in "a smouldering unclean yellow." Richard Matheson's 1950 short story "Born of Man and Woman" is set entirely in a claustrophobic basement, emphasizing the gloomy captivity of its pathetic narrator, a deformed child caged by its parents.

Real locations are found less often in horror, but can be equally effective, if used correctly. For example: Anne Rice's use of New Orleans as the setting for parts of *Interview with the Vampire* underscores the age, style, and decadence of her eternal bloodsuckers. Sometimes an existing place's reputation can be put to good use as well: Goethe, for instance, played on folklore beliefs surrounding the Brocken (a mountain in Germany) when he chose to set a wild witches' revel there in *Faust*.

In my own novel *The Castle of Los Angeles*, I created a fictitious building—the Castle—and set it in a real place—downtown Los Angeles. The Castle is based in part on the real-life Los Angeles artists' community known as the Brewery; but of course had I chosen to set my story within the real Brewery, I would have not only possibly run afoul of legal action (I'm sure the Brewery's owners would rather not perpetuate the notion that murderous ghosts haunt its halls), I would have risked raising the eyebrows of everyone who had ever visited the Brewery and knew quite well that it was not in fact haunted. Creating the Castle also allowed me to control the geography of the story—it was important to me that the building have a huge celebrity penthouse, which the real Brewery doesn't. Setting my Castle in virtually the same area where the Brewery resides, however, allowed me to suggest that the Castle—and its spectral residents—certainly *could* be real.

EXERCISE

Think about your own home and the neighborhood where you live. Is there an area reputed to be haunted? Or someplace where something dreadful happened, perhaps a place that has since been abandoned as a result? If you don't know much about the history of your town, you might try checking out the local library or talking to friends who've delved into the area's folklore. Exploring online can be helpful too; most towns now have Facebook groups or discussion boards for people who are interested in the town's provenance.

Once you've found or decided on an area, visit it in person, then write a detailed description. Note as much about it as you can—the streets, other buildings, even plants, architectural details, or furnishings.

Now imagine characters in that area, how they'd move around it, what they'd think of it. Would it initially present a nice place, somewhere they'd like to stay? Or is it a spooky place right from the start, but some other part of the action compels them to stay there? Does it present possibilities for shocks—branches that can suddenly snap, pavement that might cave in, structures that could collapse?

A word of caution: As much as description can add to the terror, don't overdo describing your setting to the point where you begin to slow down your pace. After visiting and researching your location you'll probably have plenty of notes, but you should pick just a few of the most evocative bits to lay out your setting for the reader. Several carefully chosen items—just a rotted step and a broken window, for example—will usually work better than filling up pages with every small observation catalogued in detail.

JAN KOZLOWSKI

Bringing Horror Home

JAN KOZLOWSKI first fell in love with horror in 1975 when the single drop of ruby red blood on the engraved black cover of Stephen King's *Salem's Lot* hypnotized her into buying it. Her short stories appear in *Hungry for Your Love: An Anthology of Zombie Romance* and *Fang Bangers: An Erotic Anthology of Fangs, Claws, Sex and Love*. Her novel—*Die, You Bastard! Die!*—debuted in 2012 as part of the new horror imprint, Ravenous Shadows.

I'm a big fan of Stephen King. As my bio says, it was the paperback version of his second book, *Salem's Lot*, that turned me on to horror back in the mid-seventies. Why King, though? Why not Lovecraft or Poe or any of the dozens of other paperback/pulp horror writers who filled the revolving wire rack at the local drugstore? Why didn't any of those other guys (and they were all guys in those days) hook me the way King did?

The answer, for me anyway, has always been that not only did Stephen King's best stories scare the hell out of me; they did it by proving that horror is not something that just happens in creepy Transylvanian castles or in far-off alien worlds. King's horror happened to people just like me, who were suddenly plunged into terrifying situations as they went about their normal, everyday lives.

I realize that this type of story might not be everyone's cup of tea. Perhaps you prefer evil government agencies running amok, jet-setting serial killers, or sparkly vampires, but personally, King's style of "suburban horror" is not only the kind of story I'm willing to plunk down money to read, it's the type of story I prefer to write myself.

The exercises below are ones that I use when I'm trying to generate plot and character ideas. Thanks to Ray Bradbury and his fabulous book *Zen in the Art of Writing: Essays on Creativity* for showing me the value of using word association lists as writing tools.

EXERCISE

1. Make two lists. First, write a list of places you go or things you do on a regular basis, like picking up the dry cleaning, dropping off the dog at the groomers, or getting stuck in traffic on the Arrigoni Bridge.

   Second, make a list of your fears and phobias. Mine, for example, include a paralyzing terror of natural bodies of water that I was able to plug into for the swamp scene in my novel, *Die, You Bastard! Die!* Check out The Phobia List at phobialist.com if you need ideas or inspiration.

   Once you have the two lists, pick one entry from each and give yourself five minutes to write down everything that comes to mind, no matter how "out there" it may seem. After time is up, read over what you've got. Is there a story germ there? A character, setting, or possible plot line that clicks for you? Explore it. If nothing worked, try another pairing.

2. The next time you're stuck in a line somewhere, instead of sitting or standing around fuming, try imagining what is the worst thing that could happen to you *right now*. The Hindu demon Rakshasa laying waste to your local coffee shop? A flaming tractor-trailer barreling down on you as you're stuck in line at a tollbooth? A serial killer lurking in the movie theater restroom? Let your fears and phobias come out to play, then write it all down, paying particular attention to the emotions that crop up.

BUILDING WORLDS

"I didn't think; I experimented."
—ANTHONY BURGESS

"We're not in Kansas anymore . . ."
—DOROTHY, IN *THE WONDERFUL WIZARD OF OZ,* BY L. FRANK BAUM

E. E. KING

Fact into Fiction

E. E. KING is the award-winning author of *Dirk Quigby's Guide to the Afterlife* (Exterminating Angel Press) and *Real Conversations with Imaginary* Friends (27th Dimension Publishing). Her newest novel is *The Card Game*, which was serialized at IsotropicFiction.com. She has received international writing, biology, and painting grants and worked on various biology projects around the world.

I remember the first time and place I did it consciously. It was in Bucyrus, Ohio. I had just written a perfect "flash." Flash fiction is usually defined as fiction under 1,000 words. When I am reading aloud, performing what I refer to as literary stand-up, I prefer 200 words. That way, if the piece isn't going well at least it's over quickly.

Publishing however is a different matter. My favorite length of fiction is too long to tweet and too short to story. If you sell by the word, it's a starvation diet.

When I was invited to share an exercise I use when writing, I did not want to create one. I desired to share an insight. Something I do, each and every time I write. When I write, even micro-flash fiction, I use fact and I research, the longer the piece, the more extensive the research.

The following is the story that made me conscious of what I was doing.

THE SANDS OF TIME

In the sands of time, which lie between the past and memory, a small boy travels. He'd begun the journey an unpleasant, snot-nosed brat.

*By the time he arrives in his mother's reminiscences, he has turned
into a prince, handsome, smart, and valiant. In the distance between
reality and his father's recollections, he has become obedient, loving,
and a fabulous athlete. Now a man, he listens to his parents' stories.
When the little boy manages to cross the desert to his fully grown self,
he remembers his parents' memories. He had indeed been wise beyond
his years—brilliant, altruistic, empathetic, true, kind, and a wonder
at sports. His sister Carol however, still remembers him as an unpleasant, snot-nosed brat.*

Done! But, though easy to publish, good for resume building, I
wanted to expand. I decided to follow Carol. She was obviously unhappy and resentful. Why? She had probably been thwarted. She had
ended up in some small, almost certainly unpleasant, oddly named
town in the Midwest . . . Ohio possibly . . . I began a search and stumbled into Bucyrus, Ohio, Bratwurst Capital of the World. It's a real
place. In the Roaring Twenties, Al Capone used to stop off in Bucyrus
at an underground speakeasy. For decades, the speakeasy was forgotten; a tangled network of underground tunnels weaving twisted
roots under the streets of Bucyrus. Now, it is used as a storage space
by Cooper's Cider Mill. They keep apples there, fermenting between
walls so thick, even the spray of Tommy gun bullets couldn't pene-
trate.

That was when I realized, for me, that research and fact are where
I go for inspiration.

Perhaps it's because I am a biologist. Perhaps it's because all good
tales, be they fantasy, sci-fi, or horror are constructed on a frame of
truth. Truth is not stranger than fiction because it is odd, but because
it is true. Ocean reef fish change sex at least once in their lives. Slime
molds have more than 750 different sexes.

And biology doesn't even touch on the relatively recent (pun intended) worlds of quantum theory, infinite realities in the spiraling
strings of space. Another reality could be less than a tissue paper's
width apart from the here and now, or even in the same space but
upon another dimension. Two paths diverge in a yellow wood; you
take them both at the same instance.

Although I love fantasy, I am married to fact. Where does your tale take place? Even if it's an invented city, or an imagined planet, reality and science will aid you.

EXERCISE

1. First, always write down ideas or lines, even if they wake you at 2:00 a.m., especially if they wake you at 2:00 a.m. You may think you will remember, but you won't. Ray Bradbury, my mentor, said: "Throw it up in the morning and clean it up in the afternoon."

   Example: *"He was a tailor/psychiatrist. He designed suits to keep in all those messy emotions."* This is a jumping off point. Now you have to decide when and where your tale takes place. Maybe it's in a small town on Mars? Research both small towns and Mars, and you will create some very real fantasy.

2. Are there flowers in this world? What do they look like, and most importantly how do they get pollinated? Consider the drive behind every living thing . . . reproduction! Birds do it, bees do it, flowers and trees do it . . . and they do it in millions of weird and wonderful ways. It doesn't matter if you are not writing about sex. Creation is not just about passing on one's genes. It encompasses the transmission of ideas and visions, a piece of art, attempting to control the world. Same drive, different outcome.

3. We see only a small percent of color and a fraction of smells and sounds. What do other animals see, hear, and smell? Do a little research and the world will supply ideas.

DAVID ANTHONY DURHAM

Think Historical

DAVID ANTHONY DURHAM is the author of six award-winning works of historical fiction and fantasy. The first of his Acacia epic fantasy series was a Prix Imaginales finalist and won the John W. Campbell Award for best new writer of science fiction. His novels have twice been *New York Times* Notable Books, won two awards from the American Library Association, and been translated into eight languages.

Before embarking on an epic fantasy series (the Acacia Trilogy), I wrote three historical novels. A lot of folks asked, "Why the dramatic change?" Wasn't writing fantasy totally different than dealing with historical material? I didn't think so then, and I still don't.

As a writer of historical fiction, you're bringing to life a world that no longer exists anywhere but in your imagination. It may seem foreign to readers, with different cultural norms, technological levels, spiritual beliefs, and knowledge of science. The exact same things can be said about speculative settings.

Often, the same issues that trip up historical writers can prove troublesome for science fiction and fantasy writers. In historical fiction, we struggle with how to world build, what details to convey, how to avoid anachronisms, and how to chronicle the events that have shaped the time we're writing about. Again, all the same things are true of science fiction and fantasy. As a speculative writer, you may be making facts up instead of researching them, but you still need to find the best ways to convey the details of your world to readers.

Also, world building in historical fiction isn't just about reciting historical facts, names, places, makes, and models. Those may be the things of history books, but fictions set in history have to breathe life into them. Settings need to feel grounded, lived-in, real. They need to be filled with details that are the small stuff of life. With that in mind, I offer the following exercise.

I suggest approaching this as a series of four timed-writing exercises. You can come back and revise later. For the first attempt, I want you to set a timer for three minutes (for each part), turn it on, and start writing. Don't stop until the timer goes off. Keep your pen moving the whole time. If you have to write nonsense, do it. But keep refocusing on the topic even as you let the first things that come to your mind pour straight out of your pen.

Let's give it a try. This exercise is one I first developed for writing historical fiction. For our purposes, I've recast it for the speculative genres.

EXERCISE

1. Take three minutes and describe the interior of a building, a room from some specific time or place. It could be recognizably Earth, a variation on Earth, another planet, or a fantasy world. Don't tell us the location overtly. Instead, just describe visually the things that appear in your mind, large details and small. Try to just let pour the things you imagine you would see and feel and smell in your room—wherever in the universe it is.

2. Take three minutes and write a description of a character who's in the room you've just described. Make him or her someone you're interested in, someone with traits of the specific setting but also with things that are unique to her or him.

3. Let's hear your character talk. Have him or her begin with some small talk, speaking to someone else he or she knows, and going wherever it goes thereafter.

4. Now get to the meat of the conversation. Introduce the problem that's been behind your character's small talk, something that has been influenced by the setting, something you've never faced in your twenty first-century life, but which will hit the reader in the gut in some way. What is the troubling situation that's about to spark where this story goes?

MARK SEBANC

In Xanadu . . . Grounding the Fantastic

MARK SEBANC is the co-author of the Legacy of the Stone Harp fantasy series with James G. Anderson. The first two novels in the sequence are *The Stoneholding* and *Darkling Fields of Arvon*. Both are published by Baen Books. Sebanc has also worked as an editor and translator.

In the realm of folklore, a special, oftentimes sinister, significance is attributed to the in-between places, the earthen boundary between forest and ploughland, for example, or the in-between times like dawn and twilight, which mark the slow-stepping progressions of day and night towards one another.

At the same time, these places and times of shape-shifting uncertainty are suggestive of mystery and hopeful possibility. In many ways such boundaries stand as a metaphor for the dangers and ambiguities that mark the frontiers of human experience in all its enigmatic fragility, things like birth and death, sickness and health, loss and gain, wayfaring and homecoming, and so on.

Similarly, in an uncanny echo of this vital aspect of our humanness, fantasy as a literary genre occupies the uncertain, frontier area between what's "true to life" and soaring flights of the imagination that beckon the reader toward the unfamiliar and the strange. For those of us who practice the craft of words, fantasy can pose some serious artistic challenges, precisely because it occupies such perilously unsure ground.

Writing speculative fiction can be a tough row to hoe, one that requires the exercise of high standards of good judgment, as we try to negotiate our way through the pitfalls and dangers of the ground that lies between a sturdy realism and the figments conjured by our imagination. Like all writers from time immemorial, what we're aiming to induce in the reader is a *willing suspension of disbelief,* a term coined by the nineteenth-century English poet Samuel Taylor Coleridge.

According to one school of thought, writers should write about what they know, i.e. their own life experiences. When it comes to the genre of fantasy, this rule of thumb clearly needs to be revisited and qualified. To give a notable example, Elves and Orcs did not stem from Tolkien's practical knowledge of the world. This is because Tolkien wrote quite properly about not only what he knew, but what he was able to envision by way of his fertile imagination. In so doing, he attracted vast legions of readers. But it wasn't all about his imagination. In the end, it was about balance. Tolkien succeeded in spectacular fashion because he portrayed perfectly the homey, reassuring realities of everyday life, while setting them in a compelling imaginary world quite out of the ordinary. The key thing about Tolkien's imagination is that it is not arbitrary, nor is it a faculty untethered from reality.

As fantastic and extraordinary as the outpourings of his imagination are, they are marked by an overarching coherence and groundedness. They resonate with the reader because they exhibit a two-fold strength. On the one hand, they are placed in a matrix of ordinary life, many of whose aspects we recognize as normal and human. In this respect, Tolkien wrote about what he knew and experienced. On the other hand, his creative approach is steeped in his vast scholarly knowledge of old England and the medieval world of northern Europe, which he embroiders with his own flights of genius and inventiveness. In this respect, Tolkien's imaginary creations illustrate the proverbial wisdom inherent in the statement that truth is stranger than fiction.

Of all genres, fantasy most requires the touchstone of truth as an aid to the reader in the suspension of disbelief. Just as electrical devices need to be grounded, so too does speculative fiction. Otherwise, it risks becoming literally incredible, a phantasmagoria of the bizarre. In our Legacy of the Stone Harp series, my co-author Jim Anderson and I have made it a key principle that our invented world of Ahn Norvys should in vital ways mirror the laws and constraints of the real world.

Of course, the actual nature and extent of this grounding in the real varies from work to work and is in the end a matter of artistic judgment and preference. Jim and I are convinced, however, that by pursuing a fairly rigorous exclusion of plot devices that depend on the miraculous, we have added plausibility to our portrayal of Ahn Norvys. This is not to say that we do not have thematic elements that are arrestingly strange, evocatively suggestive of the miraculous.

The theme of *songlines* that we use in our series is a good example. It's an idea that was sparked when I read travel writer Bruce Chatwin's book on the importance of this concept for Australian aborigines. The concept of ley lines is also very similar to that of songlines, suggesting fresh, new, even haunting, ways of regarding the world around us.

For me, travel writing and historical nonfiction have always played an important role as stimulants of my imagination. I'm thinking here in particular of the thought-provoking theories of alternative archaeology proposed by a writer like Graham Hancock, or the fascinating accounts of ancient Mongol and Chinese civilization tendered by John Man, for example. It's all wonderful grist for the mill and serves to keep our work within the limits of credibility.

In "Kubla Khan," one of the most famous poems of the Romantic period, Coleridge provides another excellent illustration of what I mean here. An important commentator on the role of the imagination in literature, Coleridge begins with a lavishly fanciful, indeed fantastic, description of Xanadu, the summer palace of the Mongol emperor from whom the poem takes its name. While in the poem Xanadu is actually much more reminiscent of Coleridge's native Somerset than it is of northern China, we learn that he drew his inspiration for the poem from a passage in the writings of Samuel Purchas, an Elizabethan geographer.

EXERCISE

Consider an area of the world that you're interested in or some place by which you feel intrigued. Then go on a search engine like Google for twenty or thirty minutes, looking for historical information or travel blogs on the subject. Keep your eyes open for any tidbit that might serve as an example of truth being stranger than fiction, and that might be used as the keynote of an alternative world.

The Web being such a vast and wonderful place, odds are you'll find more than enough material that strikes your fancy. After that, spend fifteen to twenty minutes framing out a one- or two-paragraph outline that could be used as the basis for a novel.

MELISSA SCOTT

Humming the Sets: World Building
That Supports the Story

MELISSA SCOTT is the author of more than twenty science fiction and fantasy novels, and has won Lambda Literary Awards, Spectrum Awards, and the John W. Campbell Award for best new writer. Her recent novels, written with Jo Graham, are *Lost Things* and the sequel *Steel Blues* (Crossroad Press).

There's an old joke about musical theater that seems perennially relevant to discussions of world building in science fiction and fantasy (SFF): no matter how good a designer you are, no one leaves the show humming the sets. While this isn't entirely true in SFF—there are books that are loved as much for their worlds as for their characters—the fact remains that, in most cases, the worlds you spend months creating remain sets, settings in which the characters and the story are lovingly displayed. Even novels that are noted for their elaborately worked-out worlds—*The Lord of the Rings*, for example—wouldn't have attracted so many passionate readers if it weren't for the characters and their story.

Of course, the details of your world are vitally important because of the basic nature of SFF. Most work in the genre is written as though it is in fact a realistic novel, using all the conventions of realistic fiction; however, the world described is entirely imaginary, and often impossible. The reason behind this is to give readers a way into a vast array of wildly differing fictional worlds: No matter how peculiar the world, how far-fetched the science, you're using a frame that readers understand. They know how to interpret the forms; you're just filling them with unfamiliar information.

This is part of persuading readers to suspend their disbelief: the buildup of solid, consistent details that seem to follow logically from the choices you've made; and to make it work, you have to know your imaginary world inside and out. The weirder your central premise, the more solid your supporting details have to be. Even if the point of the story is the discovery of something new, or the exploration of a strange place, so that the characters (and thus the readers) are learning about the world as they explore it, you as a writer need to know more than they do, so that you can select the perfect detail that directs (or misdirects) the reader's attention.

The other reason for knowing your world in detail is that it helps you learn about your characters. The world shapes your characters; it sets limits on what they can do for a living, on how they live, on what they can imagine, even on their physical bodies. The more you know about the world, the more fine detail you can add to your picture, the better you understand how to shape your characters' lives and choices.

For example, in writing *Dreamships*, I knew that the population of Persephone, where the novel is set, was split between Freyan "coolies" who had been brought in to work the lower-level jobs, and corporate employees from the Urban Worlds, who control most of the managerial functions. There would be a distinct linguistic split between the groups, and the coolies—a relatively small and impoverished population even on their original home world—had a large deaf population for whom sign language is their primary medium of communication. The novel's main character, Reverdy Jian, straddles both worlds: she works in the industrial upperworld, and is fluent in sign, but she was born to the midworld and educated there. She doesn't really fit anywhere in Persephone's stratified society. As I worked out more details, I realized that silence was almost always a sign of lower status, of social weakness. And that meant that Reverdy, who would not concede she was anything but a person of status, would never not say what was on her mind. That realization shaped every bit of dialogue in the novel.

A word of warning: You won't, and probably shouldn't, use everything you discover, or at least you won't put them into the story directly. However, you will know what the world looks like outside the focus of the story, what lies around the corners and in the un-entered rooms; you'll have a much better idea of who your characters are and why they make their choices. The implicit knowledge, and the consistency it creates, will make for a better story.

EXERCISE

This is an exercise that I come back to repeatedly, because it lets me work on world and character at the same time, each reinforcing the other.

1. The Ordinary Day: What do your characters do on a normal day? What do they do for a living, and how does that shape their daily rhythm? What is their ordinary, mindless routine? What are the things that they do and see and hear that they never really notice? (This is particularly useful to fill out the background of characters who are breaking out of their usual lives to get involved in the events of a novel.)

2. Take the Day Off: If, just for once, your characters have no outside obligations, what do they do with their holiday? What do they do for fun and relaxation? What do they do when they're not on duty, when no one's counting on them? What's the fanciest evening's entertainment your characters could imagine, and what could they actually afford? What would they dare to do? (This is especially good for characters whose jobs are at the focus of the story.)

L. E. MODESITT, JR.

System Rules

L. E. MODESITT, JR., has written more than sixty published novels and numerous short stories as well as technical publications in the environmental and economic fields. Although he is possibly best known for his Saga of Recluce fantasy series, with over two million books in print, and the more recent Imager Portfolio series (both Tor Fantasy), he continues to write science fiction as well.

I f you're going to write speculative fiction, that generally means that you're going to write about worlds where there is either a different level of technology or where magic exists—if not both. One of the problems that all too many beginning writers have in dealing with magic or technology is that they don't understand how a failure to structure the use and costs of either technology or magic can undermine an entire book.

I actually wrote my very first fantasy, *The Magic of Recluce,* because I was tired of fantasy novels with flawed or patently unworkable magic systems, many of which weren't well thought out, or were lifted whole from either traditional folklore or gaming systems, and clearly didn't exactly apply to what the author had in mind. When I began, I faced the very real problem of creating a magic system that was logical, rational, and workable, within a practical economic, political, and technological structure that was neither particularly exotic nor borrowed lock, stock, and barrel from western European history.

While writers today generally do a better job of creating magic systems, all too often they don't think out all the implications of the magic they invent. The following questions are designed to address those implications. Although it is structured in dealing with "magic," many of the questions also apply to advanced technology.

EXERCISE

EIGHT QUESTIONS FOR A MAGIC SYSTEM

Use these to examine how your magic system works:

1. *Is the magic system logical and practical, or illogical, or arbitrary?* This may seem like an obvious question, and it is, but the implications of the choice are not. Almost invariably, a logical and practical magic system offers the characters hope and the chance that, at the very least, they can come to terms with the world. A magical system that is arbitrary and does not follow the rules can leave characters at the whim or mercy of a capricious world. This is not necessarily bad, but it does lead to a different type of story.

2. *What is the source of the magic?* Does it come from a theological source (gods or goddesses), or does it come from the ability to exploit the structure or workings of the world? If it comes from a theological source, it has to be, by definition, less powerful than the magic of the deity who grants it and will likely have conditions attached.

    If it comes from the structure of the world, it will be limited and affected by the world itself, but will also theoretically be able to affect the world.

3. *How powerful is the magic, and what limits it?* By practical definition, magic has to have limits, because, if there are no limits, it can and will destroy the universe in which you're writing, besides which, if it's a part of your universe, the part can't be greater than the whole.

4. *Who can use magic and why?* Generally speaking, magic use can be determined by genetics (inherited ability), disciplined skill honed by knowledge and training, or "grace" (i.e., bestowed by a higher power) . . . or some combination of those conditions.

In any human society, and probably any society of intelligent beings, any skill of great power or value will be able to be mastered only by a small number of people.

5. *What is required of a magic user?* Any use of a high-level skill exacts a toll on the user. That can range from the requirement for long years of training to master the skill, to the need to live apart, or to continually use the skill to maintain that power . . . or to age more quickly . . . but there are costs, and those costs should be consistent for all users. The greater the use of any power the greater the toll on the user, although that toll can be "paid" in many ways.

6. *How is magic used in the society?* Human beings are tool users. Most likely any intelligent species is. That means that magic is unlikely to have a significant role in society unless it is predictable, replicable, and cost-effective. How it meets those tests will determine whether the magic user is essentially a poor hedge wizard (the magic being unreliable, but sometimes effective) or a power baron or somewhere in between.

   Useful magic will also most likely have an economic value, depending on what it can accomplish and how many magic users there are with the same skills. In addition, magic will affect the structure of any society because it will create another separation between haves and have-nots.

7. *What is the inter-relation between magic and the technology of the society?* Does magic enhance technology, or does technology enhance magic? Are they mutually exclusive? If so, why or under what conditions?

8. *To what degree does the ending or resolution of your story or novel depend on magic?*

   A story whose ending is determined entirely by "magic" is likely to be perceived as a *deus ex machina* ending, while one where magic plays no part risks being considered "mainstream" or "romance"or some other genre with magic just thrown in as window dressing. The best speculative fiction integrates the magic (or technology) with the human elements so that the ending is not possible without both.

So, What Do *You* Know? Deepening Your World Building Through Point of View

JANICE HARDY always wondered about the darker side of healing. For her Healing Wars fantasy trilogy, she tapped into her own dark side to create a world where healing was dangerous, and those with the best intentions often made the worst choices. Her books include *The Shifter*, *Blue Fire*, and *Darkfall* from Balzer + Bray/HarperCollins.

I remember the exact moment I finally "got" point of view. I was reading a critique of my very first novel. In one scene, my protagonist was running for her life and mentioned seeing a possible way to escape. The sentence was: "She came around the corner and saw the rowboat tied to a dock piling."

The critiquer asked: "Did she know the rowboat was there? Because *the* implies prior knowledge, and I don't think she was looking for it or knew it was there before she saw it."

Back then I had no clue what she was talking about. Prior knowledge? Huh? She went on to explain that the word *the* implied that my point of view character knew there was a rowboat there. It wasn't *a* rowboat (which implies generality, just something she happened to see) but *the* rowboat (which implies it's a known thing to her beforehand).

Something as simple as *the* vs. *a* showed how much my point of view knew about that one silly little rowboat. If she didn't know it was there, she couldn't call it *the* rowboat. She'd have no prior knowledge of it. It would be no different than any other object around. A flat detail with no meaning to character or reader.

Light bulbs went on.

What your character *knows* is a tremendous tool for describing your world and making it feel real to your reader. It can help you decide which details to show and how to incorporate them into your story in a natural way. To put it in writer terms: it can help you show, not tell, and avoid info dumps and backstory.

What your character knows helps ground the reader to your world and explains all the rules of that world. She can show them what's normal, how society works, what cultural rules apply, anything you need the reader to know. How she moves through her world is how you'll describe that world to your reader.

If you send a five-year-old girl and a forty-year-old ex-Navy SEAL into a room, they're going to react differently to what they find there. Same as if you sent in a two-hundred-year-old evil wizard and a young idealistic starship captain.

This is especially important in speculative fiction, because so much of the world is crafted and thus unknown to readers. They can't rely on what *they* know to understand the world the story takes place in. They need the *characters* to show them what's important and what things mean.

When you create your worlds and the people in them, remember that the characters who live there take that world for granted and see it as it is, and has always been. What we might consider wrong could be perfectly normal and acceptable for them.

Even if they're trying to change the world, chances are they won't be trying to make it what *we* think the world should be. They'll try to change the part that they disagree with based on what they've experienced.

If slavery is acceptable, they won't think about the poor slaves. One person might treat them like furniture; another may treat them like favored pets and think she's being kind by doing so. If backstabbing and ruthless business practices are the norm, no one will think twice about betraying a friend. Or if they do, they won't think of themselves as being bad people, just hate the fact this is what they have to do to get ahead.

Let your characters see and react to their worlds as someone living in that world would see and react to it. Fill it with lots of small details that show what's important to them, not just what matters to the setting or plot.

People see the world as it pertains to them. Take advantage of that, and your story world will be richer.

EXERCISE

Ask yourself a few basic questions and think about how your characters would answer them. How do they see the world you've created for them?

1. *What is a normal day like for your protagonist?* This is a great way to show the everyday elements of your world and how it works. If space travel is common, he might have friends talking about a trip to another planet.

2. *Where does she live?* Home environment provides opportunities to show what matters to them and what they care about. Or things they might need to hide. If books are outlawed, a character with a treasured library might go to a lot of trouble to hide it.

3. *Where does he work or go to school?* This allows you to show the economic and educational aspects of your world. If your characters are poor and hungry, they might be on the streets or in the bowels of a space station.

4. *Where does she fit on the social and economic ladder?* Comparing her to others lets you describe details that are important, but might not be relevant to the point of view character. Plot might dictate readers know who the lord of the castle is and details about him, but if your protagonist never sees him, it's hard to get him into the story in a natural way. But if the locals gossip about him, then all those details can be conveyed.

5. *Who are your protagonist's friends?* You can say a lot about a world and the people in it by how your protagonist views her friend-

ships. *Do they have common issues? Threats? Ambitions?* Friends talk, so world details can be slipped into conversation.

6. *Who are your protagonist's enemies?* (Not just the antagonist, anyone who doesn't like him or her.)

7. *What social or economic group does he belong to?* You can show class distinctions by how your characters view others and why they feel that way.

8. *What are some challenges to living in this world? What makes life harder?* Often this will be plot related, which allows you to show the inherent conflicts and lay important groundwork without a lot of exposition and info dumping. What are the things your protagonist tries to avoid on a regular basis? Maybe they're landscape elements, or weather patterns, or groups of people. It could even be starvation or keeping a secret.

9. *What are some advantages to living in this world?* Don't forget the positive elements.

10. *What's considered beautiful? What are things to aspire to? What makes life easier?* This could be a river that allows your protagonist to get around unseen or a secret ability that lets them accomplish difficult tasks.

KIJ JOHNSON

Feel Things Out

KIJ JOHNSON is the author of three novels and a collection of short stories. She is a three-time winner of the Nebula Award, and a winner of the World Fantasy, Theodore Sturgeon Memorial, and Crawford Awards. She teaches a science-fiction novel workshop each summer for the University of Kansas, where she also teaches writing and fantasy as literature.

Your science fiction or fantasy story takes place somewhere that is by definition not here and now: the future, an alien planet, Oz, the afterlife—or a world a lot like ours except that there are zombies or talking horses. It's easy to treat these places as a two-dimensional game board you can push your character tokens around on, with just enough depth and complexity to advance the plot, but they're not. They're real places, to the characters anyway. There are a million things they can see that you can't. Their bodies are moving through air (or methane or water) just as ours do.

To my mind, the trick is to show us the world "immersively"—the things the character notices *when* she notices and *in the way* she notices. How does she know who just walked into the room behind her back? By smell? By the sound of walking (or slithering)? Unless her eyes grow on stalks or there's a mirror, it's going to be something like that.

A lot of people will tell you to visualize the scene as it plays out, and I think this is spot-on. For me this involves muttering the dialogue to myself until it sounds right—though since I write in coffee shops, I try to keep it down, not always successfully. I also act out the movements; how can my character carry an unconscious friend through a doorway without bashing his head on the lintel? By ducking, maybe?

Do her knees hurt at all from that? Mine would! Might she overbalance? Or maybe she's in a hurry and she just lets him hit: no time to stop or adjust! Maybe he's dripping blood now, or maybe the bang wakes him up; either way, what might be a straightforward chase scene develops some unique elements that can make it feel more real.

But more than that: For me the greatest part of making a scene (and by extension a story) real is not what is seen or said or done; it is what is experienced. Sensation. Our character may be running from aliens or eating a banquet with gods, but whatever else is going on, she is also feeling things, sensing things, experiencing things—and not just in the "engage all five senses in a scene" way.

EXERCISE

So, try this. Pick a scene you're writing, and try to have your character engage with some of the following experiential elements. Maybe she notices one incidentally; maybe one gets in the way of her doing or saying or thinking things; maybe she has an emotional or a physiological response. Maybe her experience of these things reflects a mood you're trying to convey. Try it with these:

1. Blood chemistry. Know what a sugar rush feels like? What about a sugar drop? Adrenaline leaves you feeling sick to your stomach. Your character will get depressed once the endorphins wear off; everyone does.

2. Thirst. Two percent dehydration impairs your ability to think clearly. I didn't know this, but yeah, it's true. Let's not forget that her eyes will get gummy and she won't be able to stop chewing on her chapped lips, and the skin on her fingers will feel leathery.

3. A crick in your character's neck. Anyone who's ever had chronic pain knows it colors everything. A few years ago my back was bothering me enough that if I had been Frodo, I would have said the heck with it, and let Sauron win.

4. Ambient temperature. Obviously, being cold makes it harder to thread needles and being hot means you wear less clothes, but what about heat rashes? Winter clothes restrict movement. Your character might have trouble opening her eyes all the way if it's bitterly cold; she may miss things.

5. Ambient noise. Close your eyes. Can you hear the 60-hertz buzz of electricity? It's everywhere and it's part of your world; you would know if it was missing, even if you couldn't tell right away what was wrong. What about the air-conditioning clicking on? Your waistband squeaking when you lean forward? Instead of just telling me about noises that move your plot forward—gunfire, screams, ships landing—what about all the background sounds of your character's life?

6. Things touching her. Are any parts of you sore right now? Itchy? Ticklish? Are your clothes binding you anywhere: waistbands, bra straps, eyeglasses? Your characters' do too.

And so forth. Walk through a day observing things. When you eat, think about the food's flavor, sure; but also its color and its texture and what the heat or cold feels like on your tongue. When you walk into a new room, think not just about what you see there and who's waiting but also where the lighting is coming from. Is the air dry? Does it chap your lips? When you lie down to sleep, think about whether you can see through your eyelids or not; how your pillow heats up; whether your sheets are bunching up; how they smell.

Now extrapolate. There may be no curtains to brush against the pillowcases in your character's world, but there are other small soft noises that mean comfort. Make one up. You character walks through (or runs through, pursued by bears) her world the same way you and I do: in a cloud of sensory experiences, in a body that feels things large and small. Show me that.

CHRIS HOWARD

Building Worlds Without Boring Your Readers or Becoming the Minister for Tourism

CHRIS HOWARD is the author of several books including *Seaborn* (Juno Books, 2008). His stories have appeared in *Fantasy Magazine*, *The Harrow*, *Another Realm*, and elsewhere. His short story "Hammers and Snails" was a Robert A. Heinlein Centennial Short Fiction Contest winner. He is illustrating and writing the graphic novel edition of *Saltwater Witch*.

If you are writing science fiction, fantasy, horror, tech thrillers, or any kind of story with a speculative layer, you're probably world building and you have probably run into hazards like the "tour guide" problem, the "talkative professor" problem, or the "erudite writer" problem. I have encountered them all in my own writing. In this exercise I want to work through ways to uncover the beautiful details of your world without boring the reader or setting up barriers in your story.

I'm going to use *new world* for any variation or combination of an entirely fictional world (Discworld, Virga, Dune, Middle-earth), or a fictional world that overlays our own, but with some significant differences (the New York of Holly Black's *Valiant*, Sookie Stackhouse's Louisiana, the San Francisco of Richard Morgan's *Altered Carbon*).

New worlds, no matter how lovely, dangerous, similar to or different from our own, are still new, and that means it's going to take some time to get used to them. On the good side, readers of genre fiction expect a certain level of uncertainty. They also expect the author to come through in the end with most of the answers, and they're usually willing to wait for them. Readers expect to be taken somewhere they haven't been before, or to be shown something dramatically different about places they know well. One thing they don't expect is to have it all dumped on them at once.

Making them wait is the key.

In any story with a new world, the writer is going to struggle to hold back the interesting stuff. You want to draw the reader into your world, show it off, and you've spent so much creative time and effort on maps, background, and cultural details that they are difficult to pass by without a glance. Why can't we stop once in a while and take in the scenery, point out the spaceport, or smell those odd-looking flowers?

You can. It just takes a little patience and some guidelines. There are methods for successfully revealing the workings of your world as well as for letting you know when to cut them from the story.

Let's look at some common problems I see in books—my own included.

The tour guide problem: I know I'm not the only one who would kill to have the Fodor's or *Lonely Planet* guide to so many of the worlds in science fiction and fantasy. Chances are a first-time reader doesn't. That's usually because they haven't experienced it yet. They haven't lived in your world for three or four hundred pages. You know how wonderful your world is—down to the dance steps of the cloud nomads and how Whirligig Alley got its name—and you are dying to tell your readers about it.

Don't.

That's not a hard and fast *don't*, and fortunately writers don't fall into the tour guide trap. It's the tour guide *problem*. Traps have to be disarmed or safely destroyed. Problems are there to be solved, passed to another chapter to deal with, or at least manipulated into something that doesn't look like a problem anymore. Readers will gladly continue on if your main character—who by chapter four or five has pulled them into the story—finds himself among the cloud nomads and is asked to dance.

You've heard this before: Put down some dots and let the reader connect them.

A clearer way to put it might be: Write as if your readers have the

Michelin Green Guide to your fabulous city and seaside resort. You may have to remind them of details here and there, but unless knowing about those advanced building materials or the molecular structure of some device is essential to the plot, you should write as if your readers know the world almost as well as you do.

Solving the tour guide problem can be summed up with *don't stop to smell anything*. Keep moving and only use your nose—if you have to—as you run past. That will be enough.

The talkative professor problem: This is common in any story where technology, science, or some complicated social, magical, or technological arrangement plays a crucial role. The problem is that the professor usually has something important to say that underlies the whole world, and it usually affects the plot or how your characters make critical decisions. It's also probably complicated or requires a character with some authority to deliver. While the tour guide problem is handled with restraint, the talkative professor has to be solved by breaking up a lot of information and spreading it thinly across the story. You can't dump it on the reader in a three-page monologue. Your reader may know very little about submarines or the diseases thrown around by a particular elder god—and the particular combination of plant stems that provide immunity to those diseases, but you're going to have to get them up to speed on the details for your story to make sense.

Weaving them in is the key, and showing them in action is the most effective way to get them into your reader's head. That doesn't mean you can't have one character explain the situation to another, conveying information to the reader at the same time. It just has to be done carefully and in small amounts.

When your story requires you to convey a lot of information to the reader, think about the patience needed for gardening. If you thinly seed the details of your world, let them grow, introduce them, and reuse them in small amounts throughout the story, you will be rewarded with the most important aspect of successful world building: plausibility.

You plant a hint here and there, refer to those hints, develop them as the story progresses, and once they sprout, the reader won't be surprised to see them. The reader will accept the details of your world as if they had always been there—because in fact they have been. Plots that pivot and change direction based on the social structure, the feeding rituals, the properties of a tree's shadow during a solar eclipse, the strength of tidal forces, the way calendars are calculated, or any of the physical components of your world that have evolved steadily with your story—that fit organically into the whole—will ultimately have a much stronger foundation in the reader's mind. This is where plausibility comes from. Organic equals plausible.

The erudite writer problem: There are world details that have to be baked into the story for things to make sense. Then there are world details that really don't need to be there, and have little or no impact on the plot or character action. This is the erudite writer problem and it may be more common in alternate history or mainstream historical fiction where knowledgeable readers expect the writer to know about the rivets used to assemble Roman armor or seventh-century agricultural techniques common along the west coast of Africa. Readers may even want to learn about these. They just don't want all the heavy details served to them in one bite. My solution to the erudite writer problem is let them ask for it, or let them look it up in a glossary or notes section. Another option is to set up a blog or an email account for one of your characters and post or respond in character, showing off the amazing stuff you know. Just don't cram it all into your novel.

Here are a few more things to keep in mind before we do the exercise:

When you introduce something about your world it has to be important to the plot at the scene or chapter level, not necessarily to the plot as a whole. If sail cloth must have a specific coating to keep the local micro-fauna from eating it, that may not be important to the story as a whole, but it may be very important to the plot and the tension you will be building over the next couple chapters when your characters board a ship and are about to cross eel-infested waters.

Your purpose as a world builder has to fit with your purpose as a storyteller. You want the reader to turn the page, to wonder what's going to happen next, to sympathize with or at least understand your POV characters, to speculate on the journey your characters are going to take in the world you have laid out for them, and to be satisfyingly surprised when things don't go as planned. As a writer, you're primarily concerned with what the characters are doing, and as a world builder your primary concern is where they are doing it and how it affects or constrains what they can do. Bring those together with the right balance, and readers are going to love your world and come back for more.

EXERCISE

Everyone understands the general writing rule "show don't tell." When it comes to presenting your world it's "act don't explain." Especially in the opening scenes of your book.

Write the first three chapters of a new story (or rewrite the first three chapters of an existing one) without explaining anything about your world to the reader. That's three chapters of action without stopping to fill in any details. You will have characters moving through your world, but when you come across some fact or feature that is begging for more than a couple of descriptive words, just name it (if you have to) and move on.

Keep the guidelines in mind: Write as if your reader has already been there before. Don't over-explain. Pretend they know all this stuff. Keep the professor in the back until after chapter three. Sure, your characters are going to see things that need explaining. Hide most of it until the reader is well on her way through the story.

If there are constraining factors that limit your characters, such as a poisonous atmosphere or a curse barrier, have your characters react as if they understand perfectly well what they are up against. It's too soon to explain their actions to the reader. Just do them.

Your purpose for the first three chapters is to maintain a reasonable level of uncertainty for the reader. (See James Scott Bell on "pleasurable uncertainty" in his book *Elements of Fiction Writing: Conflict & Suspense*.) Go out of your way to withhold information. Use a brief description or name only if you have to tell the reader anything at all. There will be cases where you will have to import enough meaning into a name to get the general function across to the reader—but no more. For example, if the plaza is filled with humans, androids, and mellaliths, move on as if every reader knows what a "mellalith" is. How much you want to reveal in the name itself is up to you. A reader may jump on "lith" in the name and think "stone"—or not.

The idea is that you don't explain anything in detail until you are at least three chapters into the story. Wait until your readers have invested some time in your world. Wait until they are breathing a little bit of the same air as your characters before you reveal the cool behind-the-scenes stuff. Readers will keep turning pages because after a while it will come down to needing more of that air.

NANCY KRESS

Follow the Money

NANCY KRESS is the author of thirty-one books, including twenty-four novels, four collections of stories, and three books about writing. Her work has won four Nebulas, two Hugos, a Theodore Sturgeon Memorial Award, and the John W. Campbell Memorial Award. Kress frequently teaches writing, and for sixteen years she was the fiction columnist for *Writer's Digest* magazine.

S ometimes the most useful critique session of one's work-in-progress is also the most painful. More than twenty years ago I attended a workshop called Sycamore Hill, at which seventeen science fiction professionals submitted stories to be critiqued by their colleagues. The workshop took an entire week and was helped along by a lot of white wine. I had brought a novella that I knew was not among my best, but I thought it was at least passable.

Bruce Sterling did not think so. One of SF's best writers and sharpest critics, Bruce took strong issue not with the writing in my piece, or the characters or even the events, but with my future society. "It doesn't make sense," he said, at great length and in devastating detail. "And if it doesn't make sense, I can't believe it, and then the whole thing falls apart. How does this space colony work? Who makes the rules? Who holds the power? Where is the money?"

Bruce was absolutely right. Enterprises—colonies (terrestrial or not), spaceships, scientific expeditions, wars, cities, even families—are all based on economics. The economics may take the form of money, of barter, of cooperative manufacture (see Ursula Le Guin's wonderful novel *The Dispossessed*), or of anything else you can come up with. But to create a convincing future or fantasy society, it needs to possess a convincing economy. Even a single person lost in the wilderness got his boots and knife from somewhere. Even a primitive society of cave-men has a system for gathering and sharing resources (see Jean Auel's ingenious novel *Clan of the Cave Bear*).

But (you ask) what if my story has nothing to do with economics? It's a story about personal relationships in the future. Fine; speculative fiction needs those. But that future in which your characters are relating to each other does not exist in a vacuum. Each character needs a place to live, food to eat, clothing to wear, rocket fuel, steel swords, hydroponic vats or vials to put the magic potions in, or whatever else is appropriate to your society. The more you know about how these things came into existence, the richer and fuller your story will seem.

I would, however, like to note two exceptions to all this. First, if your story is present-day or very near future, you can simply borrow the existing economy, which is what your readers will assume you are doing anyway. Then you don't need to explain where your heroine got her cell phone or her Toyota. Second, if your story is very short—say, 3,000 words—you may not need to give too much thought to its economics because your focus will be tightly on one or two scenes. Think of a close-up photograph of a flower; it doesn't matter to viewers where the flower is positioned when the picture was taken. But if you use a wider lens—a whole field of flowers—framing the picture with background becomes more important.

After I recovered from Bruce's dissection of my novella, I thought long and hard about economics. "Follow the money," Bruce said, and I tried. The next thing I wrote won both a Hugo and a Nebula: *Beggars in Spain*.

So, as a general rule: The longer your speculative fiction story, and/or the farther removed from us in time or space, the more thought you need to give to the economics behind your society. How do you do that?

I can't overemphasize the value of knowing the answers to these questions before you proceed very far into your story. Not only will the novel be richer and more plausible, but thinking about its economic underpinnings may suggest plot lines you want to develop. If, for example, interstellar war has cut the supply of goods to an extraterrestrial colony from Earth, what will your characters now lack: replacement parts for robots? Terra-forming equipment? New clothing? Will they try to develop substitutes, raid other colonies for the goods, make alliance with the enemy to get them, or what? And how will your hero be involved? Does that involvement make him braver, bent on revenge, or a turncoat?

Ultimately, all stories of all genres come down to the characters. But characters interact with their environment, and their environment is shaped by economics. The richer your created economics, the stronger and more plausible your story will seem.

Even if Bruce Sterling never reads it.

EXERCISE

Considering the society of a story or novel you are working on right now, make sure you can answer each of the following questions:

1. What level of technology does this society possess? If it is a roughly medieval fantasy society, do they have gunpowder? Crossbows? Steel or just iron? Glass? If it is a space ship, what are its weapons? Does it have a faster-than-light drive? (If not, you need wormholes or a generation ship to get very far away from the solar system.) If this is a future or off-Earth city, what level of transportation do they possess to move around goods and people? Can you see it?

2. Where did the raw materials for this level of technology come from? Swords require mining. Spaceships have to have been built somewhere with sophisticated, extensive, and well-defended facilities. Even clothing must be woven or manufactured from raw materials. And everyone must eat. Do you need farms, hydroponic tanks, factories? Where are they? And who works them: slaves, serfs, peasant families, a laboring class of citizens, robots? Who builds habitats (tents, houses, cathedrals, castles, settlements)? One reason that Kim Stanley Robinson's novel *Red Mars* is a classic

is because of the plausible and fascinating details of building a human civilization on Mars.

3. Now for a biggie: Who controls all this sword forging, spaceship funding, colony building, food growing, expedition mounting? Is it a government, and if so, what kind (monarchy, oligarchy, republic, totalitarian state, theocracy)? Is it a corporation, and if so, how does your corporation fit into the larger economy (national, global, intrasolar, interstellar)? Is your economy capitalism, socialism, libertarianism, some blend of those, something else entirely? (Walter Jon Williams created a fascinating economy based on calorie use.) What this means is: Who makes the big decisions in your society? And, just as important:

4. How is that economic control maintained? Through force (army, cadre of men-at-arms, police force) or laws (which usually need to be backed up by force), or social controls (loyalty, patriotism, the threat of hell, the need to support one's family, the desire to advance in one's profession)? In what combination?

5. Who is trying to hang on to or increase their control over everybody else? (There is always somebody trying this.) How?

THEME AND MEANING

"Science fiction encourages us to explore . . . all the futures, good and bad, that the human mind can envision."

—MARION ZIMMER BRADLEY

"A writer is, after all, only half his book. The other half is the reader and from the reader the writer learns."

—P. L. TRAVERS

HARLAN ELLISON®

First, There Was the Title

HARLAN ELLISON has published more than 1,700 short stories, novellas, essays, and more. He was editor of two groundbreaking science fiction anthologies, *Dangerous Visions* and *Again, Dangerous Visions*. He has written and performed as conceptual consultant for TV shows such as *Babylon 5*, *The Outer Limits*, and *The Twilight Zone*. Ellison has won numerous awards including multiple Hugos, Nebulas, and Edgars.

L ike most comfortable, familiar old-shoe clichés, there is an important and irrefutable kernel of truth in this one: people, schmucks though they may be for doing it, *do* judge a book by its cover. Even I do it once in a while. I bought a paperback, *Apeland*, because of the cover. There was a mystery novel I spent seven dollars to purchase, in hardcover, because of the cleverness of the cover art. It was called *Dead Piano*. It wasn't that good a novel, but what did the author or the publisher care by that time . . . they had me. Not to mention my seven dollars.

And after judging by the cover, readers judge by the title. Many times they read the back spine of the book, or the title on a table of contents if it's a shorter story in question, so it's judged *before* the cover. What you *call* a story is important.

I'll try to tell you why. And how to do it well.

Here's a sample group of titles. I've made them up on the moment.

Say they're arrayed on a contents page, each bylined with a name you don't know, so you have no preference based on familiarity with an author's previous work. Which one do you read first?

The Box

Heat Lightning

Pay as You Go

Hear the Whisper of the World

The Journey

Dead by Morning

Every Day Is Doomsday

Doing It

Now, unless you're more peculiar than the people on whom I tried that list, you picked "Hear the Whisper of the World" first, you probably picked "Doing It" next, and "Dead by Morning" third. Unless you've led a *very* dull life, you picked "The Box" next to last and would read everything else before selecting "The Journey". If you picked "The Journey" first, go get a bricklayer's ticket, because you'll never be a writer. "The Journey" is the dullest title I could think of, and believe me I *worked* at it.

It wasn't the length or complexity of "Hear the Whisper of the World" that made it most intriguing. I'll agree it may not even be the most exhilarating title ever devised, but it has some of the elements that *make* a title intriguing, that suggest a quality that will engender trust in the author. S/he knows how to use words. He or she has a thought there, an implied theme, a point to which the subtext of the story will speak. All this on a very subliminal level as far as a potential reader is concerned. And (how many times, to the brink of exhaustion, must we repeat *this*!?) trust is the first, the best thing you can instill in a reader. If readers trust you, they will go with you in terms of the willing suspension of disbelief that is necessary in *any* kind of fiction, but it is absolutely mandatory for fantasy and science fiction.

The second thing it possesses is a quality of maintaining a tension between not telling too little and not telling too much. Remember how many times you were pissed off when a magazine editor changed a title so the punch line was revealed too early: you were reading along, being nicely led from plot-point to plot-point, having the complexity of the story unsnarl itself logically, and you were trying to outguess the writer, and then, too soon, you got to a place where you remembered the title and thought, *Oh shit, so* that's *what it means!* And the rest of the story was predictable. The title stole a joy from you.

So a title should titillate, inveigle you, tease and bemuse you . . . but not confuse you or spill the beans. Titles in the vein of "The Journey" neither excite nor inform. "Hear the Whisper of the World", I hope and pray (otherwise it's a dumb example), fulfills the criteria.

The *Blank* of *Blank* titles are the kinds of titles away from which to stay, as Churchill might have syntactically put it. You know the kind I mean, *The Doomfarers of Coramonde, The Dancers of Noyo, The Hero of Downways, The Ships of Durostorum, The Clocks of Iraz.* That kind of baroque thing.

Naturally I've picked examples of such titles that include another sophomoric titling flaw. The use of alien-sounding words that cannot be readily pronounced or—more important—when the reader is asking to purchase the book or recommending it to someone else, words that cannot be remembered. "Hey, I read a great book yesterday. *The Reelers of Skooth* or *The Ravers of Seeth* or . . . I dunno, you look for it; it has a green cover . . ."

Asimov believed in short titles, because they're easy to remember by sales clerks, book buyers for the chain stories, and readers who not only don't recall the titles of what they've read, but seldom know the name of the author. On the other hand, both Chip Delany and I think that a cleverly constructed long title plants sufficient key words in a reader's mind that, even if it's delivered incorrectly, enough remains to make the point. Witness examples, "Time Considered as a Helix of Semi-Precious Stones", "The Beast That Shouted Love at the Heart of the World", "'Repent, Harlequin!' Said the Ticktockman" or "The Doors of His Face, the Lamps of His Mouth". There is a strong argument both ways. "Nightfall", *Slan, Dune* and "Killdozer" simply cannot be ignored. But then, neither can *Do Androids Dream of Electric Sheep?*

The rule of thumb, of course, is simple: if it's clever and catchy enough, short or long doesn't make a bit of difference.

But try to avoid being *too* clever. You can bad-pun and out-clever yourself into annoying a reader before the story is ever considered. *I Never Promised You a Rose Garden* makes it, but *Your Erroneous Zones* simply sucks. The original title for Roger Zelazny's "He Who Shapes", published in book form as *The Dream Master*, was "The Ides of Octember" which seems to me too precious by half, while the title Joe Haldeman originally wanted to put on his Star Trek novelization— "Spock, Meshuginah!"—caroms off into ludicrousness. But funny. I know from funny, and *that* is funny. Thomas Disch is a master at walking that line. *Getting into Death* is masterful, as is *Fun with Your New Head*. But the classic example of tightrope-walking by Disch was the original title of his novel *Mankind under the Leash* (the Ace Paperback title, and a dumb thing it is), which was originally called *The Puppies of Terra.* (That's its title in England.)

Arthur Byron Cover has a flair for the utterly ridiculous that is *so* loony you have to buy the book to see if he can pull it off. Witness: *The Platypus of Doom.*

Until the very last tick before production, the title of Margaret Mitchell's *Gone With the Wind* was "Mules in Horses' Harness"; and though I truly love the hell out of it, sufficiently to have appropriated it half a century later for an essay I wrote, I think F. Scott Fitzgerald was well-pressured when his publisher badgered him into retitling Trimalchio in West Egg as *The Great Gatsby.*

The name of a character, if interesting, can be a way out when you're stuck for a title. It's surprising how few science fiction novels have done this, indicating the low esteem most traditional sf writers have placed on characterization, preferring to deal with *Analog*-style technician terms such as "Test Stand", "Flashpoint", "Test to Destruction", or "No Connections". We have so few novels with titles like *The*

Great Gatsby, Babbitt, The Adventures of Huckleberry Finn, or *Lord Jim.* Delany scored with *Dhalgren,* I've had some success with "Knox", and Gordon Dickson's best-loved story is "Black Charlie".

Ideally, a title should add an extra fillip when you've finished reading a story. It should capsulize it, state the theme, and make a point after touchdown. It should, one hopes, explain more than you cared to baldly state in the text. Judith Merril's "That Only a Mother" is a perfect example, as is the double-entendre of her "Dead Center". It is an extra gift to an alert reader, and makes the reader feel close to you.

By the same token, you dare not cheat a reader with a clever title that doesn't pay off. The one that pops to mind first is "The Gun Without a Bang", one of the best titles from the usually satisfying Robert Sheckley. *Great* title. The only thorn on that rose was that it was a dumb story about some people who find a gun that didn't make any noise, which says a whole lot less than the symbolic, metaphysical, textual, or tonal implications passim the title's promise.

One of the most brilliant title-creators sf has ever known is Jack Chalker. I'm not talking about the actual stories, just the titles. Beauties like *Midnight at the Well of Souls,* and *The Devil Will Drag You Under, Pirates of the Thunder,* and "Forty Days and Nights in the Wilderness" are to die for.

But when—way back in 1978—Jack saw publication of a short story with the absolute killer title, "Dance Band on the *Titanic*", everybody wanted to assassinate him. First, because the title was utterly dynamite; and second, because the stupid story was *about* the dance band on the *Titanic*!

"No!" we screamed at him, "You great banana, you don't waste a prime candidate for beautiful allegory on a story that is about the very thing named in the title." Man was lucky to escape with his life!

For myself, I cannot begin a story until I have a title. Sometimes I have titles—such as "The Deathbird" or "Mefisto in Onyx"—years before I have a story to fit. Often a story will be titled in my mind, be the impetus for writing that particular piece, and then, when I've finished, the title no longer resonates properly. It is a title that has not grown to keep pace with more important things in the story, or the focus was wrong, or it was too frivolous for what turned out to be a more serious piece of work. In that case, painful as it may be to disrespect the spark that gave birth to the work, one must be bloody ruthless and scribble the title down for later use, or jettison it completely. That is the mature act of censorship a writer brings to every word of a story, because in a very personal way that is what writing is about: self-censorship. Picking *"the"* instead of *"a"* means you not only exclude *"a"*, but all the possible storylines proceeding from that word. You kill entire universes with every word-choice. And while it's auctorial censorship, it is a cathexian process forever separating the amateurs from the professionals.

I cannot stress enough the importance of an intriguing and original title. It is what an editor sees first, and what draws that worthy person into reading the first page of the story.

No one could avoid reading a story called "The Hurkle Is a Happy Beast" or "If You Was a Molkin", but it takes a masochist to plunge into a manuscript titled "The Wicker Chair".

I leave you with these thoughts.

Right now I have to write a story called "The Other Eye of Polyphemus".

EXERCISE

1. Start collecting a list of possible titles for stories. Do any of these spark new story ideas?

2. Come up with three alternative titles for a current project. Include a short one and a long one. Which best suits the heart and soul of your story—hinting at theme without giving anything away, catchy without being too clever?

   Ask five or six people to be honest about which of the three titles they find the most intriguing. Include at least two who have read your story, and a few who haven't.

PEN DENSHAM

Writing into the Spiritual Unknown

PEN DENSHAM is a writer, producer, director known for writing and producing films such as *THE DANGEROUS LIVES OF ALTAR BOYS, BACKDRAFT, ROBIN HOOD: PRINCE OF THIEVES*, and television revivals of *The Outer Limits* and *The Twilight Zone*, as well as writing, producing, and directing MGM's *MOLL FLANDERS*. He has won and been nominated for multiple awards, including two Oscar nominations for his short films.

As a creator I have never pursued a "genre"; instead I have always been drawn to call from myself that which is visionary and most compelling.

I have written and directed a historical character study like *MOLL FLANDERS*, because I shared having a daughter with my wife and this story seemed to come from needing a way of illustrating to our child that the imperfections that life brings out of us in no way disqualify us from deserving love and admiration.

Harry Houdini fascinated me—a man whose persona was so powerful, that magicians today are still competing with him. And yet he could never find enough adulation to feel that he could value himself. A state of compulsion that I think many artists/performers share.

Over my career, from re-envisioning Robin Hood, a historic adventure, to *LARGER THAN LIFE*, a Bill Murray movie in which I wrote about a man who inherits an elephant, I have tried to write from my inner inspirations.

I have also been lucky enough to personally champion the re-birth of both *The Outer Limits* and *The Twilight Zone* to network television. I saw each series as a vast opportunity for myself, and others, to explore human nature under the magnifying focus of a supernatural or science fiction premise. A focus of heated, dramatic light that forced the characters to quickly strip off their protective layers to reveal their inner, human dynamics, and to change and struggle to find choices that evolved their courage in the face of awesome difficulty.

I am in development on one script that truly haunted me, *Night-Shifts*. It was scary at times during the writing—something I'd never felt before. It is about a young female resident doctor, forced to work dozens of hours, who starts to fear one of her patients trapped in a coma is trying to possess her body. (I lost my mother when I was eight—my father brought psychics to the house and held séances.)

I describe myself as a romantic skeptic, as I have found little evidence of a life after death. Except in the oddly unexplained but well-documented phenomena of the near death and white light experiences—which are universal in history and culture. And they tied back to the warning I was given as a child by one zealous "psychic" that when we sleep: "Our souls float out of our bodies. Be careful, because malicious entities can take them over."

Joseph Campbell regarded myths as living things, meant to reflect the immediate, social experiences and lives of those who created them . . . I think I was exploring that child in me—who still retained self-protective instincts about not losing control while asleep. Like my young doctor, who finds she is doing bizarre things when she tries to capture a few minutes of recuperative sleep.

I would rather this script be regarded as a modern, dark myth than just a horror story. Somehow defining a film as horror seems to disable its value. "Horror" can be a pejorative that allows one to dispense with its purpose of envisioning the inevitable mystery and cycle of life. I see *Night-Shifts* as a metaphysical journey that we all can take with Mary, its heroine. And yes, it embraces the dark currents of the horror form. Not for "Gorno" (gore-porn), but to present a series of supernatural possibilities that cause a contemporary heroine to confront the limits of her courage, make discoveries about her past, and come to examine the existence of the human soul.

And, of course, to entertain.

I firmly believe that scary movies work on us because they provoke our natural survival instincts. Films like *JURASSIC PARK, ALIEN,* and *JAWS* are what I call "avoidance of being eaten" stories. We are drawn to *THE SILENCE OF THE LAMBS* and *Dexter* because we have anxiety about being killed by serial killers. We watch disaster movies because they play out scenarios that we unconsciously use to calculate strategies that we might use in a similar situation. And movies like *A NIGHTMARE ON ELM STREET, PARANORMAL ACTIVITY, THE THING,* etc., deal with unnatural things that we conjure from our collective unconscious (like demons, goblins, spirits), that we imagine want to harm or possess us. Despite our sophisticated position at the peak of the mammal species, we still have urges and instincts from those six-million-years-ago ape-like creatures that were our ancestors.

EXERCISE

There is a simple creativity tool called Bi-sociation: taking two topics and forcing them together to create a new hybrid that incorporates values from both.

Make a list of twenty movies or scary speculative fiction books that have appealed to you. *FINAL DESTINATION—PSYCHO—THE EXORCIST—CARRIE—FRANKENSTEIN—THE OMEN—*Dante's *Inferno—ALIEN,* etc.

Then have fun and see if you can combine any two, to inspire the plot for new survival-instinct-provoking stories!

EXAMPLES:

THE EXORCIST—meets—Dante's *Inferno*

— A priest is chosen to go into Hell to rescue an innocent soul.

ALIEN—meets—*THE OMEN*

— The Devil possesses people on a space ship.

CARRIE—meets—*THE SHINING*

High school students are trapped in a snowbound hotel and the girl they haze starts to hunt them down with her powers.

DOUGLAS MCGOWAN

Catching Up with the Future

DOUGLAS MCGOWAN is the co-author of *Nature of the Beast: A Graphic Novel*. He lives in Oregon where he produces music reissues and runs the Yoga Records and Ethereal Sequence record labels.

I'm often struck by the yawning divide between the fantastic visions of the human imagination and the relatively mundane fantasies put forth by mainstream Hollywood.

In fact, reality often seems to have overtaken fantasy, at least for anyone who follows the latest headlines in science and technology.

Consider: We are perhaps ten or twenty years away from "the singularity," the point at which artificial intelligence surpasses the real, human thing. It is a moment of epochal significance that should occupy the imaginations of our greatest fantasy writers, and yet future historians—take note we may be talking about robots now—may be surprised by how little this matter seemed to weigh on the collective consciousness in the early part of the twenty-first century. Or they may not be surprised at all, given a presumably omnivorous appetite for data that would make very few things truly surprising.

Yes, there are notable exceptions like *GATTACA*, the Matrix series, *A.I.*, *ETERNAL SUNSHINE OF THE SPOTLESS MIND*, or *MOON*—stories that do more than just imagine; they speculate. But in general, it's not unreasonable to say that we creators aren't thinking about the future as creatively as we used to.

Pessimism explains much of this. It's been a tough millennium so far. And seriously visualizing our future can be a scary thing. But we conceive the future first in our minds, then set about creating it. A little pessimism is realistic; too much isn't just bad news—it's unsustainable.

Lack of originality is also a huge factor here. Much of the current field of cinematic science fiction seems to extrapolate its ideas less from the real world than it does from other movies and comic books.

If the goal is to create something striking, look anywhere *but* the movies and pop culture for inspiration for your visionary science fiction ideas.

And if you must use the movies for inspiration, make sure you know what you're up to—make sure you aren't just treating someone else's fiction as some sort of given reality. And yeah, make sure you're not just lifting from existing works.

If one focuses a little more on the science, the fiction might start to write itself.

EXERCISE

For this exercise, begin by paying closer attention to what is happening on the cutting edge of real world science right now. Subscribe to a blog such as slashdot.com, blogs.scientificamerican.com, or weliveinthefuture.tumblr.com. Find a story that inspires or connects to some radical idea of the future, and research it more closely.

Now extrapolate the impact of whatever change you see coming. For example, what will it be like growing up in a world of advanced artificial intelligence? How will young people relate with their families, their teachers, and one another when the "voice of authority" comes to them through a seemingly all-knowing smartphone, neural implant, or teddy bear? How will a creative person survive in a world like this? A tutor? A grifter?

Make sure that your idea represents more than just one step from where we are. You may have to create a whole backstory just to explain why an object, a custom, a saying in your fantasy story is the way it is. It can be hard work, but this sort of richness of detail is close to a universal feature of the best science fiction.

Take a story from the present or the past and put it in the future defined by a development you think will affect the way we live. For example, retell your childhood in this new world, or transpose a fairy tale into the world of this new development.

Finally, contrast your sci-fi idea with modern day reality. Explain to yourself, and anyone you count on for criticism, what is truly futuristic about your idea. Draw a line winding from the present moment to whatever future you're imagining, and prove why it's more advanced and more compelling than what is already happening at this very moment. If you can do that, you're probably onto something.

MARC SCOTT ZICREE

Creating Your Own Science Fiction

MARC SCOTT ZICREE has written for most of the major networks and studios, with hundreds of hours of produced credits. He is currently co-writing *Guillermo del Toro's Cabinet of Curiosities* with Guillermo del Toro for Harper Design and writing, directing, and producing *SPACE COMMAND*.

I still remember the first time I saw *The Twilight Zone*. I was eight years old, down in the garage with my stepfather. Two old black-and-white TV sets were propped high on a shelf. One only got picture, the other only sound.

Suddenly, strange images appeared on the silent set on the left, three men inside a spacecraft, landing on an alien planet, finding a wrecked duplicate of their ship and, inside it, incredibly, horribly . . . their own dead bodies.

I didn't know then that the episode was called "Death Ship," or that two of the three men were actors named Ross Martin and Jack Klugman, or that the writer was Richard Matheson, or even the name of the show. And I certainly didn't dream that I was beginning a journey that would span more than forty years of my life and lead to my career as a writer, director, and producer in television. Nonetheless— I was hooked.

I grew up watching *The Twilight Zone*, along with *Star Trek* and the original *Outer Limits*. They formed much of who I am, my beliefs and what drives me, my moral sense, my ethics.

When I got out of college, I knew I wanted to be a writer working in TV, but was challenged how to learn that trade and learn it well. I decided that by studying how a classic show was made, I might find how to emulate it.

I started looking for articles or books about *The Twilight Zone* and found there were virtually none available. I realized I would have to write the book I wanted to read. So at age twenty-two, I started writing *The Twilight Zone Companion*, a book that is still in print all these years later, with more than half a million copies sold.

Shortly after that I sold my first script, which led to hundreds of hours of produced network shows and my rise from story editor to executive producer. It all started with learning from a great example.

Over the last several decades, I've spent a great deal of time contemplating what makes a successful science fiction show. I've contributed to some notable ones, including *Star Trek: The Next Generation*, *Star Trek: Deep Space Nine*, *Babylon 5*, and *Sliders*. Early in my career I developed *Captain Power and the Soldiers of the Future*, a dystopic, live-action children's show that was actually written for adults and led directly to the creation of *Babylon 5*.

Beyond this I've written numerous science fiction pilots, including "World Enough and Time," the independent *Star Trek* episode I made with George Takei that was nominated for the Hugo and Nebula Awards. Right now, I'm creating *SPACE COMMAND*. The project was funded by the audience via Kickstarter and will be released as a series of films and half-hour episodes. It's a bold new adventure, impossible prior to the age of the digital camera, computer editing software, and the Internet.

So how do you go about creating a science fiction show? To begin with, it's the same as any TV show—it's about the characters. Whether it's Kirk, Spock, and McCoy or the characters in *Fringe* or *Doctor Who*, you're essentially creating a surrogate family the audience will want to spend time with on a regular basis.

You also have to tell exciting, well-structured, surprising, and entertaining stories with each episode.

More than that, with science fiction you're creating an entire universe. If it's an especially far-reaching and imaginative universe, it can spin off hundreds of stories with dozens of characters, as in the Star Trek and Star Wars franchises.

The trick with creating your own science fiction show is marrying characters and themes you care about with an evocative and believable science fiction landscape. And there has to be an element that's fresh to it, something we haven't seen before.

That's a tall order. So where to start?

First of all, educate yourself as to what's been done in the genre. That way, you'll know if the premise of your show is overly familiar, even cliché.

Second, look at characters and situations that intrigue you, get your character voices distinct from each other, and make sure your science (or pseudo-science) seems plausible.

Lastly—and this is crucial—make sure your idea has enough breadth to actually make a series. The way you know this is by seeing how many storylines you can spin off from it. If it won't last at least a hundred episodes, it's probably better suited as a movie, or even a novel.

Be mindful too that there are two kinds of TV series now—ones in which each episode stands alone (as with the original *Star Trek*) and those where there's a series arc—a larger over-arcing storyline that covers an entire season or number of seasons.

Thanks to the advent of home video, series arcs have become popular and are even desired by the networks. This is a big change from the old days.

Your science fiction premise can be set in the future, the present, the past, or jump around from one time frame to another—even take place on parallel worlds. However, be mindful of production realities and make sure what you're proposing can be done on a realistic television budget.

A great plus to creating your own science fiction show is that the fan audience tends to be very loyal, and even after the show has left the air it can live on in reruns, books, comic books, you name it. And then of course, like *Star Trek*, *STAR WARS*, *Doctor Who*, and *Battlestar Galactica*, it can return in ever-newer versions.

Finally—and most important of all—tell your truth. You're writing about your own life and experience, whatever imaginary cloak you put it in. Authenticity is what resonates with an audience. My dear friend and mentor Ray Bradbury told me always to look inward rather than outside myself for stories. It was good advice. But in reality, everything you are, everything you read, see, hear, experience, is grist for your mill.

Just make sure that what you create has something uniquely yours in it, something you care deeply about and are willing to invest years in bringing to fruition, and you'll be way ahead of the game.

When I was thirteen, a friend gave me a gift of a trip to the original *Star Trek* set during filming of the show's last episode. Now I'm building spaceship sets for *SPACE COMMAND*. I still feel the same excitement standing on the bridge.

Here's another thing Ray Bradbury told me, when he was in his eighties: "I have a secret to tell you," he said, and motioned me close. "I'm thirteen years old."

It was true. For that's the age when our sense of wonder is most pure, and he'd kept that intact, nurtured it, safeguarded it. I take that lesson to heart, and I urge you to do so too. Send that thirteen-year-old self into the future, the past, out to the stars and beyond.

It's an exciting universe . . . and it can be all yours.

EXERCISE

1. Start by thinking of what kind of science fiction show you might want to create. What in the real world excites you, gets you angry? What do you want to comment on? Extrapolate from there.

2. Think of five characters who might be your leads. They can be from real life or other sources, but real life helps. Make them distinctive and different from one another.

3. Put these characters in your science-fiction world. Start generating story ideas, springboards of a sentence or two. Try to generate at least twenty or thirty of these.

4. Read over what you've written and come up with five ways to make these ideas fresh and novel, different from what you've seen.

5. If you're particularly daring, outline several of these stories—beginning, middle, and end. These outlines should be no more than five pages each.

6. If you're really daring, write up a series bible—a concise description of your show, its characters, the world and the storylines, maybe even the series arc. Then write your pilot script. Now you've got something you can take out and sell. Good luck!

RICHARD BLEILER

Teaching Robert Heinlein's *Starship Troopers*

RICHARD BLEILER is the humanities librarian for the University of Connecticut, where he also teaches a class on the history and development of science fiction. He was editor of *Science Fiction Writers* and *Supernatural Fiction Writers: Contemporary Fantasy and Horror*; he was co-author of *Science-Fiction: The Early Years* and *Science-Fiction: The Gernsback Years*. He was nominated for a Bram Stoker Award for Best Nonfiction in 2002.

You do not have to like the works you are teaching, but you should respect them, and one of the works I most respect is Robert Heinlein's *Starship Troopers*. It is more than fifty years old, and yet it remains vital in an astonishing number of ways. It operates successfully on many levels and should be read by anybody wanting to write or understand American science fiction. It is one of the landmark works of science fiction.

Starship Troopers is first and foremost an exciting and tense adventure novel, and if one takes nothing else from Heinlein's narrative, this enjoyment from reading a thrilling adventure story should not be underestimated. Nevertheless, *Starship Troopers* is so much more. It is a statement about the nature and future of humanity; it is a traditional *bildungsroman* merged with a *tendenzroman;* and it is a monster story. It is also a remarkable combination of tendentiousness, provocation, and debatable political philosophy that too many students have swallowed whole without first wondering what it is they're chewing.

When I teach the novel, my classes tend to have two levels: call them *understanding* and *overstanding*. It is only through the *understand-*

ing of the text that the *overstanding* of it can be reached, and the way I like to begin to reach a common, shared understanding is by requiring as homework a brief—no more than one page—paper on the novel. This paper is not graded and is for them to answer a basic question: What makes the novel science fiction? There are many definitions—by this time in the class we have covered some, as well as discussed the list given in "Science Fiction and This Moment," the introduction to Istvan Csicsery-Ronay's *The Seven Beauties of Science Fiction*—so the students have started to recognize some of the problems inherent in attempting to define the genre.

Next, I do not lecture but instead ask them to describe what they have read, and not simply to summarize the story as it occurs in the novel. Rather, they are to put the novel's events in chronological order, describing briefly the motivations for action and the results. (At its most elemental, this confirms that they have read the book and not a Wikipedia entry.) In *Starship Troopers* a description of the narrative is actually fairly difficult, for one of Heinlein's narrative tricks is akin to making the reader focus on one thing and believe it is significant, while actually diverting attention from the other and more significant issue. In addition, Heinlein cheerfully withholds information: He avoids the dreaded info dump by almost never explaining anything, dropping hints and oblique statements that become important only in retrospect.

The class, forced to gather evidence, fill in gaps, answer questions and make assumptions, becomes embedded in understanding the story at a level that would not be possible if the narrative was linear, spelled out, and explicit. They are encouraged to correct each other but to be polite. It is surprising how few students recognize that Heinlein's Earth is under what may be seen as a benign military rule, its population divided into two groups, civilians and soldiers. They likewise often fail to recognize that only soldiers can vote in elections, run the country, and teach the class on history and moral philosophy; too often they fail to note that the soldiers tend to regard the civilians as sheep. And too often they have accepted, at face value, the arguments put forward by Mr. Dubois and others during the course of the novel;

i.e., "*Required*: to prove that war and moral perfection derive from the same genetic inheritance. Briefly, thus: All wars arise from population pressure."

Nevertheless, once a shared level of understanding has been reached, the questions that lead to a critical assessment—the *overstanding*—can be asked.

Next: linkage and contextualization. The first novel read by the class is Edward Bellamy's *Looking Backward, 2000—1887*, a book whose ideas and proposed solutions provoke discussion and dissension though the narrative is stodgy by today's standards. I point out that *Starship Troopers* is as argumentative and contentious as *Looking Backward*, which generally comes as a surprise to my students before they realize that Heinlein was the superior storyteller with a more contemporary voice. Still, like Bellamy, he was criticizing society and offering solutions to what he perceived as its problems.

Finally, after the novel is finished, I like to give students a piece of relevant criticism. I ask them to read Thomas Disch's deliberately outrageous "The Embarrassments of Science Fiction" and address the issues Disch raises about science fiction in general and Heinlein in particular. This always generates discussion: The students find themselves having to defend a novel whose ideas and conclusions they do not necessarily accept.

EXERCISE

Read Robert Heinlein's *Starship Troopers*.

To deepen your understanding of the book and issues of concern to science fiction writers in general, here are a few questions to consider while reading or after you finish. First, the "whys":

1. Why are there almost no women visible in *Starship Troopers*, although the scene at the conclusion of the first chapter and in the recruiting station in the novel's second chapter leaves no doubt that they are competent and tough enough to serve as starship

pilots? What reasons can be extrapolated from the society described by Heinlein?

2. Why does one get one chance only to serve as a soldier in Heinlein's society? Why is there no room for personal growth, individual maturation, and second chances?

3. Why does Heinlein's first chapter include a lengthy passage that calls to mind a human in the birth canal? What is being born here? If it is birth, what matures during the course of the novel?

4. Why are the soldiers fighting the "formics"?

5. What conclusions can be drawn from Johnnie's revelation that Tagalog is his native language? Why is this intriguing piece of information not given at the beginning of the book? (I present Samuel Delany's reaction upon this revelation which was, essentially, "Oh my, this isn't one more novel featuring white Americans saving the universe. The main character is brown—like me!")

And then there are the questions that address the philosophy presented in the novel:

6. Mr. Dubois heaps scorn on the idea that "violence never settles anything," arguing that violence has settled more issues in history than any other factor. Is this true? Is violence the only way a conflict can be settled? If so, what does this say about humanity? And if you disagree, figure out where Mr. Dubois was using "weasel words" and undermine his argument.

7. Mr. Dubois argues that there are no unalienable rights and takes exception to the phrase, *life, liberty, and the pursuit of happiness*. His counterarguments show that he equates physical laws with political laws. He likewise deconstructs the phrase *juvenile delinquent*, arguing that there is no such thing, that they are only juvenile hoodlums. Is his argument valid?

8. And of course, the statement about "all wars arising from population pressure." I challenge my students (and you) to duplicate

Johnnie's supposed research. Can you find demonstrable exceptions to the rule?

Do you think Heinlein believed his own arguments? Or was he just playing with ideas? After all, in science fiction playing with ideas is encouraged.

I hope that examining this work shows that you can write a sophisticated novel of ideas and still make it exciting and worthy of respect.

BRIANNA WINNER

Understanding Yourself Better Through Creative Writing

BRIANNA WINNER and her identical twin sister Brittany are America's youngest multiple-award-winning authors and writing teachers. Their first novel, *The Strand Prophecy*, became a national best seller on their thirteenth birthday. They have now written four novels, a graphic novel, and a writing book. They were recognized as prodigies by The World Council for Gifted and Talented Children.

D o you remember playing pretend when you were a child? Though you did not realize it at the time, those pretend games helped you better understand your environment and yourself. Storytelling is an important part of being human. It is instinctual, a way to understand why the world works the way it does, and a way to overcome our fears and problems. As we get older, some channel that creativity into art, acting, directing, and music. But storytelling is embedded into our lives, whether visually or in words.

Every writer consciously or unconsciously puts elements of themselves and their lives into their work. After all, you create your ideas, and your ideas are a combination of everything you experience and dream about. It may be the places you have been to or wish you could go, the way you wish the world was, or the person you strive to be. We have come to realize that story ideas are a reflection of events and feelings we experienced in our lives.

I have loved storytelling my entire life. When the other children stopped playing pretend, I chose to continue. I loved storytelling too much to let it go. My identical twin sister and I created worlds filled with science fiction characters, planets, and rich history. Our characters and story arcs were complex and compelling. We could spend all day completely content just dreaming about our stories and the worlds we created. Those stories helped us to cope with the harshness of school. Storytelling was not only our passion, but our escape.

Storytelling helped me filter through emotions and lessons I learned by trial and error. Through it I could explore the person I wanted to become and the parts of myself I wanted to change. It gave me an escape from my problems and a way to empower myself to overcome them. Playing pretend as a child and storytelling as an adult are not that different, but what is different is your age. The biggest difference is when you are older you write your stories down. Essentially every author plays pretend.

My identical twin sister and I are now authors and our love for storytelling has only grown. We continue to think about the relationship between reality and fiction and look back at our stories from when we were younger. We decided to "reverse engineer" what we all do when we are young, using emotions and memories and fictionalizing them consciously, not only as a filter for our emotions, but as a way to create new story ideas. Here is an example:

I found a quiet place and brought with me a piece of paper and a pencil. I thought back to a defining memory and tried to visualize it in as much detail as I could.

THE CARDBOARD BOX

I wasn't as nervous as I should have been. The hill was large and I was very small. I was only ten years old then, but even for a ten-year-old I was smaller than most. My friend and sister had already done it and nothing went wrong. Clearly I had no reason to be afraid. My sister handed me the cardboard box and I sat inside. She pushed the box and I went sliding down the hill. For the first couple of seconds it was fun; it felt like a roller coaster. But the dirt, rocks, and leaves were making the box swerve back and forth. I tried my best to keep it straight, but the more I kept pulling on the box, the more unstable it became. The sides began to fall off, and I was left holding onto the bottom of the box, screaming at the top of my lungs. When it came to a stop at the bottom of the hill, I was so afraid I just sat there for a minute in shock. If the box had rolled over, I would have scraped the side of my body on sharp rocks. I never did it again, and I am still wary of large hills.

I wrote down my answers to these questions on my piece of paper.

1. *Why did I choose this memory?* I chose it because it helped me realize that I was mortal.

2. *How did it make me feel?* At first I was a little worried but I ignored the fear. When I started down the hill it was exciting, but it soon became terrifying.

3. *What did it teach me?* It taught me to think through my actions and to not ignore my gut feelings just because other people say there is nothing to be afraid of. It also helped me understand there were repercussions to my actions.

Now I fictionalize that story, using my memory and my answers I wrote down as a source to create something new. I enjoy science fiction, so my story will be set in the far future in space.

THE SPACE SHIP

Ten-year-olds had no right flying spaceships. She knew this, but that didn't stop Anna. Her sister and friend had done it, and they said it was fun.

The space station where she lived was located next to an asteroid field. In school all children learned how to fly spaceships and were given their own little spaceship to practice with. But they were only allowed to fly their ships under adult supervision.

All the children had their ships parked next to their bedroom windows. So Anna took her new hacking skills she learned earlier that day and hacked into the console to open the window to her small access tube. She climbed through it and into her ship and turned it on.

She felt uneasy, but she decided to ignore it and to keep going. She took a deep breath in and flew toward the asteroid field.

The asteroids were large and jagged. At first it was fun flying in and out of the asteroids, but the asteroids began to move. Two large asteroids on either side of her ship began to move toward each other. She tried to accelerate her ship but it wasn't fast enough. The asteroids crashed against the sides of her ship. The metal screeched and the emergency oxygen mask came down from the top of her ship. She quickly put on the mask and kept accelerating. The asteroid punctured holes in her ship, and it was about to crush her. She barely made it out the other side before the asteroids slammed together. She sat for a minute in shock and then flew back to the station. She never flew in an asteroid field again.

EXERCISE

Get a piece of paper and a pencil and find a quiet place to write.

Now close your eyes and think of a defining memory in your life. Visualize it in as much detail as you can. After you have chosen your memory, ask yourself these questions.

1. *Why did I choose this memory?*

2. *How did it make me feel?*

3. *What did it teach me?*

Write your answers on your piece of paper.

Now fictionalize your story, using your memory and the answers you wrote down as a source to create something new.

It must be a genre you enjoy writing in.

Close your eyes and imagine a scene in your genre of choice. Get in touch with your inner child and get lost in the world you are creating. Then write your scene down. Keep dreaming and writing.

DEVORAH CUTLER-RUBENSTEIN

Giving Sentience to Ordinary Objects—
An Object's Purpose

DEVORAH CUTLER-RUBENSTEIN is an adjunct professor at USC's School of Cinematic Arts. A former studio exec, she began her career helping supervise Roger Zelzany's *DAMNATION ALLEY* for 20th Century Fox, and co-wrote the horror thriller *ZOMBIE DEATH HOUSE*. Recent credits include writer/producer/director on *Tattoo-U* for the FX Channel and co-writer/director "Peacock Blues" for Showtime's *Stories from the Edge*.

As children we plagued adults with endless "what if" scenarios. *What if the sky fell? What if the ocean dried up? What if my dead parakeets buried in the orange grove came back as zombie birds?*

My first poem at age nine was a classic case of what if: "Pink Cats with Purple Tails," which I recited to an enthralled audience of two: my parents. By eleven, my parents divorced and everything got a bit darker. My short story about an unhappy rebellious boy who turns his strict parents into butterflies beat out the adults in a citywide competition. A little encouragement goes a long way, and for better or worse I continue the tradition by helping others, hoping to ignite that child-like spark of imagination. Living inside all of us there's an unbridled kid genius posing the big "what if." What if every day can be a play date with our imagination?

One of the best ways to get ourselves "imagineering" is to engage in a slightly modified version of the "what if" game, looking at the purpose underlying your central character—a central character that's not necessarily or always human. How do you take an ordinary person, place, or thing and imbue it with believable supernatural powers, horrific potential, or otherworldly properties?

Successful stories have a main character with a strong sense of purpose. In speculative fiction it's often pretty simple—two opposing forces duke it out for power over the world they inhabit. Not surprisingly, underneath this massive power play there's an even larger purpose, almost spiritual or anti-spiritual in nature. This "super objective" is the hidden fuel that drives any great story forward. If you can identify that purpose—constructed from the agar of your big idea—your story suddenly has legs, eyes, maybe even sharp teeth.

My exercise is about giving consciousness to an ordinary object and figuring out the inner purpose of the now-sentient object. What does it want? What would be the most interesting thing it could possibly want? What might it want that surprises and excites you? What could it want that we've never seen on a page, stage, or screen before?

To give an object special properties for horror, sci-fi, or fantasy, you as the writer need to hook into your own passion or curiosity about an object you might pick up from a sandy shore or out of a dusty drawer. Wherever your object comes from, it should have some kind of "pull" for you. Your fascination doesn't have to border on obsession—plain ol' curiosity works.

For instance, I love microscopic or invisible worlds. When I look at anything normal, I wonder what I am *not* seeing. A few years back I heard about a special rock you could buy for your aquarium, an X Rock. It arrives sealed in bubble-wrap with a birth certificate from the UACA (Unique Aquatic Creatures Association) assuring you that your X Rock has a multitude of sleeping creatures in its nooks and crannies—much like Magic Monkeys—just add water and watch as strange, odd-looking shrimp and one-eyed kelp appear. I am sure your imagination is already going into overdrive.

The "what-if + purpose" game in speculative fiction is especially critical. It's a necessary component to exploding open your imagination. It allows your mind to surf the logical or illogical extremes of a thought . . . to skateboard down the alleyways of your mind and step into an altered universe of your object's unstoppable desire.

Let's put some sentience into the mix. What if the rock is a creature, an alien, or perhaps just another type of consciousness that can worm its way into the mind of its host? And a psychotic-symbiosis between creature consciousness and host slowly begins to take over the host's life—like any scary modern-day virus story. Could its purpose be to drive its host insane to the point of forcing its own liberation? Or did it just need the arms and legs a human could provide, that its existence trapped in a rock shape denies?

Why does one person choose a particular person to paint and another a landscape? It doesn't matter. It's your imagination calling. Whether this exercise leads to a new story or you use it to practice warming your imagination by the fire, if you're sitting in a café in Paris just remember, "what if . . ." What if the Eiffel Tower was put there by aliens as a guiding rod? And your character has to find their hidden GPS before Earth is destroyed? Cliché? Maybe. Keep working it. Have fun and don't forget to pack your imagination.

EXERCISE

1. Take an ordinary object from your home, school, office, local antique store, nearby landfill, or pond. Choose something that seems innocuous and forgotten, but for some reason you are curious or attracted to it.

2. Next, on a piece of paper, do a timed writing exercise. Take at least ten minutes and describe what it is very simply. What is the material it's made out of? Does it have sharp or dull edges? Round or square shape? Color or gray toned? Textured or smooth? Smell. Weight. Size. Be specific. What is it normally used for? Set this aside because your imagination is collecting paint on the divine palate of your child genius brain, which it may or may not use.

3. Next, sit somewhere comfortable and let your mind wander. Imagine what could happen to your object if it had a purpose other than the one it seems to have been designed for. For instance . . . what if an ordinary fork was a lightning rod for a dark and invisible

force? What if it was the opposite—it had the power to heal with one bite? What if this antique fork (make it unusual with its own backstory or future story) seems to be a portal for some sort of agenda? Perhaps you discover, going back centuries to the metal-smith in Salem, Massachusetts, that it was made using Satan's spit. Perhaps it taints the food that comes in contact with it, turns it black, singes it, smokes it . . . Take your "what if" and twist it and turn it to surprise yourself with the possible variations just by changing its divine (or evil) purpose. Now, what could go right? What might take the curse off a cursed fork? Or, if it is a healing fork, what could go wrong? What or who could have had first contact with it, and what legacy or curse needs to be undone, or what lesson learned? NOTE: In order for your choices not to be cliché, continue to think about why you like it . . . what attracts you to the object? And besides what could go right or wrong, to create further complications, ask: What possible problem could your character-object have that develops, builds, and progresses? The purpose can grow and change too.

4. Now write down a few ideas you liked from the exploration you just did. You may have the beginning of a story—just based on an ordinary object that you chose moments ago.

5. Before you lock in on it too quickly, allow yourself to think genre too. Add that to the blend. For instance, if you are doing hor-ror, that has one flavor to it. Or if you do a mixed genre, horror-comedy for instance, that has a different application. Each genre offers a different tone to the object's same purpose—just with a different spin.

Here is the equation: Object + What If + Purpose = STORY-SQUARED!

Examples:

A Rock + Can Think + Wants to Control Its Owner.

A Rock (meteor) + Can Make You Hear the Truth
(when you touch it) + Frees People to Do What They Are Scared Of.

(The latter was the basis of *Starfall*, the first story I got optioned by NBC's Operation Peacock, and it got me my first agent!)

Variation: Have someone choose an object and put it in a paper sack where you cannot see it but only feel it. Set the timer for five to ten minutes. Write about what it makes you feel as you begin to guess what it is—and what it might do to you once you figure it out.

WENDY MEWES

Leaping into Landscape

WENDY MEWES has written numerous books and articles, including *Discovering the History of Brittany*, a travelogue *Crossing Brittany*, and the Footprint travel guide to the region. Her most recent work is *Legends of Brittany*. Her two novels are *Moon Garden* and *The Five of Cups*. Current research is for a new work, "The Mirror of Landscape."

I'm on the side of legend although history is my day job. I filter ideas through the landscape, that great melting pot of man and nature. Legends grew from the need to come to terms with our environment. It's a way of controlling fear of the unknown, by leaping right in and reinterpreting the world in a new guise. Mysterious lights on the moor at night, the flicker of movement half-seen in the forest—we give these shadowy presences identity so we can meet them in our minds and devise strategies for dealing with the threats they pose. The most compelling fantasy is only just beyond the tipping point of reality: The two need connection.

Here in Brittany I live at the heart of Celtic legend, tales springing from forests and moors, rocky crags and misty marsh, landscapes that breed all manner of creatures in the imagination. A skeletal Ankou searches for souls to seize for Death, huge black dogs roam lonely paths, and at their peril do travelers respond to the call of nocturnal washerwomen . . . For malignant beings peopling harsh, eerie vistas we have only to think of *The Lord of the Rings*, where Tolkien raises landscape almost to the level of character.

Currently I'm working on the concept of the Mirror of Landscape.

Legends emanate from somewhere beyond the surface reality of man's land management: To reach those recondite layers you have to look through this mirror, to a place where our own psychological reflection meets the source of ancient creativity. It's archaeology of the imagination.

Take forest, with a dual personality fruitful for fantasy. Both dangerous and protective, it harbors hermits and monsters, criminals and refugees alike, light and shadow are its essence. Shelter becomes concealment, and the forest's semi-magical powers of transformation and regeneration challenge our very sense of self. Hidden from the sun, we literally lose direction and the balance of life suddenly shifts.

In the fourteenth century, Dante offered the first literary midlife crisis with this metaphor: *"Midway upon the journey of our life, I found myself within a forest dark / For the straightforward pathway had been lost."* The sudden descent into fear, confusion, and helplessness fits the often-bewildering geography of forest, with its twists and turns, narrow views, and unknown edges. Forest also dwells within.

The primitive aspect of forest stirs an instinctive response: Before civilization was forest. It represents something outside normal values, the haunt of giants and savage beasts. Dark Age monks cleared the land of trees to establish organized communities. This felling is symbolic of control, destroying the old pagan beliefs with stories of saints driving out evil monsters from their land. Good and evil play out in the landscape.

Forest is full of fantastical tales, from tragic *Babes in the Wood* to Shakespeare's light comedy of tricks and disguise in the Forest of Arden. Merlin's magic was powerless against the wiles of Viviane in Brocéliande, and knights who had been unfaithful to their lovers found themselves trapped by walls of air in the Valley of No Return. Such tales enhance an already exceptional landscape: They spin fantasy from Earth's layers, forging a connection between Nature and the world of man.

Forest is never destination, but a step on the path, a setting for adventure and challenge. We all need to be lost from time to time.

EXERCISE

Get in the habit of observing landscape and your own reactions to different environments. How do your moods relate to your surroundings? Watch for movements of all kinds and the changes wrought by the seasons. Keep notes and photos, think colors, sounds, and shapes.

Create fantasy characters to represent different elements in the landscape. Start with keywords that are simply descriptive (mountain—tall, forest—dark) and then try to make psychological links, something that reflects your own experiences and instincts—water may be inviting and relaxing or dangerous and unpredictable, and forests may be deeply peaceful or unpleasantly confusing.

Let's go into the forest and think about turning your emotions into situations and characters.

1. You find yourself tree-locked under a thick canopy that cuts out much of the light. Start by writing a physical description of your surroundings.

    Move on to show how your own feelings are reflected back from the forest. Does what you see make you calm, anxious, or frightened? What are your instincts about this situation?

    Suddenly there's a mysterious noise and you sense movement nearby. What can it be? Rationalize. What do you fear it is? Imagine.

    Describe your attempts to find a way out of the forest. How do physical obstacles translate into emotions? How does your body react to the situation? What do you hear and touch and sense? Are you really alone? Maybe you hear voices. Do you seek help? Will you survive?

    Conjure up a fantasy character that represents forest (not a tree!). Give a detailed physical description and character analysis. Then use this in a short story called "Death Comes to Dragon Forest."

    Go inside. Find forest.

ERIC STENER CARLSON

Finding Your Spirit in Speculative Writing

ERIC STENER CARLSON is the author of three books including supernatural mystery *The Saint Perpetuus Club of Buenos Aires* (Tartarus Press, 2009). He is also a human rights advocate, having investigated the mass graves in Argentina as well as human rights violations in the former Yugoslavia.

Writing is not like dancing on a stage along with other dancers, more or less in solidarity with you, and in front of a clearly defined jury. It is not a competition where the best writer wins, based upon some uniform criteria.

Writing is like dancing in the woods, alone. It is like dancing until your toes bleed and your joints ache. It is performing when there is only the hope that God sees your performance. It is performing in the hope that there is, indeed, a God, and that, publish your novel or not, He is pleased by it.

And after years of performing this ritual of writing in the hope that, someday, someone will want to share in it, years of sleepless nights, years of broken social engagements, you finally have a 400-page manuscript in hand, you pop it in the mail along with a SASE, and you wait for a response.

That's when the writing stops. Writing, as opposed to publishing. The older I get, in fact, the less connection I see between the quality of writing and the success in publishing.

Writing is a supreme act of faith, a grasping for the universal. Publishing is a roulette wheel.

So, it makes me believe that we need to rescue the spiritual aspects of writing, the act of writing itself, if we're going to have any satisfaction in the finished product.

Of course, because we live in a material world, and we all dream of making a living out of writing, we want to publish our work. And, therefore, as any good writing teacher says, we have to bear in mind our audience. Writing is not just a private conversation with ourselves, but a public conversation, albeit with someone else who doesn't arrive until several years after we've finished speaking.

But, in the interim, between the years we spend writing our speculative novel and the moment when the first reader cracks open the book, we have to find some way to bear the solitude. I am sure other writers will recommend "workshopping" or "blogging" or "sharing with your peers."

And, yes, other people outside the woods can help you in certain technical aspects of the ritual.

But that's not writing. My view of writing is like my view of religion—there is just you in a direct relationship with God, and no "blogging," just as no priest, can intercede for you.

As John writes, "In the beginning was the Word, and the Word was with God, and the Word was God." Writing, therefore, is not just talking to God. Writing actually *is* God.

Writing is suffering, yes. Just as I believe that, to some extent, religion is about suffering. But writing is also about finding infinite beauty. It is about discovering that clearing in the woods where something astounding is taking place, a gathering of fantastic creatures no one else has ever witnessed. It is the clear result of human feeling made manifest. It is the sublime expression of your soul.

As such, writing is more important than taking that lunch break with your colleague from Accounting. It's more important than those two hours of watching some "reality" television show you're never going to remember, or wasting your life in increasing your number of illusory friends in your "social network."

That's why I like the Greek word *eudemonia* to express how I feel about writing: It's often translated as "happiness," but it means, actually, "having a good guardian spirit" or, which I prefer, "finding your spirit" (or demon, but in a positive sense).

That's why, when you write about a character, for example, who wants to sell his soul to the Devil or contact a loved one from the spirit world, we shouldn't divorce ourselves from our own experience of writing. That is, our soul is so important to us that it should be equally important to our characters.

Every time you scratch a pen against paper or sit down in front of your computer, every noun, every verb you write, should be a prayer. It should be dedicated to finding your spirit. (It should *not* be geared toward publishing—toward imagining what other people want— which, as I've said, seems to have almost no relation to the writing process.)

This is not to say that, every time you write, you're going to channel the spirit of Marcel Proust. Some prayers are angry and full of profanity and incomplete and quickly crumpled up and thrown in the garbage can. Some of the best prayers, I think, are like that, because we pray hardest in moments of supreme desperation. But that doesn't make them less worthy.

And although I've made a number of Christian references, please don't think I'm trying to sell one interpretation of writing or one interpretation of God. Like the path to God, there are many paths to finding your spirit through writing.

You may belong to an organized religion. You may have your own personal religion. You may not have a religion at all. You may not even believe in God.

But the reason you feel a burning desire to carve out at least half an hour to write every day, out of the humdrum of your routine of calculating spreadsheets or writing code or waiting tables or plastering posters on telephone poles, is because there is something very spiritual, very deep, and very beautiful inside of you that you are driven to express. I call it God. You may call it something entirely different. But there it is, nonetheless.

Therefore, you do not need to go outside yourself to imagine a struggle between angels and demons. As a writer, you're already involved in that struggle. You just have to tap into it.

To access this spirit, especially when we are talking about fantastic literature, where I feel belief is much more important than structure, I suggest three simple exercises below. Take the good. Leave the bad. And don't let anyone tell you how you are supposed to write. Especially not me.

EXERCISE

1. *On finding the spirit:* I keep a book of prayers on my bedside table written by the Armenian St. Gregory of Narek, *Speaking with God from the Depths of the Heart.* Written more than a thousand years ago, I find his lamentations so inspiring, that I take great comfort in them. When I become overcome with thoughts about deadlines and recognition and (oh, yes) the possibility of royalties, I read one of St. Gregory's prayers, to remind me that writing is essentially a spiritual exercise. Whatever book is important to you, whether it's religious or profane—perhaps it was the first book that inspired you to become a writer of the fantastic (by Poe or Le Fanu or Machen)—keep it close to you. Reread fragments now and then to remind you that you are engaged in a dialogue that goes far beyond any you're ever going to have with your publisher.

2. *On the nature of the soul:* I don't believe the most important part of a "ghost" story is the shock value or the gore. Rather, it is the fundamental question of the human soul. If there are spirits trapped on this earth, what does that imply about God? What does that imply about justice? Again, if your character is considering selling his eternal soul for something immediate—either gaining worldly possessions or saving his child—for there to be something terrible about that transaction, there has to be something incredibly precious about the soul. And if the soul is not just a poker chip to be cashed in for something more convenient, but something our character lives and breathes, then I suggest we first ask ourselves what our soul means to us. Do you believe in a soul? Where does it go when we die? And would we sell it just to get published?

3. *On describing evil:* I remember quite clearly a moment in the Caribbean one night, when I woke up with the distinct feeling there was

an evil presence in my room. Not a hypothetical, read-it-in-a-book sort of evil, but Evil, right there, crouching next to me. I turned on all the lights, and I searched through my room, until I found a prayer for protection. And I read that prayer, over and over again, until the dawn. If the evil we describe in our books is to have any resonance, then we should recognize the role it plays in our own lives. For me, that night in the Caribbean, as well as my work in the mass graves in Argentina and my investigation of war crimes in the former Yugoslavia, remind me that evil—whether from the devil or the person sitting next to you—is real. If we examine our own lives (or even just turn on the nightly news), we can find enough evil on which to build believable characters. But for our own piece of mind, once we've finished writing about evil, the comforting thing is this—if the Devil exists, then so does God.

MEMORABLE HEROES, VILLAINS, AND MONSTERS

"Two hours of writing fiction leaves this writer completely drained. For those two hours he has been in a different place with totally different people."

—ROALD DAHL

DIANA PETERFREUND

Start with the Name

DIANA PETERFREUND is the author of nine novels, including the Secret Society Girl series, the killer unicorn novels *Rampant* and *Ascendant*, and the post-apocalyptic *For Darkness Shows the Stars*. Her short stories have appeared in *Locus*'s Best of the Year list and included in *The Best Science Fiction and Fantasy of the Year, Volume Five*.

I'm a bit of a name nerd. I can't get a handle on a character until I've chosen the perfect name, and don't get my husband started on how long I fretted over the name of our firstborn.

Character names are one of the more useful tools in the writer's toolbox, a fact that has long been exploited by genre fiction's brightest stars. Want an on-the-nose depiction of the character's personality? Look to naming masters like Charles Dickens (Ebenezer Scrooge is an unbeatable classic) or J. K. Rowling (Draco Malfoy is a personal fave). Want to play with the reader's prejudices and expectations? There's a reason Joss Whedon named his cheerleader-turned-vampire-slayer the valley girl classic Buffy Summers. Want to indicate right off the bat that your story takes place in a world very different than our own? Jasper Fforde's Tuesday Next or Neal Stephenson's Hiro Protagonist drives the point home like nothing else.

What's in a name?

- *Personality*: From the name alone, you get an idea that a man named Albus Dumbledore is going to be goofy and whimsical, and one named Uriah Heep is going to be noxious. This can work especially well for minor characters and walk-ons.

- *Background*: After all, the name was ostensibly picked by the character's parents. I used this trick in *Rampant*, where reluctant teen unicorn hunter Astrid Llewelyn resents the Valkyrie warrior name chosen by her heritage-obsessed mother.

- *World building*: You know from the start that a man named Bilbo Baggins and one named Thorin Oakenshield grew up in very different societies, with different expectations and values for their citizens. And the marriage of a familiar name with a more unusual one will signal to the reader that your fantasy characters are human (Lord Eddard "Ned" Stark in *Game of Thrones*) or that your futuristic spacefarers have Earthly roots (like Frank Herbert's Lady Jessica Atreides, from *Dune*).

Rumplestiltskin (another awesome handle!) was right: Names have power, and properly tweaked, names can fix all kinds of important details in the reader's mind with one or two words. The writer's rule of "show, don't tell" shines clarion bright in a well-chosen moniker.

Don't discount the additional power that can be derived from a name the character chooses himself. Though Orson Scott Card's Andrew Wiggin picks up "Ender" through childish mispronunciation, it becomes a darkly appropriate nickname as his devastating talent in military strategy destroys an entire race of aliens. Even the title of the book, *Ender's Game*, plays on the phrase "endgame."

Paul Atreides, the exiled nobleman of *Dune*, knows exactly what he's doing when he chooses the tribal name of Muad'Dib—which is a Fremen word for both the highly adaptable and tough mouse who silently thrives in the desert and the name of the mouse-shaped shadow that dominates the planet's moon. As Muad'Dib, Paul secretly consolidates power in the desert, and uses it to wrest control of not only the entire planet, but also the universe.

I utilized this trick in *For Darkness Shows the Stars*. In that novel, the underclass slaves are given a single, one-syllable name, which makes them easily distinguishable from their multi-syllabic and surname-bearing masters. When freed, they adopt long names to honor their past, their family members, or qualities they wish to embrace. An explorer named Kai by his slave father Mal becomes Malakai Wentforth when he has the freedom to choose for himself.

Though fantasy novels are often the brunt of jokes when it comes to their more ornate naming conventions (i.e., letter salad with too many Zs, Ks, and apostrophes), you don't need to give your characters a weird or overly long name to make a statement. (Think of Tiny Tim, Jonathan Strange, or the aforementioned Ender Wiggin.) Often, giving a character a prosaic name can ground him as the everyman thrust into a world beyond his imagining (like Harry Potter or *THE TERMINATOR*'s Sarah Connor).

And one of my favorite tricks when I have a character who isn't quite gelling is to shake things up by changing his name. Once, a "Victor" I'd been struggling with for several chapters became "Vincent" mid-sentence, and thereafter clicked into place as the smoother, more charismatic leader I'd wanted from the start. Try it.

EXERCISE

Look at the names you've chosen (or may choose). Are they doing the work you want them to?

Make a list of your main characters and next to each name, ask yourself: What does this name say about the society this person came from? The people who gave the character this name (and probably had an impact on his or her upbringing)? Is the name one the character likes? Tolerates? Hates? Would the character ditch it in favor of a nickname of his own choosing (or, if a nickname, is he trying to get people to call him by his real name instead)?

Pay attention to the name the character is actually called in the text. Is it a last name? First name? Nickname? Title? It's all very well that you named your character Nobility von Trueheart Smith, but if everyone calls him Mr. Smith or "Red," your message isn't necessarily getting across. I once wrote a character named Jamie Orcutt, but his dour, sinister personality was wrapped up in his nickname: Poe.

Similarly, don't rely on the meanings often listed next to names in baby name books. Few readers know that Leslie means *garden of holly*. And connotation is as important as definition. After all, Adolf means *noble wolf*, but think twice before bestowing it on your heroic werewolf prince, since most readers would tag it deeply sinister.

Now look at your minor characters. Can you cut a lot of tiresome description of their personality by giving them a name that does the work for you? Instead of telling us that the walk-on in chapter four is a spoiled trust-fund baby, can you call him Alistair Winston Carlisle IV? Can the down-home farmer be Buddy-Ray instead of Mike?

Don't be afraid to change a character's name for a few chapters and see what becomes of them. After all, "find and replace" is only a few clicks away if you decide you want to go back, and you may discover the new, secret name holds a power all its own.

KAREN MCCOY

How Characters Drive Plot

KAREN MCCOY is a librarian who's been writing full-time since 2008, including reviews for *Children's Literature* and *Library Journal* and a feature in *School Library Journal* "What Teens Are Really Reading." She writes YA sci-fi/fantasy novels and is seeking representation.

> *"The story . . . must be a conflict, and specifically, a conflict between the forces of good and evil within a single person."*
> —Maxwell Anderson

Characters, whether they are protagonists, antagonists, minor or secondary, should be as multi-dimensional as possible. This is especially true for sci-fi, fantasy, and horror stories.

J. K. Rowling's Harry Potter books have intricate plots, sophisticated world building, and a great sense of humor. While these are all great elements to include, what makes the Harry Potter books most memorable are the complex, layered characters. If Harry was flat and one-dimensional, it probably wouldn't matter if he lived in a world where pictures move and owls carry the mail.

Take the multi-dimensional Severus Snape. While his true motivation isn't revealed until the final book, his actions always keep readers guessing. His bitter nature and moral ambiguity set him apart, allowing his character to stand independent of the plot and remain interesting.

As agent Vickie Motter stated on her blog, "Often at conferences, I'll ask a writer to describe the main character. They will then proceed to tell me what happens to them in the plot. No, no, no. I asked about the character. Who is your character? Why should we care? What makes them tick? What will draw readers to them?"

These are all necessary questions to ask while shaping multi-dimensional characters. Here are some other important elements to consider:

Characters must have a voice—don't make them speak; let them speak. When I first started writing, my dialogue was terrible. Part of this had to do with my unwillingness to let go of formal language, but the other problem was I was trying to *make* the characters speak, instead of *letting* them speak.

Now, when I go through revisions, I'll study the dialogue and ask, *Would so-and-so really say this?* If the answer is no, I let the character tell me what they want to say instead.

It's also important to make sure your character's dialogue is distinctive, especially if you're writing a first-person story with multiple POVs. If someone sounds just like everyone else, his or her diatribes won't be unique enough to keep a reader's attention.

But be careful of thick dialects. A common inclination is to change entire sentences to make a character sound different. Changing one or two words here and there (like *yer* for "your" or *an'* for "and") will do the trick.

Characters must have a motivation (even if it's not always obvious to the reader). There has to be a compelling reason for your characters to see a plot through. To ensure they won't walk away from a death-defying situation, even if they have every reason to.

In an interview, J. K. Rowling put forth a good question to ask characters: "Why fight?" (Why should Harry kill Voldemort? What does he have to gain?)

This "fight" question is a really good one to ask—not only will it help determine your character's motivations, but it's also a good element to include in a query pitch.

And it doesn't always have to do with actual fighting. A character might be compelled to help someone because of love.

A good example of character motivation is found in Janice Hardy's *The Shifter*. In the very first chapter, Nya is put into a dangerous situation because she's hungry. While battling guards, she reveals a unique set of magical abilities.

If Nya hadn't been motivated to steal food, she wouldn't have used her powers to get out of danger, and the plot would have been more stagnant at the beginning. In this way, character motivation drives plot (not the other way around).

Let's say your plot is already mapped out. No problem, just think about why your characters go places, how they interact with what happens to them, and what their motivations are.

Characters must have unique mannerisms/tics that make them who they are. When developing characters, it's often best to avoid stereotypes. Detective-type descriptions are a surefire way to leave your characters dead in the water. (And I'll bet readers won't care if your protagonist is five-foot-eight with size-seven shoes, unless these characteristics are necessary to the plot.)

When writing out scenes, study the actions of your character, whether he or she is tying a shoe or baking a cake. Does your character complete these actions differently than someone else would?

Terry Pratchett, author of the Discworld series, does this best. In his book *Wyrd Sisters*, he uses unique description to make an otherwise ordinary duke different than usual: "The duke had a mind that ticked like a clock and, like a clock, it regularly went cuckoo."

A final note of caution when creating memorable characters: Beware of too much backstory in the narrative. Background is appropriate when creating character sketches, but by the time the final draft of your manuscript is done, the character's childhood, mannerisms, and idiosyncrasies shouldn't be so overbearing that they bog down the rest of the story.

EXERCISE

Take a character from one of your completed novels or works-in-progress and pretend that he or she is sitting down to an interview. Ask this character the following questions:

What makes you happy?

What do you consider your biggest flaws? Why?

What are you fighting? Why?

What annoys you more than anything?

Who do you hate? Why?

Who do you love? Why?

What are your hopes and dreams? What will you do if you don't achieve them?

ERIC EDSON

How We Feel a Story

ERIC EDSON is a professor of screenwriting and author of the book *The Story Solution: 23 Actions All Great Heroes Must Take.* He has written seventeen feature screenplays on assignment for companies including Sony, Warner Bros., Disney, CBS, and Showtime. He is director of the Graduate Program in Screenwriting at California State University, Northridge.

W riters create fiction so they can touch people's hearts.

Blurting it out that way may sound a bit cornball. But compressed to its essence, human truth often comes out sounding sentimental. Doesn't mean it isn't true. We don't write just to preach high-toned themes about saving the planet or how we should all treat each other with a good deal more kindness. No, we seek to construct an emotional experience that leads readers to discover for themselves the real merit of our unspoken themes. In order to be effective, all stories—whether written to be read only or to be read and then filmed—must impart emotion.

One of the big challenges for writers in the "what if?" genres of horror, fantasy, or sci-fi is keeping stories focused from the start on what the lead character is experiencing emotionally, and not let the tale get too lost in the dazzle of the special world going on in the background. Because the very first step for all storytellers is to create a bond of sympathy between the reader and the hero or heroine. Readers need to care deeply about the central character before they can be brought to feel deeply in the story.

To connect with any hero a reader must first, on one level or another, like him. So the most crucial job when beginning your story is to introduce the hero in a way that fosters immediate character sympathy. This remains true no matter if your lead is a classic good-guy type or some moody, morally questionable anti-hero.

Constructing a lead character we care about does not mean inventing a flawless person. We see more of ourselves in people who are eccentric or defensive, who say the wrong thing at exactly the wrong moment. But writers must always remember to balance character flaws with strengths. For a reader to connect emotionally, the heroine's strengths must outnumber her failings.

An actual recipe exists, a list of nine ingredients that elicit sympathetic responses when connecting readers to your hero. The more of these nine character attributes you include, the more emotionally effective your story becomes. Using six is good. Seven is even better. So here are the personality traits and plot circumstances that have been creating sympathetic heroes for more than two thousand years:

1. *Courageous.* Not optional. Your lead has got to have guts. We identify more readily with flawed people, yes, but those flaws cannot include a lack of courage because only brave people take action, and only action can drive a story forward.

2. *Unfairly Injured.* After courage, the second quickest way to bond a reader to your heroine is to place her at the outset in a situation where blatant injustice is being inflicted upon her. Few things stir our passions like injustice. Being unfairly injured also demands that the heroine *do* something in response—an excellent place to start any story.

3. *Skilled.* We admire people who possess the grace, expertise, and mental acumen required to become masters of their chosen work. Doesn't matter what your hero's field of endeavor might be— tinker, tailor, CEO—as long as he's expert at it.

4. *Funny.* We warm to people who make us smile. We're naturally drawn to folks with a humorous view of the passing parade. So if you can possibly bestow upon your hero a robust and playful sense of humor, do it.

5. *Just Plain Nice*. We can easily care about kind, decent, helpful, honest people, and we admire those who treat others well, relate with respect to people in humble walks of life, and who defend the weak or stand up for the helpless.

6. *In Danger*. If when we first meet the heroine she's already in a situation of real danger, it grabs our attention immediately. Danger means the imminent threat of personal harm or loss. What represents danger in any particular story depends on the scope of your tale. In fantasy, horror, and sci-fi, it's almost always the life-or-death kind.

7. *Loved by Friends and Family*. If we're shown right off that the hero is already loved by other people, it gives us immediate permission to care about him too. How many movies have you seen that begin with a surprise party thrown for the hero by a room full of adoring friends, or some other get-together taking place where affection gushes from a doting mom, dad, sibling, mate, child, or best friend?

8. *Hardworking*. The heroines and heroes we care about have an enormous capacity for work. People who work hard create the energy needed to drive a story forward.

9. *Obsessed*. Obsession keeps brave, skilled, hardworking heroes focused on a goal, which is enormously important for any story. Driving obsession creates an active plot.

There are other qualities of character that can help create a hero we want to root for, but these are the never-to-be-ignored basic nine. Use them liberally.

At the start of the sci-fi/horror film *I AM LEGEND*, hero Robert Neville (Will Smith) is portrayed as a Courageous man who is In Danger, Unfairly Injured, and Hardworking, while he is Loved by Friends and Family, Nice, Funny, highly Skilled as a medical researcher, and Obsessed with achieving victory over an epidemic of vampires. Nine out of nine. And the movie was a huge hit.

Early on in the mega-budget sci-fi film *GREEN LANTERN*, hero

Hal Jordan (Ryan Reynolds) is portrayed as a childish, irresponsible man often lacking in real courage, who constantly messes up and displays little genuine skill, is lazy and unreliable, thoughtless and unkind, a test pilot who uses his wing-woman as a decoy during a combat exercise then thinks it funny when he gets her "shot down," who crashes his own fighter jet unnecessarily with no thought about its half-billion-dollar cost to the nation, a man whose humor is mean and snarky, and whom few people really like or trust. That's zero out of nine. And this movie was a mega-bomb at the box office.

Invite your readers to care. Then they will eagerly climb aboard for your story ride.

EXERCISE

Get the DVD of any commercially successful American movie with one hero or heroine in it. You can check for the level of box office success at BoxOfficeMojo.com. Commercial success here just means the story worked emotionally for lots of people. Picking a one-hero film simply keeps this exercise focused and clear.

From the point where the hero first enters the story, study the next twelve to fifteen minutes of the movie. Write down both character strengths and weaknesses demonstrated by the hero. Then answer the following questions:

1. How many of the nine sympathy tools are used to establish the hero?

2. How are the hero's weaknesses presented so as not to harm sympathy?

3. Are any sympathy tools used besides the nine listed here?

4. After spending these opening minutes with the hero, are you drawn to keep watching the film or not? Why?

5. If the hero is portrayed by a movie star, what personal characteristics of the star him- or herself help bond you to the hero?

BRUCE MCALLISTER

The Black Unicorn

BRUCE MCALLISTER published his first science fiction story at age sixteen. He is the author of two science fiction novels, *Humanity Prime* (Wildside Press) and genre classic *Dream Baby* (Tor Books), a literary fantasy, and a career-spanning short-story collection. He's served on top genre fiction award juries. His short fiction has been a finalist for the Hugo, Nebula, and Locus awards and received a National Endowment for the Arts award.

One of the traits of a successful fantasy, science fiction, or horror writer is an awareness of what's come before, and that means what's become clichéd.

What's wrong with a cliché? Don't people want the familiar—don't they want the things they know and already love? Yes, but they want them fresh, not stale. Stale is death; stale is the reader's boredom and disappointment, and the writer's failure to tell a story that carries the reader away.

How did I learn to make clichés new when I was starting out—fourteen years old, child of the Cold War and a peripatetic Navy family—determined to move from being a wide-eyed reader to capturing on the page the same magic my favorite authors made me feel?

I did it early on by "love," that is, by immersing myself—addicted as I was to speculative fiction—in the stories and novels I loved, rereading them, copying them out, outlining them (as writers always do, though they often won't tell you). But I was also lucky enough in college to meet a mentor, a wise old writer who'd learned all the magic tricks I wanted to learn years before I was born. That wonderful soul, my Yoda and Obi-Wan—who wasn't in the science fiction and fantasy field but was open to the "fantastic" in life, because he'd lived such a fantastic one himself—was the one who gave me the exercise I want to share with you. It transformed my fiction forever.

In writing, clichés can be deadly. Written clichés are expressions, characters, mythological creatures, settings, situations, and even ideas that are so familiar to us that they no longer have the power to move us, to make us feel or think what the writer wants us to feel or think. If you're bored reading a vampire novel, it may be because the vampires in it—and the story's situations—are clichéd; that is, because they're so familiar and predictable to you that they don't make you feel anything other than boredom. If you can't stand the typical happy ending in a Hollywood movie, that's because the happy ending, at least the way it's handled in most Hollywood movies, is a cliché. It's imposed on the movie like a formula; it's predictable; and once again you're bored and probably ready to scream by the time it arrives. If you want to scream every time a Mafia hit man who loves opera appears in a movie, that's because he's a cliché that refuses to be fresh and interesting. Clichés are very disappointing.

Professional writers—novelists, short story writers, and screenwriters—have, for at least two centuries now, had to make clichés new in order to tell stories that move and hold their readers. A science fiction writer who uses a UFO that looks just like one from a 1950s movie is going to bore us. A fantasy writer who uses the same old white unicorn is going to put us to sleep or make us want to do bodily harm to the poor beast. A crime novelist whose characters are straight from all of *THE GODFATHER* is going to bore us to death too. Because a professional writer's greatest fear is losing the reader, professional writers have come up with an exercise that turns clichés into fresh, interest-holding stories. They call it "The Black Unicorn Exercise."

EXERCISE

Take a cliché you really hate from novels or movies. To keep it simple, make it a character cliché or a mythical creature cliché: an elf, troll, pixie, unicorn, centaur, vampire, witch, werewolf, dragon, brawny hero, pretty and delicate princess, angel, demon, wicked stepmother, Mafia hit man, bad CIA operative, redneck sheriff, on and on. The choice is yours.

Once you've chosen your detestable cliché, make a list of the traits of your character or mythical creature that make it the cliché it is. Use these three categories of traits:

1. Anatomy/physical appearance (including dress and possessions).

2. Physiology (what it eats, drinks, etc., to stay alive).

3. How does it behave; what does it do? (Feel free to ask others to help you put the list together. Usually we can't remember everything that makes the cliché what it is!) A unicorn, for example, is white, has a single long horn with magical properties (so everyone in the world wants it and tries to get it), associates only with virgins (only a virgin can touch it), drinks from a pond in the moonlight, and is otherwise (we suppose) like a shy, delicate horse that somehow never manages to get dirty.

A dragon, for example, is reptilian and big. It breathes fire and flies. It is pretty much immortal unless the right hero (or heroine) can kill it. It's got scales. We're not exactly sure what it eats (if anything). Maybe it's nice; maybe it isn't. In any case, it's pretty boring if we're not madly in love with dragons.

A vampire always seems to be an adult. The vampire is immortal but not happy. He feels unloved by God, and has reason to: He does bad things. He needs blood, human blood. He runs around attacking men and women who, when he bites them and sucks their blood, turn into vampires too. He dresses nicely. He's got a cape probably. He doesn't like daylight; it burns him or does something otherwise unpleasant to him. The only way to get rid of him is with a stake through the heart. (A silver bullet is for werewolves, not vampires.) Oh, yes, he sleeps in a coffin.

The Mafia hit man is big and neckless and has a raspy voice. He's Italian. From Southern Italy. He likes good Italian food and opera. (There was never a real hit man, Italian or otherwise, this boring.)

When you've got your list of traits, what makes your character or mythical creature what he, she, or it is, start tampering with the traits. To make your character or mythical creature fresh and new, change at least one major trait to its "opposite," or to something that contrasts somehow with the clichéd trait. Make your white unicorn black. Make your Mafia hit man Irish. Make your dragon fireless.

But do more than that; change other traits as well. As you do, you'll discover what professional writers have discovered for centuries: When you change one or more clichéd traits of a clichéd character or mythical creature, you'll start to see wonderful fresh story possibilities.

If the unicorn is black, not white, and he's missing a horn, what's going to happen? Is he going to start looking for his horn? Is he an outcast among unicorns because he is black? Is he even technically a unicorn? What does a black, hornless unicorn do? He probably doesn't hang out with virgins. In fact, he may (given low self-esteem) be happier hanging out in the slums of the world. And he's probably going to set out to get a horn—whether in the end he decides to keep it or not.

If the usual unicorn is a male or neuter (no gender at all), make it a she. Who does a female unicorn hang out with? Geeky virgin guys? Priests? Who? Is she the only female unicorn ever born? What happens if she meets a horse that can fly (Pegasus) and falls in love? Where will they live—heaven or earth? Will he sacrifice his wings for her? Will she bring heaven and earth together with her love?

Change the traits of your Mafia hit man. If the usual, clichéd Mafia hit man likes opera, your Mafia hit man hates opera. Why? Because he associates it with something unpleasant from his childhood. So he likes hip-hop. He's got a pink smartphone. He wishes he could be a kid again and just tweet all day. He didn't have much fun as a kid. In fact, he's so into social media he's losing his reputation. Maybe a contract has been put out on him because he didn't kill someone he was supposed to . . . and the only way he can save himself is with the help of his Facebook friends . . . or a LinkedIn associate who makes furniture out of driftwood. (And, by the way, the raspy voice was fake all along; he just thought he needed a voice like that to be taken seriously. His father was Italian, sure, but his mother was Irish. It's hard to build up a reputation as a Mafia hit man when you've got a red-haired mother.)

If most vampires are adult, yours is a child . . . and he meets an unbitten girl . . . and wants to be human again. Which makes the Elders very unhappy . . . so he's visited by the Oldest Drinker, who is, we learn, the son of you-know-who and who wants to be human too . . .

If all dragons breathe fire, yours does only if _____ (fill in the blank). Or your dragon can't fly, but wishes she could, and the hero (or heroine!) who has come to kill her takes her to a wizard who can help her learn to fly—which she needs to do if she's to save not only her scaly kind but the wizard's people as well.

You get the picture. Jump in, have fun, and watch your writing bloom when you make what's old and stale brand-new and full of the wonder every reader (and writer) deserves.

JEFFREY A. CARVER

Create a Power!

JEFFREY A. CARVER is the author of the Chaos Chronicles series, the Nebula-nominated *Eternity's End* (Tor Science Fiction), and many other science fiction novels and stories. His online course for aspiring writers is available free to all at writesf.com.

My career path has wound through a lot of writing workshops, where I've worked with aspiring writers of all ages. It strikes me that the same challenges seem to hit everyone in the face, whether they're high school students (New England Young Writers Conference), university students (MIT), or adults trying their hand at something new (the Ultimate SF Writing Workshop I co-host with fantasist Craig Shaw Gardner). Probably the biggest single challenge after "What's my story about?" is "How do I turn my great idea into a story?"

That last is a key question, and it's not always obvious to the new writer. It wasn't to me, when I was first starting. I had lots of great ideas—at least, I thought they were great. That was fine as far as it went, but it took me a long time—and many rejections—to understand that the idea was only as good as its effects in the lives of my characters. Or to put it another way, it only came to life when it triggered some kind of conflict, because conflict is the heart and soul of story.

It might help to think of an idea as a starting block, or a coiled spring waiting to be released. A story is what happens in that release, when we see the cause and effect of the idea unfold in the lives of characters. It's when you start thinking through the consequences of your idea that you begin developing a real story.

Now, there are as many ways to discover your story as there are to trip over a dog in the kitchen—and some of them feel about as planned. But sometimes exercises can help. There is one I have found consistently useful in workshops, and that is the prompt that Craig Gardner and I call the "Powers" exercise. I don't know who first came up with it. Craig borrowed the idea from a long-ago class he attended as a beginner, taught by the late great Hal Clement, and we've fiddled with it over the course of many workshops. Hal is gone, so I can't ask him if he made it up or borrowed it in turn from someone else. Wherever it came from, it's been responsible for starting more stories and propelling them to completion than any other exercise we've used.

EXERCISE

Imagine a character who has a power. It can be any power at all, as long as it sets your character apart from everyone else. It can be a superpower, like Superman's. It can be extraordinary training, like Batman's. It can be a gift from an alien or an angel. It can be scientific, supernatural, extrasensory, mental, emotional, or technological. Anything at all.

Now, ask yourself:

1. What is the single most important benefit of this power? There might be several, but probably one or two will really jump out at you. List as many as you can think of. Find one that trumps them all.

2. What are the negative consequences? For Superman, it might be Kryptonite, and social isolation. What would it be for Batman? What would it be for your character? Think even harder about this than you did about the positive, because there's a good chance this is where you'll find your most interesting conflict. List all that you can think of.

Now write a scene. Write it so that it reveals something of the power, and also the downside. How does one flow from the other? Don't info dump it; let it play out in action. Show it in relation to other people; show the emotional consequences.

With a little luck and hard work, you may find yourself with not just a scene, but the kernel of a story. Your work has just begun!

DEREK TAYLOR KENT

FUNdamentals of Writing

DEREK TAYLOR KENT is an author, screenwriter, and performer. His Scary School book series (under pen name Derek the Ghost and published by HarperCollins) won an award for Funniest Chapter Book of 2011 from Children's Literature Network. Derek teaches children's and young adult writing for Writing Pad in Los Angeles.

Hello writers! My name is Derek Taylor Kent (AKA Derek the Ghost), author of the middle-grade series Scary School from HarperCollins. I am sure that soon you will have your own great success in writing. How do I know? I'm a ghost and we have psychic abilities. Also, by committing yourself to doing writing exercises, you've proven that you're willing to put in the time and effort it takes to get there.

I had been writing children's books since I was fifteen years old, and didn't get my first book deal until I was thirty. I've talked to several very famous authors who had written ten novels before they finally got one published. So stick to it and keep writing!

Aside from writing books, I also teach children's, YA, and adult fiction writing at Writing Pad in Los Angeles. I was very excited to be asked to contribute a writing exercise to this anthology because writing exercises are a central tenet of the Writing Pad method. Our students will do one or two writing exercises every class, and about 90 percent of the time, the stream-of-consciousness writing that comes out under a ten- to fifteen-minute time constraint ends up yielding gold that they incorporate into their books.

So for this exercise, I want you to give yourself a fifteen-minute maximum time limit.

The theme of this exercise is *fun*.

When writing for children or a middle-grade audience like I do, fun is the key word. If you write a book that's fun to read, it will probably get a book deal. If kids have fun reading it, you will probably have a hit book on the shelves. If you have fun writing it, it will probably be fun to read.

One of the questions I get asked the most is: "I don't think my book is fun enough. How do I make it more fun?"

There's a very simple answer to that question: Just make sure your characters are having fun!

When writing our plots, the characters get tangled up in a series of conflicts, problems, and obstacles to overcome. They go through so many trials and tribulations, there hardly seems to be time for them to have any fun, right?

WRONG!!

If we don't see your characters having fun, we won't know what they do for fun, and they won't be well-rounded.

Take, for instance, Harry Potter. What does he do for fun? That's right. Quidditch. J. K. Rowling knew that Harry needed an escape from being hunted down by a murderous dark Lord, so he gets to escape it all in every book with some awesome games of Quidditch. The games of Quidditch usually have nothing to do with the plot; though sometimes bad things happen that lead to character development or a new twist in the story. But while Harry is up in the sky seeking that golden snitch, it's all about him having fun.

I remember an amazing moment in THE LORD OF THE RINGS movie. Gollum gets to have a moment where he's swimming in a pool, singing to himself, and then he catches a fish and bites into it. It's the most fun he can have and the happiest he ever is in the movies. It's a great moment because the whole time Gollum has been beaten down and sulking in his awful predicament, but seeing him having fun swimming in the pool shows us that deep down there's still a fun-loving spirit, which makes us feel for him all the more.

When writing a scene in which your character is having fun, the reader has just as much fun reading it as the character is having. That's right! Reading about characters having fun is super-fun.

You know the other great thing about it? It doesn't have to have anything to do with the plot! You can totally forget about your plot for a while. Plot is boring. Characters being themselves is interesting. Characters changing is interesting. Character development is fun to read.

EXERCISE

1. Take one of your main characters from whatever project you are working on and make a list of things that they do for fun. Mark one that would be the most fun.

2. In fifteen minutes or less, write a scene in which the character is having the most fun he or she can possibly have. Do not inject any plot elements. Just let the character be him- or herself in your chosen environment. Give it to someone to read. If they smile while reading it (which they will), you've done your job.

JESSICA PAGE MORRELL

The Villain's Handbook

JESSICA PAGE MORRELL is the author of five books for writers. She works as a developmental editor, writes columns and articles about the writing life, and contributes to anthologies. She lives in Portland, Oregon, where she's surrounded by writers and the oft-gloomy skies bring on imaginings she usually keeps to herself.

I was scared a lot as a kid. Of monsters lurking in my closet and tigers pacing under my bed, and the Wicked Witch of the West who came to snatch me in my nightmares. It didn't help that my older brother and I would attend horror films at our local theater. After the films we'd walk home in the dark and every shadow seemed to leap out at me. Decades later I can still recall my heart-racing fear.

Because I spent my early years quaking beneath my blankets, monsters and villains have always fascinated me. Because I teach writers, I'm convinced that how a writer populates his or her fictional world is the ultimate skill test. And villains need to be the crown of a writer's creation. Slippery, evil, dangerous . . . villains are the chess masters of the fiction world. It's not enough that they are adversaries; the villain should bedevil, terrify, and cause suffering.

Villains run the gamut of vile criminals, warlords, incarnations of Satan, fallen angels, sociopaths, and monsters. But just because a villain has the job of wreaking havoc in the story world, it doesn't mean you have a license to simply create a character or creature that is solely evil without much thought about how he, she, or it got that way. If your villain is human, you need to know why he cannot relate to people normally. If you find that you've created a one-dimensional villain or a killing machine or golem with no motivation, then it's likely you've written a melodrama.

Let's say a word about monsters here before we go further. Monsters are a subset of villainy—usually nonhuman, bestial, and demon-like. Monsters exist to prey on our most primitive, childlike fears. Monsters are the *other*. The always whispered about bogeyman, beast, mutant, ogre, zombie. They typically star in horror, sci-fi, and fantasy, and something in their makeup is malevolent and savage.

Since monsters have been around since the beginning of time, they are usually archetypal. They will always bring chaos, the story world is an aberrant or dangerous place, and it seems as if there is no escape. In times past, monsters were soulless with rare exceptions such as Frankenstein's monster.

However things are changing. In the Twilight series the were-wolves and vampires are hunks. While this trend rages, remember that there is nothing like a potent monster. Before you create a monster, decide if it is truly monstrous or, instead, sympathetic. Real monsters create horror in the reader; sympathetic monsters bedevil us, but their potency is diluted.

All villains must be potent, believable, yet evil. The more sophisticated the plot, the more sophisticated the villain. The odd aspect of villainy is that these characters express the worst of our world. They frighten us because their evil machinations make the implausible seem all too possible.

Here's a handbook for creating a villain who will haunt your readers' days and nights.

Decide if he is sympathetic or bad to the bone. When it comes to sympathetic, it doesn't mean you'd invite a villain to dinner. Sympathy means understandable or even relatable, a presence that makes for a more realistic and nuanced story. They evoke a response from readers that goes beyond fear and loathing. There may be pity, yes, but also a creepy identification, and maybe disquiet at this insight. And although readers might understand a sympathetic villain, they must also understand the threat he poses. Your villain might genuinely love his family or desperately long for the love and approval of his father. A sympathetic villain might be hoping for redemption.

With an unsympathetic villain, readers root for his defeat; with a sympathetic villain, our feelings are more ambivalent. We often want to see him redeemed, or our hero to feel a sense of tragedy at his demise. It's easy to smugly hate the bad guy, but if we wonder if we might have taken the same wrong turns, if we question our own morals and honor, then the sympathetic villain has served his purpose.

Make your villain real. Often the most frightening villains are human, the more so for they may walk among us. Yes, it is the human side of such characters that make the hairs of your neck stand on end.

Craft an appearance that is fascinating and rare. Generally villains who blend into the landscape won't loom large in your reader's imagination—or nightmares. Maybe your villain has chalky skin, catlike yellow slits for eyes, spidery fingers.

Know how he/she/it takes up space. Elegant? Hulking? Slithery? Deformed? Avoids sunlight and scuttles around in gloomy places? Most villains try to appear larger than their actual size, but no matter their actual dimensions, they must somehow loom larger-than-life.

Stir in deviancy or the bad-ass factor. Find extra-creepy ways to prove that your villain is a true bad ass. Perhaps he's a charming sociopath like Tom Ripley, or a cannibal stew of savagery and sophistication like Hannibal Lecter. A female who doesn't display motherly nurturing is always frightening because it turns upside down our notions of gender roles—she becomes the witch or evil stepmother of countless fairy tales.

Nail down your villain's psychology. Narcissism is typical in villains' makeup. Thus they rarely fight battles they cannot win. They put their own interests first, believing themselves the most important creatures in the universe. But of course feelings of deep inferiority feed a need for endless power. Does your villain have the extreme elements of narcissism or other sociopathic tendencies in his makeup? Is he mad, or does he pretend to be?

Know why he wants what he wants. Villains without understandable motives come off as papery. The more horrific their villainy, the stronger must be the motive. A thirst for revenge, greed, anger, lust for power, and jealousy are typical drivers. Combine and personalize them, and they become even more powerful. For example, a villain wants to take over a kingdom and is also secretly in love with the hero's betrothed. Adding a further motive on top of "more power" makes them an even better character.

Make your villain unstoppable. Since villains are highly motivated, they are also unstoppable. Villains range one step ahead of your protagonist, and the world in general. Far thinking is a typical attribute of villains. When the hero arrives on the scene, the villain's power base must be established, a plan in place. Realize that if the reader doesn't believe in the threat your villain represents, you have comedy rather than horror.

Give your villain allure. Often villains have pulled in others with cunning and craft. This could be through sexual prowess, rewards, power, and flattery. The spice of control. The feeling of being on the edge of grasping even a tainted dream.

Let your villain relish the fight. In real life most people avoid conflict, preferring to make nice. Not so for the villainous. They're up for the fight, with a chess master's farseeing eye for strategy within the world in which they maneuver, and they know their own powers. But step beyond clichés. Is he plodding yet indestructible? Or devious, always coming up with new ways to bring the pain?

Create a troubled, complicated past. A villain's backstory is often filled with bile. They have a need for power to compensate for the pain of their early years. The reader will always want to know why. Somewhere in their past, they were overlooked, ridiculed, neglected, abused, lived in the shadow of a sibling. Then they took a wrong turn that led to the disintegration of their soul.

Have your villain progress step by step. Usually effective villains are a long time in the making. They first score small successes, then move on to bigger victories and strategies. Patience is often their prime trait. If your villain is rash, he probably won't make a good villain. Know his rise to power that propelled him to aberrant greatness. And let the reader watch as that power grows to hubris, which in turn leads him to his deserved doom.

Undone. You need to know how your villain can be brought down and plan for it as you plot each scene. Sauron is undone by one of the smallest creatures in Middle-earth. The best villains fight to the death;

they don't screw up so the hero can win. A villain who stops to explain his diabolical plans, and in so doing gives the hero a means of escape, just doesn't cut it.

EXERCISE

1. Begin with a potent name. Names are powerful tools. Used correctly, they'll invisibly support your story, enhancing and underlining your plot and themes. The best villain names have firepower. An unsympathetic villain's name should reflect menace, coldness, and/or strength. Think Gollum, Darth Vader, the Borg. Not exactly names you'd find in a baby book. Look into the meanings and the history of those who've shared the name, so you can subtly enrich your story by choosing names that are a commentary or secret clue to the action. You just *know* they're on the wrong team. S sounds like Snape suggest something slithery and shivery. The Borg sounds like a collective nightmare. James Moriarty sounds like both a worthy nemesis and a professor. Morgoth sounds evil. You might want to choose hard consonant sounds like K or unusual names like Xykon from the Order of the Stick.

2. What are your villain's main personality traits? These traits will create the foundation for your character and will be put to work in the story. They should be evident in every scene and appear in your character the first time we meet him, her, or it. A criminal mastermind needs to be intelligent, cunning, and ruthless. The White Witch from *The Lion, the Witch and the Wardrobe* by C. S. Lewis is beautiful, proud, cruel, and she possesses a smoldering rage.

   Tie these key traits to a backstory that explains how they were developed. Think of the shadow of every power trait: the dark side that may spell the villain's doom.

3. Your character's first impression on the reader is do or die. Decide if your aim is to terrify the reader, or foreshadow villainy to come. How does he slide onto the page the first time? In disguise? Raring for a fight? Without warning?

STACEY GRAHAM

Oh, the Humanity: What Makes Monsters Tick

STACEY GRAHAM has spent a good part of the last twenty years sitting in dark attics waiting to poke the paranormal and see if it giggles. When not wrestling ghosts, she enjoys writing zombie poetry, humor, and ghost stories. Graham is the author of *The Girls' Ghost Hunting Guide* and the *Zombie Tarot*.

Trying to scare people these days is harder than it looks. Vampires sparkle, werewolves glisten where they should be hairy, and zombies can be almost charming as they stumble and drool. What makes a reader turn the page of a story when society is becoming immune to fright? It's the little niggles in the back of the readers' brains that within those monsters still lay the foundation of being human—that the monsters were once just like them. Finding the humanity within your monster creates a hesitation to hate it outright. Suddenly it has depth and you question, *Why is it there? Where does it go after it leaves? Will it be back and what drives it to return? Are there more like it, and are they good dancers?*

Speculative fiction dealing with the paranormal nurtures the uncertainty that we're not really in control, that there are forces we can't foresee or wrestle to the ground when confronted. As the writer, your job is to exploit that doubt and turn it into something that makes the reader check the closet twice before he or she turns off the light at bedtime.

EXERCISE

I love a good ghost story. Trapped between two worlds I wonder if they can hear us, are they trying to communicate or plot revenge, or do they simply want you to hit the snooze button on your alarm clock faster?

Write three scenes:

1. Put the reader in the ghost's place: What's his backstory? Was he a victim of a crime of passion? Illness? Does he know he's dead? How does he interact with the living? Is he an adult or a child? If a child, how does your protagonist react to him? Describe the ghost's first few days after the realization of his death. Is he terrified or excited by the freedom being a ghost may offer?

2. Create a setting: While spooky abandoned mansions spring to mind, ghosts don't always hang around such gloomy digs. Ghosts have been reported on city buses, in restaurants, at daycare centers, and in fields. Take your story out of the familiar venues and see where it leads you. In this scene, use the inanimate surroundings to convey a feeling of being haunted without the overt presence of the ghost.

3. Make the familiar terrifying: Ghosts who succeed pull an emotional response from the reader. If they display traits that make the reader identify someone they know, it makes the story sharper and more memorable. Write a scene that takes place in your neighborhood. Use that backdrop to create a ghost from a mixture of people you know to create layers. What trait is most sinister? What seemingly benign characteristic is really hiding a secret instead?

MARK SEVI

The Uncanny Valley

Mark Sevi is a screenwriter with more than nineteen feature films produced including *PTERODACTYL* and *ARACHNID*. His latest, *DEVIL'S KNOT*, stars Reese Witherspoon and Colin Firth. Sevi teaches screenwriting and is founder and president of the Orange County Screenwriter's Association.

> *"To sleep, perchance to dream—ay, there's the rub."*
> —Hamlet in *Hamlet*, Shakespeare

> *"We are such stuff as dreams are made on."*
> —Prospero in *The Tempest*, Shakespeare

I'm a nuts-and-bolts writer (some would say nuts and a dolt, but they're just haters). But in some things I'm as "new agey" as Shirley MacLaine's spirit guides. The writer's subconscious mind is one of those areas where I want to say "Ommmmm" with gusto and sincerity.

We are dreamers, we writers, especially those of us who dabble in speculative fiction. We dream large and in all directions and dimensions. I've always been a fanboy of sci-fi and known that it, more than all other forms of fiction, must do the same things as other works— make someone laugh, cry, fear, etc.—but it must also put those emotional responses and tight plots on a lunar colony, a spaceship, a bubble in an ocean, or a haunted house on Earth. Speculative fiction must do everything that Hemingway did, but backwards and in high heels (to paraphrase newswoman Linda Ellerbee).

We speculative writers must ask what, how, why, when, how much and turn those questions into answers that make sense to our characters.

Shakespeare understood this. Consider *Hamlet*, which starts with talk of a ghost. Imagine trying to sell that to his publishers. "A what, of who? Are you serious, Bill?" But The Bard understood that dreaming is connected to a world we barely understand and can't, and shouldn't, look at directly. However, that world, the "uncanny valley" of our subconscious is rooted wholly in the familiar.

So how do we express ourselves properly in worlds or situations that don't exist? Putting our characters in bizarre locations and situations that must ring true? We go digital. And how is that happening?

We live our lives in analog, minute by minute, surrounded by the familiar but we dream in digital. Nothing is too random, outrageous, funny, or frightening in our subconscious state. We can be riding a skateboard that floats on water one second and the next be talking with dead relatives about a recipe for potato salad at a picnic on a volcano.

Practitioners of lucid dreaming learn to take control of their dreams in order to gain a better or different outcome. They "insert" themselves into their dreams and take an active role rather than allowing the dream to unfold as it will. Interesting. Sounds a lot like daydreaming to me. So what I propose is to lucid dream backwards in a manner—starting the process awake, not asleep.

Transcendental Meditation (TM) teaches us how to achieve a level deeper than sleep that is conscious and yet not, a place of "somewhere in-between." No less creative giants than the Beatles practiced it and if you strip away all the mumbo-jumbo crap some have tried to foster about TM, you get a physiological phenomenon. A way to dream while awake. Lucid dreaming in reverse.

The idea is to *not* control the process of the dream, but to allow it to unfold as a flower would. Lest I get too touchy-feely for you, let me emphasize again that what I'm trying to pass on to you is a way for you to tap the dreamer in all writers, especially those who want to be in the speculative fields—and to learn to trust your subconscious like never before.

When I head to L.A. for story meetings or pitch sessions, I have prepared my material the night before, but on the way up in my car I don't rehearse anymore or think much about what I'm heading to. I feel like my mind should be mostly focused on the incredibly complex and frighteningly random freeway experiences we have here in SoCal, but I also want to give my subconscious time to focus its insights and present them to my conscious mind when I walk through the doors of that meeting. It's never failed me yet.

You must dream and then trust that the dream will come to you when you need it. TM helps (for me) but when I don't have time to meditate, simply allowing my mind to run rampant on the field of creation is the best thing I can do.

Practice on a conscious level all your skill set like any good musician or athlete—actually writing is the only way to make you a better writer—but at some point, you must also learn to trust your subconscious mind and build that trust to a point where you believe it will deliver when necessary.

Everyone's process is necessarily different. If you want to try mine to find those dreams and tap into them, here's an immersion exercise I call "Be the Killer."

Too many times we horror writers settle for the quick and easy thumbnail of the killer. I need total immersion to write with veracity. In order to know I'm inside my killer's head, I need to begin dreaming like him or her. To get to that point, I need to know the killer completely.

EXERCISE

Be the killer: I don't advise this for everyone, but for those writing horror it helps to be inside the killer's head. Smelling everything, seeing things that he or she (or it) sees. These types of villains ring false unless you have a more perfect understanding of them. Unless we're totally insane, we (humans) typically have a rationale for what we do, including killing. Climbing inside the head of your slasher makes that slasher much more frightening, because you have a better understanding of that character.

1. *How do you interact with neighbors? Are you shy, surly? Do you dislike the people around you? Is that barking dog going to be a victim of poison some dark night?*

2. *What is your job? How do you pay rent? What's your car like? Are you capable of caring about anything besides yourself?*

3. Go to a grocery store and buy groceries that your killer would like. Go late at night and pick out a victim.

4. Surf the Web with your killer's mind—what would be interesting to him besides porn?

5. Sit quietly and imagine your victims and their surroundings and how you're going to get into their house. Put yourself in the moment of break-in. *Is it cold? Will your exhaled breath give you away?*

6. *What does the hammer feel like in your hand? Is the tape you bought as part of your rape kit sticky enough? Or because you bought it at the ninety-nine-cent store, is it melted and crap? How hard is it to carry an adult to a car? What does your victims' fear smell like? How do you handle the bloody mess? Do you feel anything—excitement, disgust— when you shove a knife into a body, or are you numb?*

7. *Is your apartment clean or dirty? What does your toilet look like? Do you have a medical problem that you need to resolve? Are you meticulous with personal grooming or do you not care? Are your teeth disgusting or pristine? Do you have teeth?*

8. *What do you dream of . . . ?*
    Write. And dream. The answers are there inside you. All you have to do is learn to allow them to come freely to you.

BRAD SCHREIBER

Metamorphosis

BRAD SCHREIBER is author of six books. Schreiber adapted Ray Bradbury's "The One Who Waits" for National Public Radio (NPR), winning an award from National Audio Theatre Festivals. His Philip K. Dick adaptation "Sales Pitch" also aired on NPR. He's taught at the American Film Institute, the Directors Guild of America, CalArts, USC, and Pixar Animation.

The great Franz Kafka used to do readings of his dark, menacing, fantastical fiction in Prague, and it's said that sometimes he would publicly involuntarily laugh at the most disturbing images or situations in his prose. Now, you can call him a freak if you must, but Kafka was a great writer, not because he thought up the weird idea of a man turning into an insect in *The Metamorphosis*, but because he explored the internal thoughts of a man who has turned into an insect, and because he made important observations about society when the other characters had to deal with the horribly transmogrified Gregor Samsa.

And while a strong and imaginative premise is most desirable in science fiction and fantasy, that is not the only thing the writer must provide. The strangeness or terror in these genres is amplified by recognizable human reactions to the given premise—whether in thought or action—that makes it all the more real for us.

Kafka made poor Gregor alternately pathetic, humorous, frightening, and philosophical, as he confronted the reality of his new form. It would be valuable to infuse your major characters with thoughts and actions that fully explore the ramifications of the wild and unnatural situations you conjure up for them. That is the intent of this exercise.

EXERCISE

Create a scene in which a character has been radically altered in physical appearance. It might involve a change that resembles another living person, a historical or literary figure, partial mechanization, or an appearance that resembles a living animal, plant, or even an inanimate object. The transformation can be partial or complete.

First, write the scene for this changed person with a high level of danger.

Explore this same physically transformed character in scenes that are alternately philosophical, humorous, pathetic, melancholy, transcendent, contemplative, or self-destructive.

COMMUNICATION
AND RELATIONSHIPS

"I was very much interested in the way people behaved, the human dance, how they seemed to move around each other. I wanted to play around with that."
—OCTAVIA BUTLER

REGGIE OLIVER

"He Do the Police in Different Voices"

REGGIE OLIVER is the author of five collections of supernatural terror stories—the latest is *Mrs. Midnight and Other Tails* (Tartarus Press, 2011). His novel, *The Dracula Papers, Book I: The Scholar's Tale* (Chomu Press, 2011), is the first of a projected four. An omnibus edition of his stories was published by Centipede Press as part of its Masters of the Weird Tale series.

> *"He do the Police in different voices."*
>
> —Betty Higden, in *Our Mutual Friend,* by Charles Dickens
>
> (also the alternative title to T. S. Eliot's *The Waste Land*)

I am always astonished by the confidence with which some writers instruct other would-be writers in their art. A couple of publications and they see themselves as having acquired the status of "author," and possibly they have, in a way. Personally I have never seen myself as a "writer" at all, let alone an "author," though I do seem to have had a surprising amount of stuff published; I am simply someone, like you, who writes. I have no cunning expertise to hand down from the exalted heights of Mount Parnassus. And neither have these other writers, really, but there you are.

The fact is, I write, not because I have acquired some mystical skill, and certainly not because I ever wanted to be a writer. I'd much rather not be. The world is far too full of them as it is, and they are far too full of themselves. I write because I have a story that simply must be told. That is the only possible excuse that any of us have for occupying bookshelves and the attention of others. I have always rather admired the attitude of Lord Foppington in *The Relapse*, a comedy of 1697 by Sir John Vanbrugh:

"To my mind, Madam, the inside of a book is to entertain oneself with the forced product of another man's brain. Now I think a man of quality and breeding may be much better diverted with the natural sprauts of his own."

Lord Foppington is of course a monster of arrogance and affectation and is a great comic creation, but, as Leigh Hunt pointed out in his perceptive essay on the play, he has a point. ("An idiotic one, but a point," as Addison DeWitt [George Sanders] says of Claudia Casswell [Marilyn Monroe] in *ALL ABOUT EVE*.)

And this is my point, perhaps my only one: Vanbrugh (a brilliant architect by the way) wrote only one really good play, *The Relapse*, and even this play only comes fully alive when Lord Foppington is on the stage. You can't get enough of him. His talk reaches the heights of absurdity but yet, on his own bizarre terms, as in that extract, he is eminently reasonable. Vanbrugh had somehow managed to get inside Lord Foppington, had found his voice, and the stuff just came pouring out in glorious Technicolor. He couldn't help himself.

T. S. Eliot's great poem *The Waste Land*, perhaps the greatest poem of the twentieth century, is only understandable as a collage of different voices, hence the alternative title. Those seem to have come welling out of him, all of them somehow echoing, in their own way, the neuroses of the modern age.

My feeling is that writing is only worthwhile if you can find these voices: your own voice, certainly, but, just as importantly, perhaps more importantly, the voices of others. Because, let's face it, the only good writer is the one who can somehow make other human beings come alive in his or her imagination. All the rest is window dressing. That's my view anyway, but don't take my word for it. You're just as much a "writer" as I am.

But if you do agree, try this. It's something I often do:

EXERCISE

1. Find a character, not your own, based partly on the recollection of someone you know, but enhanced by imagination. Start trying to talk in his or her voice. Imitate the accent if you can, but above all the mannerisms of speech, obsessions, and preoccupations. Walk around as you do so. I find that helps. It's hard at first, but very soon you won't be able to stop the character. When anything he or she says particularly strikes you, jot it down.

2. Now create another character, as different as possible from the first. Develop in a similar way, by talking out his or her stream of consciousness. Make notes again, but only once you have really got going with your character.

3. Now bring the two together and have them argue over something. Very soon you'll have a story worth writing down. Once you get going, you won't be able to stop them because they'll be alive.

4. Here's a tip from a great master. The brilliant playwright Georges Feydeau once wrote that one of the most successful devices in farce is to create two characters who absolutely must not meet and then bring them together. It is a good formula for other forms of fiction too. I can vouch for that.

JAMES G. ANDERSON

More Than Words Can Say

JAMES G. ANDERSON is a teacher, folk musician, poet, and co-author of the Legacy of the Stone Harp series of epic fantasy novels published by Baen Books with Mark Sebanc. Anderson and Sebanc are currently writing the third book of the four-part series. Anderson and his family live on the Canadian prairies, near Saskatoon, Saskatchewan, where they work with the St. Therese Institute of Faith and Mission.

When one of my readers chats with me about a story, nine times out of ten the first thing I say is, "So, you've met Gelanor." Or it might be Tromwyn or Gabaro or Bethsefra or any other of the people that populate the pages I have written. To me, the characters I write are real folk—walking, talking persons—and I derive a great joy from introducing each of them to a reader. Early in my writing career, a friend in the craft offered me the following sage advice: It is primarily the characters in a story that will capture and sustain the reader's interest, so create characters that people will care about.

Certainly, that has been my own experience as a reader: I am interested not so much in "What happens next?" as in "What happens next to Bob?" But how does one create credible characters that people will care about? I propose that the answer lies in the human ability to communicate with one another and elicit an emotional response, be it positive or negative.

In studying human speech, psychologist Albert Mehrabian identified the relative importance of the three main aspects of spoken communication in conveying meaning. He concluded that:

- 7 percent of meaning is expressed through the verbal aspect, that is the actual words spoken;

- 38 percent is by means of the tonal or vocal aspect, which includes tone of voice, pacing, and accents of speech; and finally

- 55 percent is the physiological or visual aspect, that is the facial gestures, eye movements, hand gestures, and body postures that accompany speech.

Even if we accepted a far more liberal estimate of the relative importance of the verbal component in spoken communication, say 50 percent, this still means that at least half of the meaning of anything said is conveyed non-verbally. This presents a unique challenge to writers, whose stock-in-trade is words.

Any piece of writing is, by its very nature, communication, and a form of communication that is 100 percent verbal. However, resident within a piece of writing there may be characters interacting, and when characters interact, there is another level of communication, that of dialogue. While arguably misinterpreted and misapplied in many instances of human interaction, Mehrabian's 7-38-55 formula does apply to spoken communication involving the expression of feelings, emotions, and personal opinion—and the greater part of dialogue in any story is indeed an expression of emotion or opinion on the part of the characters. If this interaction is to be believable, well-developed, and real—keeping it real is the goal in writing fiction, and speculative fiction is no exception—then it is incumbent upon a writer to afford due respect to all modes of expressing meaning in spoken communication when crafting dialogue.

The writer faces a further challenge. To the reader, a passage of dialogue should be an intimate eavesdropping, a close listening in on the characters. The task of a writer is to put the reader into direct contact with the characters. The voice of the narrator must fade into the background, allowing the voices of the characters themselves to be brought to the fore, voices that speak in words, in tones, and in gestures. This then must be of primary concern when writing dialogue, namely, paying attention to the three V's of spoken communication as suggested by Mehrabian's research: the verbal, vocal, and visual.

In terms of the verbal, a writer must think not simply of the clarity of meaning carried by the actual words spoken by a character, but also of the character's diction and any unique mannerisms of speech he might have. The character is a real person and has to speak like a real person, so the writer must be careful to put words in the character's mouth that the character would naturally say, and in a way that he would naturally say them.

Words are expressed in speech with intonation, pacing, and flow. Without tone of voice, much of the meaning of the words is lost. The vocal can be nuanced by use of the conventions of dialogue, particularly the use of the exclamation mark to express a raised voice, the ellipsis to indicate a speaker drifting off or not completing a thought, and the dash, which indicates an interruption of speech.

The pacing of dialogue is also an important part of vocalization. Descriptive beats—that is, instances of action, gesture, or description—can be used to give dialogue some breathing space and slow a scene down. Conversely, short sentences, interrupted speech, and limited use of speaker attribution (the "so-and-so said" component) can pick up the pace of dialogue.

An inherent danger in speaker attribution is the temptation for a writer to explain how a character has said something either through the choice of word used for speaker attribution or by using an adverb or adverbial phrase to modify the speaker attribution. *Said* is an invisible word and the reader's eye will ignore it. So a writer should not be afraid to use *said* and indeed, use it consistently, even though there may be a strong temptation to use other speaker attribution words for variety's sake.

Speaker attribution is only necessary to keep the reader on track with who is saying what, not *how* who is saying what. Remember, show, don't tell—it is the cardinal rule of fiction writing. To do otherwise is to impose the voice of the narrator on the scene, thus interrupting the direct contact of the reader with the character. This direct contact, this intimate eavesdropping, is vital in gaining a reader's empathy with the characters. A writer needs to win over the reader, paving the way for the reader to make an emotional connection with, and commitment to, the characters in a story. The intrusion of the narrator's voice will impede this process. Therefore, rather than saying how someone spoke, a writer should use the words themselves or, even better, the vocal and non-verbal attributes of a character's speech to express meaning. Descriptive beats can often be used in place of speaker attribution and can very effectively express a character's non-verbal or visual communication.

The visual may in fact be the most important aspect of dialogue in bringing characters to life. A writer must discover what might be called the *body-voice* of a character. What mannerisms, habitual gestures, common postures, facial expressions, or physical quirks does a character have? How will a character behave when nervous, content, angry, excited, or depressed? Body language is also subject to cultural and environmental factors, however, so it is important to research the cultural and social mores and norms relevant to a character's background. Of course, in the realm of speculative fiction, there is some latitude in this matter, the cultures and societies often being the product of the writer's imagination. Even so, it is vital to be consistent in characterization—a character should not change voice except for some legitimate and credible reason.

Discovering a character in the writing process and bringing that person to life is one of the greatest joys I have found as a writer, a joy that achieves its culmination whenever a reader connects at an emotional level with that character. The key to this, I have found, is to build credible characters through credible dialogue by careful attention to all the means of expression in human communication: verbal, vocal, and visual.

EXERCISE

Many people, particularly in the field of human relations and business, have invested ample resources in the research and study of body language. Spend some time online learning the basics of how to read body language.

Now, equipped with this knowledge, head off to a coffee shop or some other public place and practice some creative eavesdropping, paying closer attention to the vocal and visual aspects of communication than the verbal. Perhaps even try eavesdropping out of earshot, "listening" only to body language. Jot down anything you notice that might be useful in writing dialogue.

If you dare, ask a close friend to reflect back to you your own body-voice. What gestures, facial expressions, and physical habits are unique to you when you're in conversation?

GABRIELLE MOSS

Creating Convincing Communication Between Humans and Supernatural Creatures

GABRIELLE MOSS is a writer whose work has appeared on literary websites including GQ, New York Post, The Hairpin, Jezebel, and Nerve. She lives in Brooklyn, New York, where she's never communicated with a real ghost (but not for lack of trying).

What's making your demonic possession narrative fall flat? Why is your ghost story boo-ring?

It might come down to something as simple as the communications between your human and supernatural characters.

Some supernatural characters can stay completely silent, or get away with just a well-timed growl, and still be completely terrifying.

But if your plot hinges on a human character interacting with a supernatural creature—a vampire traveling across Europe, a possessed little girl, a ghost seeking vengeance for her untimely death—the choices you make regarding their style of communication can make or break the mood of your story.

For instance, using no language-based communication at all can lower the stakes in a story about a ghost's desire for revenge; conversely, a too-verbose ghost who chats away like he's on line at the grocery store can dial down the tension in a tale of terror.

But how do you find the right balance between too much and too little communication? And how do you develop a unique style of communication for your supernatural character, one that clearly conveys his aims to the reader, but also shows that he is most certainly not of this world?

Some of the most terrifying conversations ever put down on paper are those that transpire between Pennywise the Clown and his human victims in Stephen King's *It*. Pennywise often communicates directly with the book's characters, but these conversations make him more threatening, not less.

Why? Because Pennywise doesn't speak like a normal human being. He uses metaphor, poetic imagery, and phrases that we half-remember from childhood. King mixes all these elements together to set Pennywise apart as a being that does not fit into our world. In one of the book's most famous scenes, Pennywise tells a boy, "They float, Georgie, and when you're down here with me, you'll float, too." The use of the word *float* draws the reader's brain to a wide array of images and associations—a dead body floating in water, the floating balloons of childhood (which Pennywise also utilizes), a spirit floating to Heaven, a dandelion seed floating away on a breeze. This invokes a very different reaction in the reader than the phrase, ". . . and when you get down here, you'll be dead, too"—even though both convey the same general idea.

By using this metaphorical language, Pennywise not only makes clear that he is far different from the humans around us, but he also brings the reader back to the terror of childhood, a time when the true meaning of a lot of words and phrases used by adults were unclear to us. Pennywise's specific and unusual communication style is one of the key elements that makes him a great villain of modern horror.

But I'm just a regular human being, you may be saying. I've been speaking regular human my whole life. How do I crack the code for creating a one-of-a-kind communication style for my supernatural characters?

EXERCISE

1. Take a mental inventory of what makes you feel scared. Dreams can be a very good resource for this information, and keeping a dream journal, in which you take specific notes on how information is communicated to you by other characters in your dreams, can be of great help when figuring out how your supernatural

creature conveys information to your human characters. Since conscious logic flies out the window in dreams, they can also be a great place to draw inspiration from when developing supernatural scenarios overall.

2. Freewrite longhand for ten minutes on what makes you afraid. No internal censorship, no judgments, no picking your pen up off the paper. Just write down everything that comes to you, and pay particular attention to the strange things that frightened you as a child—a commercial jingle, a certain room in your house. When the ten minutes are up, go back through—what words or phrases popped up that are more evocative than logical?

3. Read poetry, and collect in a notebook metaphors that you enjoy or find particularly evocative. While your creature does not have to speak in flowery, poetic language by any means (in fact, it's probably best if he doesn't), poetry can contain strong, jarring imagery or syntax that can help inspire your creature's unusual tone and point of view.

4. Talk to some children. Yes, *human* children.* Kids who are just getting a handle on spoken language can be accidental masters of the unusual metaphor, and the world they weave with their words can be inspiring for a writer attempting to develop fresh and unusual ways to communicate information.

Spend a week collecting odd phrases, lines of poetry, even single words. Don't think about it too much—just trust your gut, and jot down any phrase or word that feels evocatively strange to you.

Then, go back to your story. Think about the specific kind of emotions you want your supernatural character to inspire. Are your human characters scared of him because he is ancient, noble, and powerful? Are they wary of her because she knows something about a mystery that they don't? Try to zero in on the exact state

---

*Please talk only to your own children or a friend or relative's—and please get their parents' permission before talking to them. Do not chase children you do not know down the street, shouting, "I just want to learn about your metaphors!"

of mind your human characters will be in when they communicate with your supernatural creature.

Then, using this information on their state of mind, go back to your list. Again, go with your gut, and select any words or phrases that feel in line with your human character's emotional reaction to the creature.

Now, write up two versions of a brief scene between your human and supernatural character(s). In the first, write a scene where your supernatural character speaks in clear, simple language ("I'm haunting you because you built a parking garage over my grave!").

In the second, have your supernatural character speak only in those evocative words and phrases you picked out from your list ("Plum-colored gargoyle taste of tears broken ocean!"). Comparing the two scenes side-by-side, you should begin to see a way for your supernatural character to communicate clearly, in a style all his own.

VANESSA VAUGHN

What's Love Got to Do with It?

VANESSA VAUGHN is the author of the popular werewolf novel *Pack of Lies* (Ravenous Romance) and has published numerous works of steampunk, vampire, and zombie fiction. Her edgy erotic stories have appeared in dozens of anthologies, including the award-winning Best Women's Erotica and Best Lesbian Erotica series.

Few things get to the core of a character the way sex can.

In many ways, sex is an indispensable tool. It can describe characters' insecurity or overconfidence, their deep-seated self-loathing, or their incredible vanity. It can help us learn about their bodies as we see their gruesome battle scars or their carefully applied lipstick, their fingers worn down by hard work or softened by years of pampering.

By imagining two characters engaged in intimacy, we not only see their bodies for what they are, but witness them opening up to one another in the ultimate way. The encounter forces a private dialogue between protagonists, even if no words are exchanged. A night together can reveal what one character truly desires from the other in their heart of hearts . . . or what they most fear.

Some writers go all the way, describing graphic encounters in their publications, while others merely hint at possible relationships. Both approaches can prove very effective. Yet whether you intend to include detailed sex in your final story or not, envisioning sex (or even just a date) between your characters is a valuable writing exercise as you plan out your characters, imagining their motivations, their dreams, their desires, and their fears.

Take for example the famous literary duo of Sherlock Holmes and Dr. Watson. At 221B Baker Street, not a stitch of clothing was ever removed, not a single kiss ever exchanged between the crime-fighting pair during their years together. An explicit sexual relationship was not intended to exist between these characters and never did. Yet, if writing about them, imagining a deeper relationship between the two could be a useful tool for understanding them and fully fleshing out their characters in your mind.

Would Holmes's famous self-centeredness shine through, even in an intimate moment? Would Holmes be subtly jealous of Watson's many female conquests? After years of living together, would the two bicker just like an old married couple?

And what about the physical side of things? Would Watson have scars from his years in the army? Would Holmes have track marks from his recent experimentation with morphine? What about calluses on his fingers and dark circles under his eyes from playing his violin late into the night?

As you attempt to understand your characters better by writing an intimate scene between them, you may even discover that they can't possibly go through with it. Take, for example, the famous flirtation between James Bond and Moneypenny. Their interactions were nothing but sexual throughout the Bond books and films—an endless parade of double entendres, sly remarks, and innuendo. Yet if faced with the possibility of real sex, it's quite possible these characters would never be able to go through with it. An author going through this exercise might realize that beneath the playful surface, the heart of their relationship was much more serious. Imagining a failed sex scene would teach the writer to view Bond's connection with Moneypenny as more of a mother/son relationship instead of a light flirtation. The writer might come to the conclusion that Moneypenny is a friendly home for the protagonist to come back to time and time again, not another casual conquest to be had and discarded.

Incidentally, this exercise is not just for allies. Envisioning intimacy between enemies can be a useful tool as well. Do the hero and villainess hate one another because they are so different, or because they are more similar than they care to admit? What do the characters fear about one another? What do they want to punish or reward? All of this and more can be revealed by imagining them in an intimate setting.

EXERCISE

Choose two characters whose relationship you want to understand better and write an intimate scene between the two of them.

Whether you intend for your characters to have a sexual relationship in your story or not, going through the exercise of picturing them in an intimate setting puts meat on their bones. It allows you to envision their bodies, perfect or imperfect, as they are. It lets you flesh out their relationship in detail (sexual or asexual, playful or serious, bickering or tender, loving or hate-filled as it may be).

So, grab a pen and spend the next hour describing a close moment between these two, whether that moment is a date or something much more physical. Have fun with it. Delve deep into both characters' psyches, watch them open up, and try to ask yourself the following questions as you are writing:

What do these characters like most about one another?

What do they hate most about one another?

What do they want from one another?

In what ways are they the same?

In what ways are they different?

Do they have any attractive physical characteristics? Any repulsive physical characteristics? Any unusual physical characteristics?

Do they feel very strongly about the other (for good or ill), or do they feel mostly indifferent?

Are they comfortable or uncomfortable being so intimate?

Do they have a lot to talk about?

Is either one aggressive? Passive?

Is there competition between them? Jealousy? Love?

Sit back, let your imagination run wild, and have fun with this one. This exercise can be quite revealing.

MARIO ACEVEDO

Love Between the Species

MARIO ACEVEDO is the author of the Felix Gomez detective-vampire series from HarperCollins and IDW Publishing. His short fiction is included in numerous anthologies that include Arte Público Press, and in *Modern Drunkard Magazine*. Acevedo lives and writes in Denver, Colorado.

L ove between humans is complicated enough. Now try to sex it up between humans and nonhumans.

To start with, you've got two types of nonhumans. In column A, you have the type that look like us, more or less. Vampires. Angels. Demons. Vulcans. Klingons. Basically, two arms, two legs, one set of private bits connected in a very human-looking arrangement. You wouldn't have trouble shopping for them at the Gap or L.L. Bean. Imagine sex with any of these creatures and you wouldn't go, "Yew, gross!" In fact, what guy wouldn't want to score an elf chick?

And what nonhuman dude wouldn't want to hit it with human babes? It's even in Scripture. The Book of Genesis tells of Nephilim (aka Giants or Angels, maybe even the Dodgers) looking down upon the daughters of men and finding them fair. *Going my way, sweetheart?*

Column B is a lot more diverse and problematic. Here you got all kinds of critters. Insect aliens. Unicorns. Dragons. Blobs. Zombies. Though zombies are undead humans, and you'd think should be considered in Column A, the whole rotting body parts and junk-becoming-detached-in-mid-copulation implies a huge gross-out factor. The Dumpster smell does little for the romantic ambience.

Not only does sex with anything from Column B conjure disgusting images, but it might even be illegal in some states.

One way around the bestiality implications is to depict a sensual rather than sexual experience. Melding of the minds. After all, we're told by psychotherapists that the brain is the largest erogenous zone (for you maybe), so some inter-mind hanky-panky avoids the grinding of body parts in a particularly icky fashion.

For example, a male astronaut falls into a vat filled with female alien goo. It becomes love at first splash. She's all like, "OMG! You understand me."

He's all like, "Oh baby, you're so hot!"

Literally. The vat is 110°F. He flails in the tank. She splishes. He flails. She splashes. And the next thing, he can't help but cuddle in the afterglow, and because she's liquid, there is no arguing over who sleeps in the wet spot.

Romance might be a little easier, because it's more about how your lovebirds feel about one another on an emotional level, where the thrust—as it were—is not about thrusting, but love.

Writing fiction is all about emotional manipulation. Readers want the vicarious experience. Don't let them down. Give the readers characters they care about, that they feel for. Make your readers laugh. Cry. Feel the angst. The anticipation. The heat of desire. Triumph. Loss. Regret.

If it's all about the plumbing, your narrative will read like a chart about the human anatomy. Okay, there's his outie. Her innie. Yawn.

But don't let me discourage you from exploring graphic human-alien erotica. Picture this scenario: A female starship captain is marooned with a brainy professor squid. She has needs. He has needs. They have chemistry. She's curious and horny. Same for him, plus he has numerous appendages. They're both consenting adults. Write that story and you might just pen the next mommy-porn mega best seller. I'll even give you the best line: *She moaned, "Oh baby, you touch me in so many different ways."*

EXERCISE

1. Write a paragraph in which your protagonist first discovers an attraction to a future lover. Use internalizations.

2. Write an erotic encounter between two different creatures only by describing emotions.

3. Sadly, everything must end. Write a scene where one of your intra-species lovers decides to call it quits. You know: It's not you—it's me.

SCENE CONSTRUCTION AND STYLE

"Words have no power to impress the mind without the exquisite horror of their reality."

—EDGAR ALLAN POE

JACK KETCHUM

Economy

JACK KETCHUM is the author of thirteen novels, five of which have been filmed, and dozens of screenplays, novellas, and short stories. He is the four-time winner of the Bram Stoker Award and was elected Grand Master at the 2011 World Horror Convention. He lives with cats.

For me, economy is crucial to really good writing, particularly at the onset of your story, and particularly in writing suspense. To hell with exposition—you can sneak that in gradually, as the story goes along. Right now, at the onset, you want to keep 'em turning those pages. You want to make them leap right in.

As Elmore Leonard famously said when asked how he got his writing so tight, "I leave out the parts that people tend to skip." Unless height, weight, hair color, or the size of his dick is crucial to your character, leave it the hell out. Unless the landscape is itself a major character, which it is in some books by James Lee Burke, Cormac McCarthy, and others, leave it for later.

I think it was the screenwriter and novelist William Goldman who advised writers to start a scene as close to the end of the thing as possible, and that Vonnegut had something to say about that too. Good idea. Skip the buildup and get to the guts of it. Here's the opening paragraph to a story of mine called "Bully":

"So it's all pouring out of him now, he's all over the place, we're done with the weather and the small talk, it's like I've set something loose inside him which he says he's not spoken of in twenty-odd years and maybe it's his own three scotches to my one but I think it runs much deeper than that. I think he's speaking about who he is and why."

This is a reporter doing an interview. We don't need to know who he is just yet or even who his interview subject is. Don't need to know where they're sitting, how he got there, what he wants to learn from this man. That comes later. We enter in the *middle* of something, and it seems important. Economy.

Note that this entire paragraph is two sentences, the first one long run-on. It's meant to race you through the paragraph without a breather. Long run-ons and short, staccato sentences are the *poetry* of suspense writing, the stressed-unstressed-stressed, the meter. Compare the above to these lines from my novel with Lucky McKee, *The Woman*:

"There is pain. Pain that pulses through her body from shoulder to knee. That beats at her body as the waves beat the shore. But pain is to be borne. This is nothing to the pain of birthing. Pain says one thing only.

Alive."

Short, choppy, nervous-making sentences. Partials. The literary equivalent of stuttering. Just like. What I'm. Writing. Now.

What do the two types of sentences have in common? Read the selections again.

Both are packed with information about the people involved.

Economy.

EXERCISE

1. Write an opening paragraph that starts in the middle of something. Make sure your first line is immediate and draws us right in, and that the paragraph that follows fulfills the promise of that line. This is not the time to go off on a tangent. This is the time to start singing your song.

2. Write an opening paragraph using short, staccato lines. Then write the same paragraph using run-ons. Reverse the process and write another.

RAINBOW REED

Using Your Senses

RAINBOW REED is the poet/writer in residence at The Wicked Come. She has had poetry published in many anthologies and enjoys exploring the darker side of existence. She is the author of the dark romantic/gothic horror poetry book *The Wicked Come* (Lost Tower Publications). She is now working on the dark fantasy novel "The Torcian Chronicles."

I write dark fantasy novels and dark romantic/horror poetry. I use the following technique for both story writing and poetry as it is a very simple but vivid way of opening up your world to your audience and drawing them into the world that you have created.

When writing, you have to convey the story, set the scene, and build up believable characters in as short a time as possible and using few words, so as to immediately engage your reader's attention and encourage them to carry on reading. Words are precious, so use them with care. Too many and your audience will drift away, too few and they will not understand your work.

One way to set the scene for your work but not overburden your audience with reams of descriptive narrative is to use the Five Senses Technique. The senses contain psychological feelings, memories, and emotions that you can exploit in your writing. You are inviting your audience into a new world so they should be able to feel, hear, see, taste, and smell it!

The Sense of Sight. This is the image your writing is creating in your audience's mind. The readers should be able to imagine their own interpretations of your world and be able to connect emotionally and imaginatively with it, so your writing should offer signposts to your world but not dictate it.

For example, in my poem "Devotion" the first verse describes a wedding day photo of a happy bride . . .

Beside your bed,
The photo rests:
Happy Wedding Days,
Soft, loving eyes,
Seas of blue,
A sunshine smile,
On an Angel's face.

Immediately, the audience is given a portal into the world I have created, that of a room with a photo of a happy bride, but they do not know exactly what she looks like, so can build up a picture in their mind's eye, creating their own "dream girl," but neither do they know who is observing the photo, even though most would imagine it to be her husband.

So by using the sight sense, the audience has their first glimpse into your world, creating their own images about it as it has not been fully explored, and they are left with questions, to encourage them to read on for more information about your world.

The Sense of Touch. As humans we touch our environment all the time. I am sure you are touching something now. We remember and identify with the objects and environments we interact with, so when writing you can use your readers' own memories to make your world feel real and draw your audience deeper into your world. Again it's better to be short and descriptive. For example, in the second verse of "Devotion," touch is introduced very simply with the pillows on her bed being, "*Sprinkled with rose petals.*"

Readers can immediately identify with their own experiences of feeling the soft but moist petals of flowers, so they are given another way into exploring your world. However, they are still left with questions: *Who is scattering petals on the pillow? What has happened to the girl in the photo? Is this a beautiful, romantic gesture?* By writing less your readers will imagine more.

The Sense of Smell. Smell is one of the most emotionally evocative senses. Your audience has experienced a lifetime of smells, which you can use to draw them into your world. The smell of death is an immediate indication that something bad has happened while the smell of scented candles will evoke more sensual memories. Smells can quickly set the mood for your story. In "Devotion" I introduced smell in the second verse, while describing an unmade bed with twisted sheets:

> *Your perfume lingers*
> *Loiters on soft pillows.*

Your readers can identify with the smell of roses, perhaps triggering a memory in their brain but still the story is yet to unfold. In the case of "Devotion" the readers have been given a hint through the smell of roses, and maybe their own experiences with being given roses, that perhaps they are reading a love story.

The Sense of Taste. Taste always provokes a personal, emotional response and is deeply associated with people's own memories and experiences, which can therefore be used as a valuable tool for getting your reader emotionally involved in your story. A good taste such as eating chocolate can be linked to a happy experience and evoke feelings of pleasure in your reader, while a bitter taste will create feelings of anger, resentment, or tension. For example, in "Devotion" in the third verse the story unfolds that the observer finds the girl's lip gloss:

> *Strawberry lip gloss,*
> *Our favorite taste,*
> *I must have.*

The audience can immediately understand and imagine the taste of the strawberry lip gloss as they sensually taste the plot unfold. However, there are questions left unanswered. *Why does the observer have to have the lip gloss? Is this the action of a husband, boyfriend, or someone more sinister?* Suddenly, through strawberry lip gloss, doubt is introduced.

The Sense of Hearing. Noise can promote all sorts of reactions from your audience. Some great iconic movie moments have been created using sound such as the theme from *JAWS*, the "Here's Johnny" call from Jack Nicholson in *THE SHINING*, and the shower scene music from *PSYCHO*. People remember sounds and they produce an emotional response. You can use this in your writing to promote positive or negative feelings in your audience. Bird songs, gurgling streams, and giggling babies will have your audience smiling, while footsteps approaching on an empty staircase should promote fear. All your readers will have heard noises that made them happy or scared, so you can exploit this in your writing. In "Devotion" I used sound to indicate a darker twist to the story:

> *You stir; waking.*
> *And through the skylight*
> *I leave alone.*

Now the reader's senses should be tingling, aware that something is not right as this is not the action of a romantic husband but someone a lot more sinister.

EXERCISE

It is very easy to use the Five Senses Technique in your writing to create your world.

At the start of any writing I write down the five senses: taste, touch, sight, hearing, and smell. Then I cross them out as they are included in the work.

The order the senses are introduced to your reader should occur naturally in your story, so use whatever order makes sense to your writing. But always make sure that you keep your descriptions clear and to the point.

Simply by using the five senses you can emotionally engage your reader in your work, using their own experiences and memories to draw them into your world, getting your readers to feel your work through all their senses, evoking feelings of fear, happiness, or foreboding . . . the choice is yours.

J. MICHELLE NEWMAN

Make It Real

J. MICHELLE NEWMAN is completing her first historical fantasy novel, "Mistaken Knights," while trying to save the world one kilowatt hour at a time: She moonlights for a company that creates green energy solutions for small and medium-sized businesses.

I believed that I was writing historical fiction until an agent categorized my novel as fantasy. To me the world of the novel was grounded in history, or at least the historical facts about the type of food, clothing, animals, buildings, and weapons known to have existed during the sixth century. I built my world from the elements of this very real sixth-century foundation by adding blocks of fantasy: time travel, characters based on a legend, magical and mythical beasts. The world of my novel became real to me with characters and landscapes that were three-dimensional. I could see clearly the landscape in each scene in my mind's eye and I could experience what the characters were feeling. I write what I love to read and I love to get lost in fiction and escape to another reality, so I never questioned whether a dragon really could exist!

The craft is to create a world where dragons do exist, and your readers become so immersed in that world that they believe anything the writer tells them, even though it may be pure fantasy. To truly get lost in fiction, the reader must be able to experience the action of the novel along with the characters, to get inside their bodies and feel what they feel and see the world through their eyes.

If you've done your job as a writer, your readers will predict and anticipate your character's behavior before they act, just as in a real world social situation. This ability to discern one's own and others' mental states such as *"Purpose, intention, knowledge, belief, thinking, doubt, guessing, pretending, liking . . ."* and to interpret behavior based on this discernment is a concept originally introduced by Premack and Woodruff in 1978 in their article, "Does the Chimpanzee Have a Theory of Mind?"

According to Lisa Zunshine in her 2006 book *Why We Read Fiction: Theory of Mind and the Novel*, our "theory of mind" or "mind-reading" tendency is the reason why we read and write fiction: *"Fictional narratives feed our hungry theory of mind, giving us carefully crafted, emotionally and aesthetically compelling social contexts shot through with mind-reading opportunities."*

As my improvisation teacher, Melanie Chartoff, always tells me, to make a scene real: Stay in the moment, get inside your body, and interact with the objects in the world. If you believe the world exists, then so will the audience. And the same holds true for writing. If your characters slow down to see, feel, and interact with their surroundings, then your readers will believe in the new reality also.

So now, the question is how to make it real. Visualize the landscape of the scene before you begin to write. Paint the world with sensory experiences, allow your characters to react to the inputs, and follow Newton's Third Law of Motion: For every action there is an equal and opposite reaction.

Make it sensory by incorporating sight, smell, hearing, touch, and taste. Be specific by providing details that readers can easily identify from their real life, so they have a base to compare with the "new" world or reality of your story. Imagine your character walking through this world and interacting with objects within the landscape rather than just listing them. If the reader can experience the world with the character, then it will be three dimensional and real. I need to see the world before I can even begin writing. If it feels real, then to me it *is* real.

Try this technique and see how it works for your story. With each revision, the scene will become richer and more believable. Don't rush. Take the time to make it real.

EXERCISE

1. Pick a specific moment within your story. Before writing, try to imagine the setting for the scene. It could be a cave in Cornwall, a castle in Northumbria, a forest in Brittany, or an office tower on Wall Street in New York City, anything you desire. Write a description of the landscape (or place) without editing. Be sure to have your character look in all directions and try to describe what they actually see through their eyes.

2. Reread it. Did you include all five senses? If not, then revise by adding sensory inputs. How does it smell? What is the temperature? Is there any background noise?

3. Did you describe the world through the character's eyes, from his or her perspective? Get inside the character's body. What would the character notice at this particular moment within the story, and why? Have your character show what he is feeling by how he interacts with the environment in the scene in the moment.

4. Did you include some real-world details to ground your reader? For instance, you could describe a thatched hut with a sleeping roll stuffed with goose feathers, a glass jar of fermented ginger, and a box filled with amulets in the shape of serpent eggs. If the reader can relate to objects from his or her real world, then you can include a fantastical element like the serpent eggs.

5. Did you follow the law of action and reaction?

6. Reread it one more time and revise again. Remember to slow down and stay in the present moment with your character.

LILLIAN STEWART CARL

Describe a Spiral Staircase

LILLIAN STEWART CARL has written multiple novels and multiple short stories in multiple genres. She was nominated for a Hugo Award for co-editing *The Vorkosigan Companion*, an overview of Lois McMaster Bujold's science fiction work. She lives in a book-lined cloister in Texas and enjoys crossword puzzles, music, needlework, and tai chi.

Many years ago I worked with a man who would tease me for using my hands while I talked. He'd grab them and say, "Now describe a spiral staircase."

So how do you use no more than words to form images in the reader's mind?

As a child doomed to be a writer, I'd verbalize descriptions of my grandmother's living room, from the bay window to the tapestry depicting a desert scene (I thought it illustrated "We Three Kings"), from the four overstuffed bookcases to a card table piled with dictionaries, newspapers, and crossword puzzles.

A twentieth-century house, a Christmas carol, newspapers—the scene is an ordinary one. A scene in a fantasy or science fiction tale, however, is not. It's tempting to catalog every sight, every smell, every noise, so your reader will know where he is before you pull the rug out from under him.

In *The Call of Cthulhu*, H. P. Lovecraft describes a statuette: "*this thing, which seemed instinct with a fearsome and unnatural malignancy, was of a somewhat bloated corpulence and squatted evilly on a rectangular block or pedestal . . .*"

Expressions such as "unnatural malignancy" and "squatted evilly" are narrator intrusion: telling, not showing. After a page and a half of adjective overload, Lovecraft begins to sound like a lecturer waving a laser pointer.

J. R. R. Tolkien in *The Two Towers* describes the road leading to the city of the Ringwraiths: "*Here the road, gleaming faintly, passed over the stream in the midst of the valley, and went on, winding deviously up toward the city's gate . . .*"

One word, *deviously*, nails the image.

Or consider instead the dialogue in *FORBIDDEN PLANET*, where Morbius compares the trapezoidal doorways in the Krell laboratory to our doorways, shaped to the human body, and leaves the rest to our imagination.

In *Memory*, Lois McMaster Bujold shows Miles arriving at his ancestral home on the planet Barrayar. "*Vorkosigan House sat in the center. . . . A stone wall topped with black wrought-iron spikes surrounded it all. The four stories of great gray stone blocks, in two main wings plus some extra odd architectural bits, rose in a vast archaic mass. All it needed was window slits and a moat. And a few bats and ravens for decoration.*"

By segueing from a straightforward description into Miles's thoughts, referencing familiar cultural images, Bujold not only shows the reader the hide-bound traditionalism of Barrayar, but also Miles's mood—he doesn't see his home as a place of comfort, but as a grim fortress.

In *The Martian Chronicles*, Ray Bradbury also uses familiar images, but twists them, ever so casually, to evoke an alien world: "*They had a house of crystal pillars on the planet Mars by the edge of an empty sea, and every morning you could see Mrs. K. eating the golden fruits that grew from the crystal walls, or cleaning the house with handfuls of magnetic dust which, taking all dirt with it, blew away on the hot wind. . . . you could see Mr. K. himself in his room, reading from a metal book with raised hieroglyphs over which he brushed his hand, as one might play a harp. And from the book, as his fingers stroked, a voice sang, a soft ancient voice, which told tales of when the sea was red steam on the shore and ancient men had carried clouds of metal insects and electric spiders into battle.*"

Here's how I set the scene in my own story "*Pleasure Palace*," nominated for a Theodore Sturgeon Memorial Award: "*Varina turned and*

glanced out a porthole. The cracked, steaming surface of Io stretched be-
fore her. Yesterday's eruption had already begun to darken into orange; soon
the crawlers would be sampling it for mineral content, for market value. A
plume of fire billowed above the far horizon, consuming the stars; deep fis-
sures glowed flickering red. Lucifer waited for the unwary, a rover slipping
down a scoriated lava slope, a crawler caving in the edge of magma pool. A
medieval Hell, painted by Bosch and orchestrated by the cries of the damned—
except we, Varina thought, damn ourselves."

Anna Jacobs, who writes historical and modern tales, provides an example applicable to any genre. Compare version A: *"The town sat in a circular valley with a river running through it. The hills around the valley were covered with woods which in summer were carpeted by wildflowers."*

To version B: *"She couldn't resist stopping the car at the lookout. She hadn't expected the town to be so pretty—wide streets, gardens full of flowers, a big square where people were strolling or stopping to chat. 'I think I shall like living here,' she said aloud. As the river below her glinted in the sunlight and a breeze rustled through the trees she could feel herself relaxing, tension flowing away. Smiling she got back into the car. This was the last place he'd think of looking for her, the very last."*

And we're off and running with the story!

EXERCISE

1. Describe your writing space.

    Never mind the desk or the computer. What details reveal your personality? I could say I keep several toys in my office. Or I could say I have a doll of Merida from the movie *BRAVE*, with her red hair and bow and arrows, and an action figure of Éowyn from the Lord of the Rings series, complete with sword and spear.

    Funny, my first published novel, *Sabazel*, was the story of an Amazon queen.

2. Describe a real place, perhaps a favorite vacation spot.

    A misty morning in Scotland with the tang of peat smoke in the air? Waves lapping a beach in the South Seas? What is happening there, and to whom, and why? Is that actually peat smoke or smoke from a house fired by an arsonist? Are the waves lapping the beach because, just off shore, the *Nautilus* is rising from the sea?

Never assume the landscape is static.

3. Use the same methods to describe an imaginary place.

Just as in poetry, in description every word counts. Be specific. Choose strong words that show not just what's there, but what the observer feels. Integrate the description into the narrative rather than leaving it in lumps. Description reveals character and motivation as well as setting the scene.

Make that spiral staircase carry the reader into the story!

JODY LYNN NYE

Breaking the *Was*-ing Habit
(and Making Friends with Your Active Verbs)

JODY LYNN NYE has published forty books, including *The Ship Who Won* with Anne McCaffrey; a humorous anthology about mothers, *Don't Forget Your Spacesuit, Dear;* and more than a hundred short stories. Her latest books are *View from the Imperium* (Baen Books), and *Robert Asprin's Myth-Quoted* (Ace Books).

Dynamic writing will bring your reader into your story in a matter of a few words. Many new writers don't realize that they are keeping their readers at arm's length by their very sentence structure. They begin far too many sentences with "It was," "They were," "He was," and so on. I know, because I was one of those new writers.

During the early years of my professional career, I worked on a project under the aegis of best-selling science fiction legend Anne McCaffrey. She drew my attention to my over-reliance on *was* and its relatives, and broke me of the habit. With a kind but firm hand, Anne showed me where I let my reader down. I had gone to so much trouble to construct my world that I had overlooked the very phrases that presented my beautiful creation to my audience. I had taken what could have been emotionally satisfying encounters between my characters and their environment, and made them too remote to enjoy. In my own defense, I didn't do it that often, just often enough to offend Anne's sense of narrative flow. She made me more aware of my verb choices.

The main trouble with *was* is that it can make for lazy writing. It leads to telling instead of showing. The most popular example of ex-cruciatingly bad writing is, of course, *"It was a dark and stormy night."* Would Sir Edward Bulwer-Lytton have been better off beginning his deathless story with, *"The rain slashed down, striking the unlucky traveler with icy bullets of rain invisible in the deep gloom of the night"*? Perhaps. It comes out just as purple, but more active. The reader will become more involved in the story when offered a visceral experience instead of a remote one. Passive verbs cause the reader to have a passive con-nection with the narrative. If the aim is to engage them actively, then use active verbs. Naturally, there will be times when you want to hold the reader apart from emotional involvement. This exercise will help you correct yourself when you don't mean to do it.

Even if you are not guilty of nonstrategic *was*-ing, it's still good to hone your chops. Here's your assignment:

EXERCISE

Write an action scene of two to five pages. You must create a setting, introduce and describe one or more characters, and describe a fight or a daring escape or a romantic encounter, all without using the words *was* or *were*. (Or, if you *must* write it in the present tense, *is*, *am*, and *are*.)

Search for an active verb that takes the place of one of the old reli-able, boring standbys. Read it over to make sure none of those sneaky verbs have crept in (except where appropriate in dialogue). You'll be surprised how much more fully you begin to picture the scene. Your readers will appreciate the difference.

SCOTT RUBENSTEIN

Surprise in the Twenty-fourth Century

SCOTT RUBENSTEIN has written thirty produced episodes for television including *Star Trek: The New Generation*, *Cagney & Lacey*, *Hunter*, *MacGyver*, *Night Court*, *Nine to Five*, and *Diff'rent Strokes*. Aside from also being a story editor on three shows, he executive produced the award-winning documentary *NOT AFRAID TO LAUGH* and *Peacock Blues* for Showtime. He taught for ten years as an adjunct professor at California State University, Northridge and USC.

It was 1988. I was staring at Maurice Hurley, executive producer of *Star Trek: The Next Generation*. A smile on my face. My writing partner Leonard Mlodinow and I were about to be on the writing staff of the most innovative show on the air.

I grew up in a family that loved science fiction. For a long time I thought Edgar Rice Burroughs and Ray Bradbury were relatives of mine. In some ways they were. Someone was always reading about "John Carter of Mars" and my mother became infatuated with *The Martian Chronicles*.

But this is an article about surprise. A definition of surprise is *"to cause to feel wonder, astonishment at something unanticipated."* The perfect way to describe *Star Trek: The Next Generation*. The show takes place in the twenty-fourth century, so it must be filled with surprises. Unfortunately, the first surprise we'll discuss here took place in the twentieth century.

A few days before our meeting at *Star Trek: The Next Generation*, our agent called and said the producers of the show really liked us, so we didn't need to prepare anything. We just needed to show up and prove we weren't very weird. We could do normal. We did show up, but after twenty minutes of normal, the producer asked us why we were there. Surprise.

I explained that we were there because we were going to be on the staff of the show. He said, "No." The show was very hard to write for and one couldn't be on staff without writing a script, and what ideas did we have? Bigger surprise.

First thought was I was going to have to call a lot of friends and relatives and tell them that we weren't writing on the show, and also that we killed our agent. I needed help from my bag of tricks as a writer and a person, and I needed it fast.

Before I tell you what happened at the meeting, I'll tell you what I had learned about surprise up to this point.

Surprise was always my weapon of choice. I learned it at a very early age. I knew that I wasn't the smartest kid in class. Laura Scheiner and Ronnie Lipkin had the co-honor. I wasn't the handsomest person. It felt like everyone other than me had that co-honor. First lesson for the writer to learn: the more awkward you are, and the more jokes you can tell—i.e., unanticipated, surprising reformulations of reality you come up with—the better chance you have at success as a writer. When you try to sell any idea—whether to Hollywood or the literary world—humor is important, but surprise is essential. Also, with a billion ideas out there, it's important to use an element of surprise to make your idea unique. Often it's good to even surprise yourself; your audience will follow.

I was at my first college dance. I had never asked a girl to dance. I saw this beautiful young woman sitting at the sidelines, moving to the rhythms of the song. Little did I know this was about to define me as a man, as well as help me succeed as a writer. I don't think she had a clue either.

I asked her to dance. She went into the crowd of dancing bobble-head dolls and moved to her and the band's rhythm. I was totally lost in my head. I realized that the entire trick to winning this woman for the night was to get her to dance with me for a second song. My history of second dances was limited. So I needed a strategy. I needed intrigue. So there was that awkward moment when the song ended and I asked her name. She told me, Melody Martin. She asked me mine. I paused and said, "Thirteen."

"Thirteen?" she mouthed. The band started playing. She paused for a moment. And started dancing. I had the rest of the dance to concoct a story. After that song was over, I told her my parents had twelve children before me and they ran out of names so they called me Thirteen. She laughed and we ended up dancing together for two months.

So the tricks I learned in life helped me in writing. But I should have known, if you don't come prepared for anything, you might end up in shit's creek without a paddle, or a boat.

And at this life-changing producer's meeting, my writing partner and I were up a twenty-fourth century creek. A group of writer-producers wondering what ideas we had for them, and we had been told by our agent, "No need to prepare."

So I started with an arena. Wesley, the young ensign, falls in love for the first time. I wasn't familiar enough with the show to know if they had done this. Every show will do this kind of episode, but newbies like us don't get to do them. For some lucky reason, they wanted us to go on. They seemed to be on the edge of their seats, waiting for an interesting storyline that I was praying for my unconscious to help me with. I continued spinning a story. I talked about a young female leader from another planet that the *Enterprise* needed to transport to her home planet. Everyone seemed to be nodding like it was okay up to that point (even my partner, who had no idea where I was going). I felt I needed some surprise and I knew whatever I came up with was going to be a surprise, at least to me. And then I smiled. The female leader turned out to be young, beautiful, and humanoid. But what Wesley learns, to his surprise, is that she is a shape shifter. There was a pause that seemed like a black hole. Then everyone was happy and we ended up working on the show and actually got to occupy Gene Roddenberry's old office as story editors.

EXERCISE

This exercise is based on assignments I give my students to get them involved in using surprise in their writing. It's also based on my own personal homework assignments I give myself. These are sneaky ways to trick your unconscious to share its untapped gold.

1. The first thing to do is acknowledge that based on feedback or your own nagging sense, something about what you have written is not working. You're either stuck or have written something cliché or perhaps too thin, superficial, and obvious. We are going to work on that section for the purposes of this exercise. So take a two- to five-page scene from your screenplay or portion of your book, and copy it to a new file or print it out. You're going to put this portion of your work into a creative boot camp.

2. If it's a drama, rewrite it as a comedy. Write it in that genre with all your heart, milking it for any comic potential. If it's a comedy, write it as a drama, digging deeper into the subtext to find the inherent lurking drama. Now read what you wrote. What about it surprises you? Is there one thing you uncovered from your unconscious that you can use to freshen up, deepen, or expand that section of the work?

3. Look at this or another section of your work. To turn it on its head and surprise yourself and the reader, try these other forms of rewriting to trick your creativity into surprising you:

    a. Write your story from a completely different historical perspective. If it's science fiction set it in the twenty-fourth century, the old West, or Elizabethan times. Again, see if you discover some element of surprise that you could insert into your original story.

    b. Change the gender of your characters, thereby surprising yourself with the choices they come up with, motivations as well as actions that, once you are done, you can mine for surprises.

c. Take a scene or a chapter and find a completely original location that makes no sense at all for your story, but write your characters and circumstances into that location. Explore what you come up with for more surprises.

Surprise always works to grab your audience and to keep you glued to your chair, writing yourself out of corners and into a professional writing life.

LANCE MAZMANIAN

Break the Compass

LANCE MAZMANIAN has many thousands of hours in the Hollywood trenches of physical production at all budget levels, and
with top directors, producers, and crew. He's spent decades behind various keyboards, where he has written a screenplay or
two. He has also spent time in the labyrinth of film and TV dis-
tribution.

Kill yourself.

Didn't expect that, did you?

For a screenwriter creating stories, or strings of words, or
characters, or environments, I believe strongly that the first task is
originality. Yes, I know, ain't nothing that's never been done (as Bill
Shakespeare once said so beautifully), but in trying for original language and worlds, we can often come at least close to two words or
two ideas that nobody else ever thought to stick together.

I'll use an analogy to demonstrate:

Let's say your script has a speeding 2013 Ferrari F12berlinetta,
silver, of course. It's driving down an average street, toward an average intersection. Light's green.

Does the Italian supercar make a left, a right, go straight, turn
around and go back, or maybe just stop?

None of the above: As the Ferrari speeds through the intersection,
it lifts straight into the sky. And disappears.

Unexpected. But it seemed like a normal day, right? And yet, flying
Ferrari.

I stress again: This is analogy; it's not meant to literally echo *BACK
TO THE FUTURE* or even *BLADE RUNNER*. It's just an illustrative

example of doing precisely what the audience doesn't expect. This same trick could apply to dialogue, character choices, transitions, locations, whatever.

Of course, if you simply try and assemble a patched-up chimera that's green on one side and mirrored on the other, chances are it not only will lack screen context, but will also fit no framework of cinematic reality whatsoever . . . not to mention it's likely to look and feel crazy, like someone shoehorned Dr. Seuss into an Erica Jong novel.

So, the trick is to create these original ideas and put them in a corridor with the familiar, the sane, the safe (especially if you're *not* writing sci-fi, horror, etc). And that's tricky, indeed. After all, they who walk the razor's edge don't always get Bill Murray.

Considering the above, four people who do this originality remix very well are QT (Tarantino), Charlie Kaufman, and, of course, the Coen Brothers. In these guys' pictures and words, we always peek through a lens that's just slightly off. It mostly works very well, and they each leave in their wake oft-imitated originality (or oft-imitated reconstructions of originality).

EXERCISE

Imagine that the Ferrari mentioned above suddenly comes crashing into your living room. No one hurt (thank God), but what's your initial reaction? What do you do?

Think of that first, gut, predictable response. Note it. Now, do something else. That is, imagine time has stopped and you actually have a few seconds to think clearly about your next possible "other" initial reaction. Do it; note it. It must, of course, be different from the first.

Now, stop the clock again, and think: What's yet another (third) possible initial reaction to this beautiful silver Ferrari suddenly appearing next to the sofa, uninvited? Note it. You might have to actually pause and consider. I mean, how many possible reactions are there to such a thing, anyway?

Okay, that's three potential reactions. One, two, three. Now take it to four.

Chances are, that number four reaction is the one you least expected to reach or execute, and then, of course, it's the one the audience will also least expect.

Why deal with this deep digging? Because predictability and cliché are always bad, and even the very best writers often produce unusable prose/ideas on a first run. Moving four steps away from our first efforts sometimes cleans any and all amateur fare from the air. Over time, it becomes an automatic, near instantaneous form of self-editing.

And now the pièce de résistance: Apply this exercise paradigm to scenes, character construction, lines of dialogue, reactions, and so on.

Call it the Four Corners rule of creating with words: First corner is the usual, obvious, "gut" choice; second corner is a little deeper into original territory; third corner is "midway through the mine"; corner number four is where the queen lives.

Of course, don't let me stop you from going to five, six, seven, eight.

Let me be clear, though, in closing: In all the above, I'm absolutely *not* saying your first words and ideas created via stream of consciousness aren't or won't be brilliant channeling. They might well be. But, they might well not.

Chances are, the first choices we make as writers are the weakest. Some of us have editors and collaborators to smoke the foul melodrama and trite soap opera from the page, thereby forcing us farther down the line to more interesting choices.

But some of us don't have editors and agents and so on, standing by. The above might help in that case.

Onward.

Paint It Dark: Creating an Eerie Atmosphere and Foreshadowing Ominous Events

SIMON CLARK published his first novel, *Nailed by the Heart*, in 1995, and many dreams and nightmares later he wrote the cult horror-thriller *Blood Crazy*, and other novels including *Stranger*, *Vengeance Child*, and *The Tower*. His latest novel is a return to his Vampyrrhic mythology with *His Vampyrrhic Bride*. Clark lives with his family in the atmospheric, legend-haunted county of Yorkshire in northern England.

Oooh, that's scary." This could be your reaction if you're enjoying a well-written horror story. Yet what is present in the text that scares? Is it when the werewolf attacked, the vampire pounced, or the monster roared? Probably not. I'm pretty sure those shivers started to trickle deliciously down your spine when you read the early parts of the story when, for example, a character first sets eyes on the haunted house.

I write horror. My job is to frighten. But I aim to frighten in a way that is enticing and pleasurable. So many writers, who are new to horror, rush their hero or heroine to a scene where there is full-blooded carnage that disgusts or shocks the reader. The truth is that gruesome excess soon becomes tedious.

If we're agreed that the best horror fiction requires some careful scene setting before the truly horrific action takes place, then I invite you to join me in the exercise that follows.

Before we reach the nitty-gritty of the exercise, I'd like to tell you why it is important to my own writing. As I've already said, my job is to frighten. So when I'm writing a description of a house, or even the weather, I'm mindful that it should not be a plain description of architecture or rain. I ask myself what trigger words I can employ that tell the reader that ghostly events are on their way, or that the hero is heading relentlessly toward danger.

The easiest way for me to demonstrate this is to present an example of the kind of fiction I write. What follow are the opening lines from my novel *Vengeance Child*:

"The midnight rain did not whisper. It struck the big house hard. Rain clattered at windows. Drops hit the patio table in a salvo of vicious bangs. Heaven's bullets. A sound like war. As if the earth had been invaded from above. Take no prisoners. Batter the house into the ground . . ."

So why did I write the first paragraph of my novel in such a way? By the time you've completed the exercises, you will have found the answer. What's more, there is a very good chance you'll be writing fiction that makes the reader shiver and murmur, *"Oooh, that's scary."*

Generally, eerie fiction will contain certain words and phrases that serve as something akin to hypnotic suggestion. That is to say, they implant in the reader's mind the notion that uncanny events are approaching, and that the characters will face danger from perhaps an inexplicable or supernatural source. The use of these key words and phrases might be termed "the language of horror."

"The Signal-Man" by Charles Dickens is well worth studying. This deceptively simple ghost story opens with the narrator visiting a signal-man who is based in his signal-box beside a railway line. At the beginning of the tale, the narrator gazes at the railway line, which emerges from a tunnel. Notice those powerful trigger words in the following:

". . . the gloomier entrance to a black tunnel, in whose massive architecture there was a barbarous, depressing, and forbidding air. So little sunlight ever found its way to this spot, that it had an earthy deadly smell: and so much cold wind rushed through it, that it struck chill to me, as if I had left the natural world."

A less talented author might have written, "The railway line emerged from a dark tunnel." The genius of Dickens mesmerizes the reader with his adroit use of words. He reinforces the fact that the location is ill-lit with the use of *gloomier* and *black*. The phrase *so little sunlight* drives the point home. He describes the architecture as "barbarous," so he's imbuing the structure with an air of violence. Again, the threat is reinforced by the smell of the earth being "deadly." Dickens evokes the cold and the eerie gloom of the place, then prepares us for the supernatural horror to come by announcing that the character feels as if he's "left the natural world."

The object of these exercises is this: to learn how to use the power of words to transform the ordinary into the extraordinary. To weave words and phrases in such a way that the description of a house, for example, becomes the electrifying evocation of a frightening, haunted place. If you practice, you will learn to use the language of horror. You will scare the reader in such a teasing and pleasant way that you leave them wanting more.

EXERCISE

Practice this technique with these short assignments (half a page each is ample):

1. Describe a haunted house. Firstly, talk about the house in plain terms. For example, "The house was built from brick. Its windows looked out over the park." Then insert trigger words to imbue the house with an uncanny aura. Perhaps like this: "The old, dilapidated house was built from bricks that were the color of blood. Its windows looked out over the park. They resembled cold, staring eyes as they regarded that forbidding and lonely realm of trees, which harbored the shadows of night."

2. Describe a sinister individual. Experiment with trigger words that suggest something is dangerously amiss with our stranger. Pay attention to the eyes. For example, "His eyes had a spectral glow." Or "ghost-lights glinted in her eyes." Or "In the stranger's eyes she glimpsed the suffering of a thousand orphaned children." Be adventurous!

3. Using the language of horror, describe a stretch of river as it flows beneath a city bridge.

4. Convey the menace of a tree where witches were once hanged long ago. Are its branches like hooked fingers clawing at the sky? Does its "brutal trunk" loom over the road? Do "monstrous patterns in the bark" suggest evil faces? Does the shadow it casts "chill the blood and darken the meadow"?

   And when the breeze passes through its leaves, what sound does it make? Sighs? Whispered voices? Chuckling sounds? Can you describe the tree so it seems that you're describing a malicious and violent monster? Or can you describe that melancholy old tree in such a way the reader feels as if they are reading about the tragic victims who ended their lives there?

Of course, you can continue to practice painting your descriptions dark. You can also vary the above prompts: Describe a cat found in an abandoned church, a truck owned by a madman, or a gold brooch belonging to a woman who poisoned her first husband—and the second, and the third!

JOHN SKIPP

The Choreography of Violence

JOHN SKIPP is a *New York Times* best-selling novelist and editor, zombie godfather, splatterpunk poster child, Bizarro elder statesman, and cheerful cultural agitator-turned-filmmaker who lives in Los Angeles, making crazed art-o-tainment for people who like that sort of thing.

I'm always amazed by how many exceptional writers have no idea how to stage an action scene. Which is fine, if you have no intention of writing one. Perhaps, having spent months weaving complex, memorable characters into a richly textured, lushly plotted narrative, you think the hard part is done.

But if that big exciting payoff your whole story's been building up to turns out to be the least exciting sequence in the book, please consider the following Rules to Kill By.

There are many ways to goof up an action scene. Most of them have to do with lack of immediacy, extraneous detail, verbal flab, and general unbelievability.

If you've ever been in a real-life violent encounter, you know how intensely, frenetically intimate and immediate its sensory engagement is. How blurred by momentum it gets. And how clearly certain key moments emerge.

This is why the cinematic vocabulary of conflict has gleefully expanded from two guys beating each other up in bland wide shots and over-the-shoulder coverage to insanely you-are-there POV (point of view) footage of the fist, the face, the knife, and the wound, alternately sped up into hyper-velocity and slowed down to micro-second increments—using every technical trick in the book.

But when it comes to writing fiction, there are no buttons you can hit that speed things up or slow them down, push in or pull out on the damage being done.

This is event-based writing, not ruminative writing. It's all in how you pace it and plan it. Using nothing more than carefully picked words. White space. Punctuation. Tight editing. And scrupulous attention to detail.

A master class example is the chapter in William Goldman's *Heat* (published in the UK as *Edged Weapons*), wherein our hero takes out two guys with guns, in eighteen meticulously detailed seconds (as I recall, roughly one brisk paragraph per second), armed with nothing but a credit card.

It's one of the most stunning action sequences in modern lit, because it grounds its startling triumph in:

1) Stripped-down, propulsive language that never strays from the point, or the physical specifics;

2) Tactile immediacy that engages the senses, with beat-by-beat choreography so scrupulously thought out that as it screens in your mind's eye, you go, *Wow! If that happened, it would go down exactly like this;* and

3) Psychological and emotional acuity expressed purely through physicality. Without digression. Without asides or remembrances. Purely focused on the action at hand.

Because that's how action is. When you're in it, you can't think about anything else.

I suggest you root your action in the experience of either a) one character at the center of the chaos; or b) several characters that you cut back and forth between, ratcheting up the stakes to your grand finale.

And believe me, there's nothing more important than a satisfying climax (and nothing more unsatisfying than the lack thereof). Whether your POV character is victorious or dies horribly, there's gotta be a payoff. And it's gotta be good.

So on top of your cunning imagination, do your homework. If you're inflicting damage, get the damage right. (Forensic pathology freaks will call you on it if you don't, and they now number in the trillions.) If you're utilizing traditional methods of destruction (guns, cars, bombs, bare knuckles, etc.), make sure you know how they actually work in violent practice.

When using monsters, of course, you have a little more leeway; but the more otherworldly your mythical creature is, the more it behooves you to ground its impact in the grittiest, most believable earthly terms.

I tend to open all my books with galvanizing action as a readerly incentive to keep on going. There's something to be said for starting out with a bang, with a punch line that punches 'em right in the heart. Or face. Or soul. Or wherever I'm aiming.

But whether you're that kind of roughhousing writer or not, these skills can always come in handy. (For the record, I treat just about everything—including dialogue—like action. It keeps the prose sharp and punchy, and therefore fun to write and read.)

EXERCISE

Construct a fight scene between two characters you know well. You can take two to three pages of buildup, just to get everything clear between them before the violence starts. (They can be friends, enemies, predators or prey, human or otherwise. Those dynamics are up to you.)

For the next two to three pages, write nothing but action. From the moment it starts, it does not stop until one or both of them is down.

Zero in on power words you feel in your gut. This is not the time to get cute or poetic, unless the poetry has real muscle and teeth. I recommend you alternate between short, staccato word bursts and flowing stream-of-violent-consciousness. In an exercise like this, it's all about rhythm, impact, and momentum.

Bottom line, action *is* character. What we do in the clinch is what exposes us in motion. How brave. How competent. How terrified. How unprepared.

Whoever we are in that moment stands revealed.

Extra Bonus Tip: If you're not a fighter yourself, make friends with some cool, smart people who are, and grill them on their strategic experience. If possible, get them to act your fight scene out for you, to demonstrate the flaws, and illustrate the more accurate realities.

Observe them closely. Ask questions. Take notes.

You'll be glad you did.

And finally: *Don't forget to kiss ass!* There is no substitute for genuine excitement. If you aren't completely riveted, no one else will be either.

Now go have fun with your stupendous action scene!

PRACTICING YOUR CRAFT

"If my doctor told me I had only six minutes to live, I wouldn't brood.
I'd type a little faster."

—ISAAC ASIMOV

RAMSEY CAMPBELL

What You Don't Need

RAMSEY CAMPBELL is acknowledged in the *Oxford Companion to English Literature* as "Britain's most respected living horror writer." He has been given more awards than any other writer in the field, including Grand Master of the 1999 World Horror Convention. His novels include *The Face That Must Die, Midnight Sun, The Darkest Part of the Woods, Secret Story, The Grin of the Dark, The Seven Days of Cain,* and *Ghosts Know.* His collections include *Waking Nightmares, Alone with the Horrors,* and *Just Behind You.*

I'm celebrating fifty years in print, which I hope means I've learned a few things worth knowing in that time (always compose at least the first sentence before sitting down to write; never be without a notebook or some other means of recording ideas as they suggest themselves; remember that however unsatisfactory your work may seem while being written, you can always rewrite . . .).

I write horror fiction, but I think some of what I'm going to say applies in a wider sense to writing generally. It's more than just an exercise for me, though it's simple enough: identifying an element I depend on and discovering what happens if I do without it. Here's how it has worked for me:

I first saw publication by imitating H. P. Lovecraft, as other writers have (Henry Kuttner and Robert Bloch, for instance). There's no shame in learning your craft by imitation—great painters and composers did—but I'm afraid I chose the easiest things about Lovecraft to mimic, not least his prose at its most empurpled (whereas a great deal of his best work is sober and controlled). Before I'd finished writing a book in his tradition, however, I decided to write one tale in a style as unlike his as possible, using only neutral language—no evocative words and very few adjectives—and narrated mostly through dialogue, with only essential actions described. I have to say the tale ("The Will of Stanley Brooke") betrays my youthfulness; at sixteen I hadn't learned to observe people, and the characters sound like strays from an old country-house mystery. Sometimes you need to wait until you're capable of doing your material justice.

At seventeen I read *Lolita* and fell in love with Nabokov's savoring of language. He's still an influence, but back then my style began to grow excessively baroque. Eventually, to counteract this I stripped it down again, applying much the same method that produced "The Will of Stanley Brooke." The result ("The Stocking") allowed me to concentrate on the interaction between the characters and clarified the prose. Let me suggest that the more stylistic modes you have at your disposal, the more eloquent your work may be. I find the naïve voice of a child narrator can convey unease very powerfully—a sense of the unsaid or misinterpreted. The greatest example in the genre is Arthur Machen's *The White People*—seek it out and judge for yourself.

Most of my tales have a strong—I hope vivid—visual component; very often the words bring the sights alive for me. It did no harm for me to jettison it in a couple of cases: "Hearing Is Believing," in which an uncanny invasion takes place purely on an aural level, and another story (forgive me if I don't identify it to those who haven't read it) where various images lead the reader to assume they're being seen by the protagonist when that isn't the case. Perhaps that's more of a narrative conjuring trick (like, for another instance, a detective story told by the culprit) but some of those are worth attempting at least as a test of skill.

I ought to acknowledge that doing without isn't always productive. Since the eighties I've refrained from plotting novels in advance; I prefer to let them grow organically in the writing once I've amassed enough material. The technique certainly paid off in a novella, *Needing Ghosts*, where I could hardly wait to go up to my desk every dawn to find out what I would write next. At the turn of the century however, I decided to find out what would happen if I worked out a plot before starting a novel. The result was the ramshackle *Pact of the Fathers*, quite possibly the worst constructed of my novels. Thank heaven (as always) for a good editor: Melissa Singer at Tor sent me an email several thousand words long that pointed out all the flaws. I put nearly all her advice into the rewrite and improved it in other ways of my own.

One piece of received wisdom is that horror fiction can't succeed without sympathetic characters. I don't agree, not least because I'd rather show the characters as clearly as I can without attempting to sell them to the reader. Admittedly most of my tales are based in character, but over the decades I've tested this tendency in various ways. "The Previous Tenant" leaves its central couple unnamed, and several stories I wrote in the mid-seventies address the protagonist directly in the second person (an echo of the confrontational narration of some of the old horror comics). A more recent story, "A Street Was Chosen," takes the exercise I'm recommending in this little essay as far as it will go. Written as a scientific report in the passive voice, this account of an unspecified experiment reduces its human subjects to names and numbers.

Can it work as horror fiction? Yes, to judge by the reactions of the audiences who have heard me read it. They've laughed at the black jokes but become visibly involved with the fates of the characters, even though in conventional terms there aren't any. Perhaps this proves a further point: Your attempts to do without an element should be made with suitable material—tales where the diminished technique is expressive.

And now this old man has droned on long enough.

EXERCISE

See what you can identify in your own work that you can lose for the duration of a tale. Might it be the influence of other writers, even possibly this one? Alternatively, if you've developed a strong voice of your own, might you try adopting a different one where it may be more eloquent? Or could you experiment with doing without sparseness of style if that's already characteristic of your prose? There's nothing wrong with taking risks in your work—they can make you more of a writer. Good luck! Just never do without writing!

DAVID BRIN

A Long and Lonely Road

DAVID BRIN is a *New York Times* best-selling author as well as a scientist and inventor. With books translated into twenty-five languages, he has won multiple Hugo, Nebula, and other awards. A film directed by Kevin Costner was based on his novel *The Postman*. Brin is also known for his Uplift series (Random House). His new novel from Tor Books is *Existence*.

Writing is about half skills that you can learn. The remaining fifty percent—as in all the arts—can only arise from something ineffable called talent. For example, it helps to have an ear for human dialogue. Or to perceive the quirky variations in human personality and to empathize with other types of people— including both victims and villains—well enough to portray their thoughts and motives. Sure, hard work and practice can compensate somewhat for areas of deficient talent, as in any realm of human endeavor. But only up to a point.

In other words, no matter how dedicated you are, success at writing may not be in the cards. Talents are gifts that we in this generation cannot yet manipulate or artificially expand. So don't beat yourself up if you discover that part lacking. Keep searching till you find your gift.

All right then. Let's assume you do have at least the minimum mix of talent, ambition, and will. Let me now offer a few tidbits of advice— pragmatic steps that might improve your chances of success, in speculative fiction or any other realm of writing.

1. The first ten pages of any work are crucial. They are what busy editors see when they rip open your envelope or click on your

submission file—snatched irritably from a huge pile that came in that morning. Editors must decide in minutes, perhaps moments, whether you deserve closer attention than all the other aspiring authors in the day's slush pile. If your first few pages sing out professionalism and skill—grabbing the reader with a vivid story right away—the editor may get excited. Even if the next chapter disappoints, she'll at least write you a nice note.

Alas, she won't even read those first ten pages if the one on top isn't great! And that means the first paragraph has to be better still. And the opening line must be the best of all.

2. Don't put a plot summary at the beginning. Plunge right into the story! Hook 'em with your characters. Then follow chapter one with a good outline.

3. There are at least a dozen elements needed in a good novel, from characterization and plot to ideas and empathy, to snappy dialogue and rapid scene setting, all the way to riveting action . . . and so on. I've seen writers who were great at half of these things, but horrid at the rest. Editors call these writers "tragic." Sometimes they mutter about wishing to construct a Frankenstein author out of bits and pieces of several who just missed the cut because they had one or two glaring deficits.

Only rarely will an editor tell you about these lacks or faults. It's up to you to find them. You can only do this by workshopping.

4. The only real difference between speculative or science fiction and all other genres is this: In addition to all the traits you need for good fiction in any other genre, you must also be able to supply two more: the same dedication to plot consistency and payoff that you get in murder mysteries . . . plus one more. Dedication to a sense of wonder toward some possible way the world might change. Some way that things might be different than the way they are. Hence, sci-fi is intrinsically harder than any other type of storytelling. Or, at least, it is harder to do really well.

5. Have you workshopped your creative efforts? Find a group of bright neo-writers who are at about your level of accomplishment

and learn from the tough give-and-take that arises. Local workshops can be hard to find, but try asking at a bookstore that caters to the local writing crowd; they might start a list. Or take the creative writing course at your local community college. Teachers of such courses often know only a little. But there you will at least get to meet other local writers. If you "click" with a few, you can exchange numbers and form your own workshop after class ends.

Another advantage of taking a course—the weekly assignment. Say it's ten pages. That weekly quota may provide an extra impetus, the discipline you need to keep producing. Ten pages a week for ten weeks? That's a hundred pages, partner. Think about that. And of course, nowadays you can join a workshop online! Critters.org and Fanfiction.com are two highly rated sites.

While I recommend taking lots of writing classes, I do not advise being a creative writing major in school. That educational specialization offers no correlation with success or sales. A minor in writing is fine, but you're better off studying some subject that has to do with civilization and the world. Moreover, by gaining experience in some worthy profession you'll actually have something worth writing about.

6. Avoid over-using flowery language. Especially adjectives! This is a common snare for young writers who fool themselves into thinking that more is better, or that obscurity is proof of intelligence.

I used to tell my students they should justify every adjective they put in their works. Write spare descriptions, erring in favor of tight, terse prose, especially in a first draft. Your aim is to tell a story that people can't put down! Later, when you've earned the right, you can add a few adjectival descriptions, like sprinkles on a cake. Make each one a deliberate professional choice, not a crutch.

7. Here's a tough one. Learn control over point of view, or POV. This is one of the hardest aspects of writing to teach or to grasp. Some students never get it at all.

Through which set of eyes does the reader view the story? Is your POV omniscient? (The reader knows everything, including stuff the main character doesn't.) Does the POV ride your character's shoulder? (The reader sees what the character sees, but doesn't share the character's inner thoughts.)

Or is it somewhere in between? In most modern stories we tend to ride inside the character's head, sharing his/her knowledge and surface thoughts, without either delving too deeply or learning things that the protagonist doesn't know.

Decide which it will be. Then stick with your choice. Oh, and it's generally best to limit point of view to one character at a time. Choose one person to be the POV character of each chapter—or the entire book. Establish point of view clearly and use it to assume things the character takes for granted, instead of telling and explaining things. The great master at this art was science fiction author Robert A. Heinlein. Whatever you think of his novels after chapter one, there is something magical about the first few pages, in which the reader becomes familiar with many strange things and situations by taking them for granted, the way a real character would.

8. Think *people*! As Kingsley Amis said:

> "These cardboard spacemen aren't enough
> Nor alien monsters sketched in rough
> Character's the essential stuff."

9. A final piece of advice: Beware the dangers of ego. For some, this manifests as a frantic need to see one's self as great. Oh, it's fine to believe in yourself. It takes some impudent gall to claim that other people ought to pay to read your scribblings. By all means, stoke yourself enough to believe that.

But if you listen too much to the voice saying, *Be great, BE GREAT!* it'll just get in your way. Worse, it can raise expectations that will turn any moderate degree of success into something bitter. I've seen this happen, too many times. A pity, when any success at all should bring you joy.

Others have the opposite problem . . . egos that too readily let themselves be quashed by all the fire-snorting fellows stomping around. These people tend (understandably) to keep their creativity more private. That makes it hard for them to seek critical feedback, the grist for self-improvement. At either extreme, ego can be more curse than blessing.

But if you keep it under control, you'll be able to say, "*I have some talents that I can develop. If I apply myself, I should be able to write stories that others may want to read! So give me a little room now. I'm closing the door and sitting down to write. I've earned this time, so don't anyone bother me for an hour!*"

Whatever you do, keep writing. Put passion into it! Make worlds.

EXERCISE

When puzzled over how to do something—dialogue for example—*retype* a favorite conversation that was written by a writer you admire. The same can hold for other elements of style, like setting, characterization, or that pesky point of view. Find a truly great example and tap it out on the keyboard, letter by letter.

Don't shortcut by simply rereading the scene. You will notice far more by retyping than by looking. This is because a skilled writer is performing a "magical incantation"—using words to create feelings and sensations and impressions in the reader's mind. If you simply reread a passage, especially one written by an expert, the incantation will take effect! You'll feel, know, empathize, cry . . . and you will *not* pay close attention to how the author did it.

So don't cheat. Actually retype the scene, letter by letter. The words will pass through a different part of your brain. You'll say, *Oh! That's why she put a comma there!* Seriously, try it my way. Don't cheat. You'll be glad.

JOHN SHIRLEY

Writing Is Seeing

JOHN SHIRLEY is the author of *Bleak History, Everything Is Broken, Demons, A Song Called Youth,* and *In Extremis: The Most Extreme Stories of John Shirley.* He won the Bram Stoker for his book *Black Butterflies.* His nonfiction work is *Gurdjieff: An Introduction to His Life and Ideas* (Tarcher/Penguin).

When I was a very young man at the Clarion Writers' Workshop, I was a fan of Rimbaud and later artistic radicals, like the surrealists. I liked their brashness and their florid manifestos. One day at the Clarion Writers' Workshop, Harlan Ellison was being encouraging (if that's the word), and asked me what my writing method was. Aglow with self-importance, I arched an eyebrow, gazed into the distance with a visionary air and said, "I eat with my eyes; I taste with my ears."

Well, this was pretentious as all hell, and sounded silly no doubt, especially as I didn't know much about writing at the time. However, it turns out that when I think back to the ludicrous behavior of my youth, when I wincingly consider my jejune fancies and mile-a-minute images and insights, I sometimes see, besides boyish foolishness, that I was, after all, quite right—at least about some of it. Being a bit of a misfit, I had nothing to lose, so I just tore open my frontal lobes and let the impressions pour in and the corresponding ideas pour out, with very little preconception. The results were highly uneven but sometimes, because I didn't know I could not do a thing, I *could* do it. And I did. And, in fact, I was right to try to "eat with my eyes"—that is, to look around me without expurgation, with the maximum intake and honesty, with the assumption that the normal way of looking at life is muddied—and that it's possible to see more, always more if one looks hard enough; if one gets out of the way of perception.

And this has served me. So, I advise writers to do the same: to start with the assumption that they're not really so conscious as they think they are; not so perceptive as they think they are. To make a conscious, deliberate effort to look at things they are used to and see them in ways they are not used to. Try to see the extraordinary in the mundane—not necessarily the fantastic, but the deeper reality. It is there if you look for it. Don't use drugs to open your perceptions— just open them.

Look around anywhere, really look, and you can see new characters, possible stories. Be a Sherlock Holmes of characterization. What does that stranger's distinct choice of clothing mean? Does that man's reddened knuckles and the bruise on his sad wife's cheek mean what I think it does? Look closely at her and make an educated guess. How about that man, in the subway—his hand keeps reflexively moving toward his shirt pocket, and drawing back. Is he reaching for cigarettes? Or something else?

My feeling is that a great deal of good writing originates in good observation. It's people-watching, sure, but it's also watching nature; it's absorbing urban, pastoral, and suburban settings. It's trying to see familiar things as you never saw them before.

One key to increasing one's observation is being aware of the degree of one's awareness in the first place. When I'm out interacting with the world, how much am I lost in some gray study, in a daydream, or in my smartphone? To what extent am I really inhabiting myself, really seeing . . . and feeling, smelling, hearing . . . what's there?

If I turn my attention toward my own level of awareness, I discover that typically I'm not very aware as I move about the world. I'm dreaming, brooding, or caught in haste, in anxiety, in petty fears. Which means I'm not seeing what's around me—I haven't got enough attention left, after all that distraction, to really look at the world I'm in. If I don't really see, I don't have material for convincing writing.

Verisimilitude, believability—that's a key to persuading a reader that what you're describing is real. Where do you get it? From observation—from observing yourself, people around you, the world around you. To get there, work on being in the moment. Step out of the usual half-aware state we're too often in. Being "in the moment" helps you see things as they are—and it may bring you insight into the human condition.

In a way, everyone is a character in a novel. A good writer can find the human dilemma, the human condition, in any situation, because it's always there, if you're really looking closely. Drama is always all around us, but usually we don't see it because we're not paying attention.

EXERCISE

1. Go to a place that's tediously familiar to you, the supermarket, or the post office, a place, perhaps, where you have to stand in line and normally can't wait to get away. Deliberately use the time there to practice observing. Turn your attention to people and things around you, as if you'd never seen anything like them before. Pretend you're from Mars, if you like. *So this is what creatures look like on this planet; so this is how they behave.*

   The main thing is to see them freshly—telling details and truths about them will likely jump out at you. Look freshly at the place as well as the people. As a writer, any environment is a potential setting. Look closely, more closely than your default setting, wherever you are.

2. Are there people in your life who drone on, and you say, "Uh huh . . . uh huh . . ."—as you only half-listen at best? Find one! Let him drone on . . . but this time really listen, no matter how genuinely tiresome it is. Think of it as a sort of homely telepathy—in a sense, you're actually hearing his free associations, unconscious concerns, and fears.

   An example: "I told Bill I didn't want to go to that doctor again, he always makes me wait, I don't think his assistant likes me . . ." What does that boring, self-pitying complaint actually say? It says she is going to the doctor, so she is worried about her health; it says that it may be that the choice of doctors is in Bill's hands, whoever he may be; it says she is a little afraid of the doctor's assistant, generally worried about being disliked, perhaps even a tad paranoid. It's an indirect, unconscious statement of fear, of anxiety, and considering the implications, might open up your compassion for that person, which might in turn give you insight into her. She, or someone incorporating her attributes, might become a strong character in a story.

3. Go to some place you like going to, perhaps a beach, a trail, the opera, whatever you enjoy—and try to see aspects of it you'd normally filter out, or not notice. Forget about "good" or "bad"—just look for what is. Linger in one spot and look at it more closely than normal. Again, try to see it as if you'd never seen it before . . . You'll be surprised at how the familiar is also the unfamiliar, and how much a deeper perception of it can enrich your writerly description.

JAY LAKE

Flashing Yourself

JAY LAKE's recent books are *Kalimpura* (Tor Books) and *Love in the Time of Metal and Flesh* (Prime Books). His short fiction appears regularly in markets worldwide. He won the John W. Campbell Award for best new writer, and has been a multiple nominee for the Hugo and World Fantasy Awards.

This is a writing exercise I originally got from short story master Bruce Holland Rogers. He didn't exactly give it to me as an exercise. This is more a case of leading by example than deliberate pedagogy, but I still want to give credit where credit is due.

Flash fiction—defined here as short stories of 500 words or less—is a wonderful vehicle for many things. One of the most basic satisfactions of writing flash is that even the most deliberately paced writers can usually finish a story in one sitting. There's something very nice about typing those three hash marks at the end of your piece. You experience a sense of accomplishment, and the joys of completion.

Easy to write, harder to sell, though there certainly are some good flash fiction markets out there. For our purposes, though, we're focused on flash as a writing exercise.

A neat thing about flash is that it generally does only one thing. At that length, complexity is a very rare luxury indeed. So a flash piece might focus on describing a setting, or offering a bit of characterization, or the fast, witty dialogue between two characters with competing agendas. But it's not trying to do that while balancing the other twelve or fourteen things required to build a good, solid short story.

Flash fiction is inherently a focusing exercise.

With that in mind, here's how I use the form:

When I'm stuck on some aspect of craft, I explore that aspect in flash.

I establish a basic opening, the classic character-in-a-setting-with-a-problem. For example, "Detective Saenz stumbled over the body in the doorway."

Then I write forward from that opening, focusing only on the aspect of craft with which I am troubled. For example, if my dialogue has been feeling wooden, Detective Saenz might have a conversation with the patrolman hovering in the hallway outside. If I want to work on my descriptive prose, he might look around the room with a detective's eye, cataloging in great detail what he sees of the crime scene. If sensory detail is the thing I'm wrestling with, I might talk about the reek of death and how unusually warm the apartment is, and the way Detective Saenz's skin is prickling on the arms and the back of his neck.

Then I do it again, from a slightly different perspective. Write the flash from the point of view of the patrolman in the hallway behind Detective Saenz. Write it again from the point of view of the corpse. Write it again from the point of view of the battered, blood-stained sofa. (I am a science fiction and fantasy author, I'm allowed to do things like that.)

Each pass of flash should only take you somewhere between a few minutes and an hour, depending on your natural writing speed. Try it three or four days in a row at whatever time your writing schedule permits. Use the limitations of the form's length and the limitations of your chosen aspect of craft to focus your efforts. This can be surprisingly liberating, and provide you with some excellent self-feedback on a short time scale. It's also useful for breaking writer's block and building self-confidence.

After all, these are stories. You might even sell a few.

EXERCISE

Time recommended: One hour (optionally over three to four sessions).
Tools: Your usual and most comfortable writing medium.
Set-up:

- Choose your weakest or most troubling aspect of craft.

- Select a character. Suggestion: *What profession or way of life did you last read about in a newspaper or magazine article?*

- Select a setting. Suggestion: *Where was the last book you read set?*

- Select a problem. Suggestion: Don't make this hard on yourself. Choose a problem that might legitimately be related to either the character or the setting.

- Write your opening line in a simple declarative sentence that encapsulates the above three items.

- Go where the story leads you from there, focusing on your chosen aspect of craft.

- Repeat two or three more times with variations on point of view or grammatical person or some similar structural change that honors the concept.

NICHOLAS ROYLE

Go for a Walk

NICHOLAS ROYLE is the author of six novels, two novellas, and one short story collection. He has edited fifteen anthologies, including *Darklands*, *The Best British Short Stories 2012*, and *Murmurations: An Anthology of Uncanny Stories about Birds*. A senior lecturer in creative writing at Manchester Metropolitan University, he also runs Nightjar Press, publishing limited-edition chapbooks.

This exercise is designed for the writer—or writing student—who is blocked. Not necessarily completely or fatally, perhaps just a little bit blocked. You don't know what happens next. Perhaps stuck is a better word for it. You are stuck. You have reached the end of a scene or chapter and you don't know what comes next.

Or you might have a problem in your work-in-progress that is delaying actual progress. A problem you may not even have identified, but one you know is lurking in there somewhere.

I do this every time I'm stuck or have a problem to sort out (in my work), and it always works. I never return home still stuck. Okay, maybe that's because you're not allowed to go home till you've fixed it? No, it's not like that. It really, really works. There's something about the mechanical act of walking that frees up the mind and the imagination, so you may even come up with completely unexpected, lateral solutions.

Nothing else does it for me. Cycling, running, driving—these are all too fast and you are constantly encountering hazards. I know someone who can do it while driving, but quite frankly I think she should have her license taken away, because there's no way you can do this kind of deep work while concentrating on the road.

I did this exercise with a group of about fifteen creative writing MA students, advising them to split up and walk off in different directions once they had left the center. Seven of them had been skeptical, the other seven more open-minded. One didn't believe it would achieve anything and didn't go. All fourteen who went came back and reported progress. Some had come up with completely new ideas. Those who had been stuck were now unstuck. All of them felt invigorated. The one who had stayed behind wished he had gone.

Works equally well for solo writers as for groups.

EXERCISE

You will need:

walking shoes (pair)

notebook

pen

Place notebook and pen in pocket. Put on shoes—make sure these are comfortable and suitable for a walk of half an hour or an hour or more. Leave house.

Walk, preferably in countryside or park, but town or city will do just as well, as long as you don't mind people thinking you're crazy, because you're going to be talking to yourself out loud.

Talk to yourself *out loud* about the problem you face in your work, whether it's a choice between first and third person narration or present or past tense, or you simply don't know what happens next.

Start by talking about what you've got so far, how you got to where you're currently at, and gradually work your way toward your problem. Talk it through. Work it out. Don't come home till you've cracked it.

It works. It honestly works.

JEREMY WAGNER

The Art of Being Horrifically Prolific

JEREMY WAGNER is an author, musician, and songwriter. His international best-selling first novel, *The Armageddon Chord*, was number four on the Barnes & Noble paperback best seller list, won a Hiram Award, was a finalist for Emerging Novelists Novel of the Year, and made the First Round Ballot for a Bram Stoker Award nomination.

pro·lif·ic /prə-'lif-ik/ (*adj.*): (of an artist, author, or composer) producing many works

When I think of prolific writers, I think first of Stephen King. It seemed he put out five books every quarter back in the 1980s. That's an exaggeration of course, but I remember you didn't have to go too long before another killer King book arrived. Speaking of Stephen King and his literary output, King's written and published around fifty novels (including seven under his pen name, Richard Bachman), five non-fiction books, and nine short-story collections.

That's an impressive body of work for Stephen King, or anyone else. I think publishing even several books—like J. K. Rowling did with the Harry Potter series—is quite an accomplishment.

Who blows Stephen King away when it comes to writing and releasing books? Try Spanish writer María del Socorro Tellado López (also known as: Corín Tellado). Corín Tellado (1927–2009) was a prolific writer of romantic novels. Tellado published more than 4,000 novels and sold more than 400 million books!

What about nonprolific writers? Many famous authors have only produced one piece of work for eternity. Example: Harper Lee (*To Kill a Mockingbird*), Margaret Mitchell (*Gone With the Wind*) and Emily Brontë (*Wuthering Heights*). One of my favorite scary authors is Thomas Harris, and he is, by definition, *not* prolific. He's published only five novels in the last thirty-six years: *Black Sunday* (1975), *Red Dragon* (1981), *Silence of the Lambs* (1988), *Hannibal* (1999), and *Hannibal Rising* (2006). I love Harris's work so much, but it's frustrating as a fan when you have to wait six to ten years for another novel by the guy. It also makes me wonder what he's doing in between novels. Is he spending his days on Miami Beach thinking of a new Hannibal Lecter book? Is he traveling the world? Is he writing under a pen name? Inquiring minds want to know!

Let's be prolific, okay? Keep your passion for writing alive *every day* and create. I spoke to some publishing folks, bestselling horror authors and horror publishers kind enough to share their two cents on being prolific, and, "How many books should a successful author release per year?" Here's what they said:

Lori Perkins (horror literary agent and editorial director for Ravenous Romance publishing): "Ebook writers publish more frequently. Our best authors do ten books a year and are making a good living from this."

Jonathan Maberry (best-selling horror author of *Rot & Ruin* and *Patient Zero*): "I write three novels each year. Kevin J. Anderson writes six. So does Sherrilyn Kenyon. And I believe Sandra Brown and Heather Graham do seven."

Yasmine Galenorn (*New York Times/USA Today* best-selling author of the Otherworld series): "I write three books a year. Don't overkill . . . do have a few months apart . . . for genre work it's a lot more common than for mainstream."

Jack Ketchum (best-selling horror legend and author of *The Woman*): "I'd space them out, at least nine months to a year apart. Build each one as an event. Let people salivate for the next one . . . even Stephen King waits about that long between novels, though a collection isn't out of the question . . ."

It's important to remember it's not always about quantity; quality is what's vital. Publishers love brand names though, and they like their authors to continually put out books on a regular basis. With this, perhaps quality might be diluted if an author doesn't take the time to put 100 percent into a work-in-progress . . . only working here and there.

Creating an original idea and then putting pen to paper (or fingers to keyboard) takes lots of work and personal time. Putting out three books a year might seem a huge feat to new writers—especially if you have a family and a day job—but it can be done and it will make you a better writer. Writing every day (and reading) is crucial to mastering the craft. Writing and releasing one book every ten years isn't realistic if your goals are to have some type of career and create a real brand. Here's an exercise designed to help you write more every day.

EXERCISE

1. Find time to write and make a regular schedule of it.

    To be prolific, *you must* write every day and you *must* make the time to write. Just like someone makes time to hit the gym or a Pilates studio with a regular routine, you need to create a routine to write. Get up earlier in the day, use your lunch break, or tell your spouse you might have to DVR your favorite TV shows for later—until you've finished your writing goal for the day. Though I recommend longer, dedicated stretches of writing time to pour out your creative energy, thirty-minute bursts of writing through-out your day really adds up by bedtime.

2. Find a place to write.

    If you have to write at the kitchen table, in an office, a cubi-cle, or in your car, do it. Finding your own space—without distraction—helps you get in your zone and helps channel your fictional vision into your work.

3. Make word count a goal.

    I mentioned a writing routine with the analogy of the gym in step 1. Use this same approach with daily word count. It isn't un-usual for full-time writers to produce 2,000–4,000 words per day, but for part-timers, let's start small. Make your word-count goal as important as paying a utility bill or a doctor's appointment—make it so you'll hit your daily word goal no matter what. Start writing 500 words per day. Bring your work-in-progress to your writing space (step 2), and add to it daily. This means progress, and your horror short story or novel will get finished.

To be clear, this isn't an exercise to make you a "book factory," but it will help you write every day. Writing every day makes you better, and writing every day equals more great horror stories for everyone to read! Being prolific isn't only helpful to your skills and bibliography, but it's also required when you sign a book deal. Publishers give writers deadlines—and deadlines are where your daily word-count goal is of paramount importance. Modern authors who maintain successful and prolific careers all have deadlines. In the words of this great writing series, I order you to Now Write! Maybe you'll get 4,000 books out the door by the next century.

DANA FREDSTI

Surviving Writer's Burnout

DANA FREDSTI's recent release, *Plague Town*, is the first of a zombie series with Titan Books. As an actress, she appeared in various zombie/horror movies and worked on Sam Raimi's *ARMY OF DARKNESS* as an armorer's assistant, sword-fighting captain, and sword-fighting "deadite."

I envy my fellow authors who are either managing to make a living from their craft or have someone subsidizing them while they work at it. I don't begrudge them . . . but I envy them. The reality is that most authors can't support themselves on their writing income alone. Most of us have to work at other jobs as well. For instance, I have a day job as an office manager and executive assistant. Still, within the last seven years, I've had seven books and numerous short stories published, as well as co-edited an anthology. I spent the larger part of two months this year promoting *Plague Town*, which involved a truly staggering number of guest posts and interviews. The publicity was great, but the work involved was intense.

I believe in treating writing as a job and "going to the office" each day. While promoting *Plague Town,* I nervously eyed the calendar—the deadline for the first draft of the sequel was creeping ever closer. I'd thought I could handle the promo, my day job, and work on the next book, but that would have required me to pretty much go without sleep. I need my sleep to be a functioning (and non-homicidal) member of society, so I had to choose how I spent my time. I can only imagine how my writer friends who are raising children manage to juggle their loads without going insane.

If you wonder if there are times when I get tired, cranky, and sick of being in front of a computer, the answer would be a resounding (put in some earplugs) "YES!" There are days I bitterly resent the need to work all the time if I'm going to meet deadlines and pay my bills. I also hit periods of total burnout where my brain refuses to focus and I slam into a wall of (for lack of a better term) writer's block.

About now I hear the screams of people who say, "There's no such thing as writer's block!" I'm rolling my eyes here, people. It's not like having writer's block means there's a cement wall erected between yourself and your ability to write. It's not a permanent condition. If it makes it easier, Oh Ye Who Have Tantrums at the Words "Writer's Block," think of it as a literary constipation (yes, I strive to add class wherever I go). A temporary blockage for which there are available remedies to help restore your . . . er . . . flow. I offer my own tried, tested, and successful home remedies against writer's burnout below:

EXERCISE

1. Change your environment. If you have a place you normally like to work but things just aren't flowing for you, you might need to try a change of pace. A friend invited me on a writing date at a local coffee shop and, to my surprise, I managed a couple of pages in an hour's time instead of yet another session of eking out maybe a paragraph or two. The people sitting and talking around us, instead of being a distraction, provided a buffering of white noise that enabled me to concentrate on my writing.

2. Change your writing tools. Always use the same computer? Try sitting outside with a notepad and pen, or even a different laptop or word processor. I have a Neo AlphaSmart, a lightweight keyboard and screen with no programs other than basic word processing. The screen only shows a few lines of text, which makes it easier to just plow on ahead rather than get fixated on making everything PERFECT the first time around. You can upload what you've written onto your computer and obsess on perfection later.

3. Change your routine. Always write at the same time? Sometimes that's a good thing. It gets your brain used to switching into creative mode when that certain time of day rolls around. However, when you hit a rut, this can be a problem, especially if you're wiped out from working a day job. I sometimes find myself getting preemptively exhausted as the scheduled writing time approaches and find myself increasingly resentful that I have to work two jobs all the time. So now I take my AlphaSmart on the subway during my morning commute and work on my novel instead of reading. Almost a thousand words in less than forty minutes. And all before coffee! My inner critic is still asleep and my brain's firing just enough to enable me to type. It doesn't work every morning, but often enough I have a chance to make up for an unproductive writing session the night before.

4. Try adding background ambiance. If you're writing in a particular genre, try putting on movies that inspire you or create a certain atmosphere that helps you get into the mood. For me, since I'm currently neck deep in spreading a zombie apocalypse in my new horror series, I have a stack of zombie movies I rotate in and out of the DVD player with the volume turned low. I've seen most of them . . . more times than is probably considered normal or healthy, but this enables me to ignore them just enough to get into my writing. And when I take a break, lo and behold, there are zombies on my TV screen to cheer me on. This does not work for everyone (and it doesn't always work for me) because of the distraction factor, so if you find yourself getting sucked into the movie instead of into your novel or story, turn it off and find some music instead. I tend to gravitate towards certain film scores that set the right mood. For *Plague Town* it was the score to *TWILIGHT* (don't judge me, people. The score is great and sans sparkles!) while for my paranormal romance/jaguar shifter novel, it was the score to *CAT PEOPLE* and anything with a Mesoamerican flavor.

5. Research. This may seem a tad obvious, but I never realized how much weird and random information I would need while writing a zombie novel, nor how many interesting additions and inspira-

tions for my book I'd find while looking up things like: what sort of tools a person could buy (or scavenge) from their local hardware store; what's on the menu of Calico County (a restaurant in Amarillo about to get attacked by the ravenous undead in *Plague Nation*); or gods and goddesses of the ancient Olmecs. And don't just rely on Google and the Internet. The climax for *Fixation* (my jaguar shifter novel) pretty much came to me whole when I went to see an Olmec artifact exhibit at the de Young Museum.

6. If nothing else works, take a break. Even with deadlines, there are times your body and mind just need to step away and get some playtime. Pick your favorite activity, be it exercise, going to see a movie, or getting together with friends. Giving yourself permission to take that break can be just the thing to shake things loose in the old brainpan!

PETER BRIGGS *(edited by Laurie Lamson)*

How to Molotov Cocktail the Thorny Problem
of Adaptions, Speculative and Otherwise
(The Screenwriting Anarchist's Way)

PETER BRIGGS has been a professional writing monkey for longer than he cares to remember. He's the credited co-writer of the movie *HELLBOY*, and has utterly failed to master the art of writing winning pleading letters to the Writers Guild of America arbitration boards on such features as *FREDDY VS. JASON*, *JUDGE DREDD*, and *ALIEN VS. PREDATOR* (his original draft was featured in a book called *The 50 Greatest Movies Never Made*).

After a pleasant experience scribbling for *Now Write! Screenwriting*, I was not a little bemused to be approached for this further helping of hopefully useful advice on speculative genres, held now in your finely manicured mitts.

A lexicon sidebar: the words *adaption* and *adaptation* mean the same thing in literary jargon, with the less-popular *adaption* first appearing a century later than *adaptation*, around 1704. I prefer *adaption* as I'm a contrarian Screenwriting Anarchist, I'm English (therefore a champion of the underdog), and also the reduced syllables roll suavely off the tongue while not sounding like one's afflicted with a stutter. Grammarist.com notes snootily that, "Adaption occurs far less frequently, mostly in publications and websites with relatively low editorial standards." Which, I would submit lends it perfect credence for the Hollywood community.

As a Screenwriting Anarchist, it's my duty to sway you from the path of level-headed theory offered by my fellow contributors, and have you throw caution to the wind by trying some utterly bonkers methodology instead. That being said, this article offers not only practical advice, but some personally learned caveats of the pitfalls involved.

Most of what I've written can be termed speculative, as I'm generally hired by film studios for projects in the fantasy, horror, and sci-fi genres. While the bulk is work-for-hire, the rest is "on spec" writing (not to be confused with "speculative genre"—in my particular cutthroat niche of the Scribblers' World, a "spec" is a slab of script you've slaved over without pay, and of your own volition in the hope someone'll be stunned by your genius). Of that spec work, a portion might be original pieces of my own invention, although on many occasions I adapt existing pieces from different media.

By and large, as a fledgling writer with no track record and little money at your disposal to "speculate" with, your adaption may originate from some existing out-of-copyright work. *Be careful here.* A savvy American reader would know that means "fifty years after the author's death." However, in Europe that's extended out to seventy years, with copyright laws further changing from country to country. I speak from bitter experience:

Just after the mid 1990s, I penned a faithful period adaption of H. G. Wells's *The War of the Worlds,* first serialized in *Pearson's Magazine* a century earlier. Indeed, in research I discovered several deleted serial chapters and an alternate, much more "Hollywood" ending, all of which went right back into the story. (Research pays off!)

Wells died in August 1946, which meant that under the fifty-year rule, his oeuvre had just fallen out of copyright as I was finishing my adaption. My agent took my freshly printed script to Paramount Pictures, where it came to the attention of Kenneth Branagh. Enthusiasm became, as they say, high. Just as we were all about to pitch into paperwork for a new *WAR OF THE WORLDS* movie, disaster struck.

The European copyright law changed from fifty to seventy years . . . and not only was the book no longer public domain in Europe, but a music producer re-upped his own option on the rights before we were even able to speak with Wells's estate. Which meant that even if we were to make a theatrical movie, we could do nothing with that movie once it left the cinema (DVD, TV, etc.) because Mr. Music had us over a barrel. We had to sit down with his lawyers and try to negotiate a deal for his rights. But he was having none of it.

The story didn't end there. A few years later I received a call from the head of development of Tom Cruise's company. I went in for what I thought was a standard meet-and-greet, only to discover Mr. Cruise was very interested in making the very same WAR OF THE WORLDS script. Unfortunately I had to burst their bubble and tell them of our earlier attempt. Not to be thwarted, the agents all went back to the negotiating table with Mr. Music, and once more tried to broker a deal. Even with the irresistible box-office lure of Mr. Cruise, Mr. Music was unswayed. The project fizzled a second time. Ironically, a few years later, Tom teamed up with Steven Spielberg, who wanted a more contemporary take on the story. I have no idea what hoops they jumped through to secure the rights on that third go-around, but their movie, WAR OF THE WORLDS, was made and hit theaters in 2005. I guess you just don't say "no" to Steven Spielberg . . .

Of course, that was just bad luck with a public domain property. You wouldn't attempt something like that from copyrighted material held by a studio, would you? Of course not. You'd be nuts. Um. Well-l-l-l-l . . .

Even earlier, at the first twinkle of my career, I'd lucked my way into developing science fiction material for Paramount Pictures in their British office. The lack of momentum for the material I was digging up, mostly existing sci-fi novels and comic books, was driving me a tad crazy. One rainy day, I stood in a comic store in North London and noticed the first issue of Dark Horse Comics' Alien vs. Predator series had hit the stands. I bought it, and over a pint of Guinness in the World's End pub across the road, a crazy notion struck me.

The separate ALIEN and PREDATOR franchises were both owned by 20th Century Fox. Not only was I not going to sell a script to Fox based on somebody else's notion, but for legal reasons the studio likely wouldn't even be allowed to read it. But that Alien vs. Predator comic premise by Randy Stradley was such a smack between the eyes, and I knew a script based on it might be such a wham-bang reading experience regardless, I calculated it stood a good chance of getting read elsewhere; perhaps by curious development fellows at Universal or Disney. I'd heard stories of spec scripts that were such strong reads that even if those scripts were never made, their authors were given plum movie writing assignments.

So, I sat down to tackle my adaption. In truth, it retained few elements from Stradley's comic books (although I went out of my way later to acknowledge his own terrific work).

Anyhoo. After six to eight weeks of friends discouraging me and actively mocking me at dinner parties, I took the finished *Alien vs. Predator* script to my unsuspecting agent's office in London. He stared at the cover, actually put his face in his hands, then queried gently, "Pete, have you any idea how hard this is going to be to sell?!" I attempted an innocent shrug.

Luckily, the stars shifted in my favor. Unbeknownst to me, Larry Gordon, one of the producers of the *PREDATOR* franchise, and a former president of 20th Century Fox, was an old pal of my agent. Two days later, he called and asked if I was sitting down.

Always on the lookout for material, and off the back of an underwhelming response to *PREDATOR 2* and their current troubled production of *ALIEN 3*, Fox had literally, just days before, asked Larry Gordon to come up with an idea for a monster team-up of Alien and Predator. My script landed in Larry's lap at exactly the right time. He read it. He loved it. He bought it. It was a million-to-one shot, but it paid off.

Just to balance karma though, the project struck pay dirt at the very same moment studio head Joe Roth was leaving, plunging it into a developmental black hole. But it started my career, gave me a whopper paycheck, and became something of a cause-célèbre in screenwriting magazines and books. Which just proves that sometimes the path of the Screenwriting Anarchist is a true one.

So, what if you find a novel, or perhaps even an existing film you're burning to take a remake crack at, but want to adopt a more sensible approach and see about legitimately securing the rights? If you're the trust fund heir of a major corporation, you can do what others have done and buy your way into the business, no problemo. Like most of us, however, you're probably pulling a day job to support your writing and don't have disposable income, so you need a more achievable approach. Again . . . watch out for those pitfalls.

Unless you've made a personal financial investment in your project, as a writer it's all too easy to get screwed by those who are only too eager to take you to the cleaners. Always get your paperwork in place: Secure the rights to the underlying material as a safety net for yourself if you can, right from the outset. You may be surprised; you may not even have to spend a lot. Some authors are keen to have their work taken out to the studios, particularly if they've languished unloved for a long time, or if you can gain the interest of a reputable partner producer to help champion the project, and your agent or legal adviser does their part.

A free option is never precisely free: You're legally obligated to spend at least $1 to say you own the rights. Bizarre as this sounds, Stephen King has granted free options to aspiring filmmakers on several of his stories, calling them "dollar babies," and to this day on his website he encourages film students to contact him. Some filmmakers, such as three-time Oscar-nominated Frank Darabont, owe a chunk of their early success to being granted a dollar baby by King, so it's certainly something to think about.

That's some of the business side of adaptions. If you take a list of movies made in any given year, a good proportion will be based upon existing properties, or as Hollywood glibly terms it, "branded" entertainment. In idea-starved Hollywood, anything that shortcuts the precarious development process is a Good Thing.

On a more craft-enriching level, adaption encourages you to hone your writing. If you're a novice, paralyzed with fear and doubts about the creation and plotting of your own original story, taking a successful story that already exists and spending time working on translating it can be freeing and educational. Once you've got a few adaptions under your belt, you'll be astonished at how readily you can pick out the poor dialogue from the exceptional, reworking structure and correcting logic gaps. Eliminating all the filler the original author couldn't bring himself to lose. Killing another writer's babies is ultimately a Good Thing, as it encourages you to free yourself up for your own future creations.

EXERCISE

1. Subject Research!

   If you're going to spend time on an undertaking like this, why not make it count? Pay attention to celebrity interviews and producers' ponderings. If in an interview, Brad Pitt (let's say) expresses a fond wish to play Howard Roark in Ayn Rand's *The Fountainhead*, your Spidey sense should start twitching. Keep a list of these.

2. Copyright Research!

   On researching *The Fountainhead*, you'll notice it was written in 1943. Hmm. You'll then look at the author. Dang it. Rand died in 1982. That means if you're going to wait for the copyright to expire, you have to set a computer alarm to notify you in 2052. And that's if you're willing to gamble on various copyright laws not changing between now and then, or the planet exploding in nuclear Armageddon. If you don't fancy those odds, maybe you should move on to researching what Robert Downey, Jr., has been itching to play . . .

3. Persevere with Tenacity! (Part 1: Writing. The Easy Part)

   Okay, so you're not letting a pesky thing like copyright law daunt you. So, let's roll up our sleeves. Getting hold of your subject matter (comic book, novel) is easy enough. *Do not* snag yourself a PDF or electronic copy of the book through Amazon or Project Gutenberg, except as a convenience. If you cut and paste the work into your word processor and start pruning passages, all you've become is a glorified copy editor. You need to type the passages yourself from scratch, with the sweat of your brow (and sticky fingerprints). This repetition will help you get inside the characters and story, allowing you to diverge where necessary. Creating a virtually identical facsimile of the original text will otherwise, like Jeff Goldblum's first telepod experiments in *THE FLY*, only have you manufacture a flavorless doppelgänger. Others will do that. They will fail. You're special. You will succeed.

4. Persevere With Tenacity! (Part 2: Submitting. The Difficult Part)

Well, you've read some of my anecdotes, so you know what you're up against. Now you have to get your work out to the people who will transform your work from a hunk of dead tree to a piece of entertainment that will enthrall the planet enough that you get ripped off by a million bit-torrent sites. This is the tricky part.

You don't have to be in L.A., but it helps. You don't need representation, but that too is a boon. With no connections at all, I managed to get read and represented at a major talent agency in London first time out of the gate, and worked solidly for years without getting onto a California-bound plane.

Lack of representation shouldn't be viewed as an obstacle. Film societies, organizations, and just plain communicating with people you meet in real life or on the Internet can reap dividends. A few years ago, at a comic book mixer in L.A., the beer was flowing freely and a fledgling writer approached me after I complimented him on his tentacle-festooned T-shirt. I broke my own cardinal rule that day when he asked me to read one of his scripts. I'm glad I did. I helped him set it up with Gary Kurtz the producer of *STAR WARS*. (It's now titled *PANZER 88*.)

Fired up? Good. Now, get out there you Screenwriting Anarchists, and start breaking some rules.

SHARON SCOTT

Writing the Series

SHARON SCOTT has created and written comic book series for over 15 years, including More Than Mortal, Makebelieve, and The Witchfinder. She wrote the first season of the *Alien Confidential* webcomic for Namco Bandai and is an optioned screenwriter. Scott also works in the videogame industry as a story lead and writer on licensed properties for Warner Bros., DreamWorks, and Mattel.

Many of the tools writers use to create stories can be applied to series writing. However, there are three areas in the development of a genre series that follow their own set of rules: the series concept, its structure, and the development of the series characters.

Let's start with concept. A stand-alone story is a single idea with a clear end point. *A doctor must find a way to cure his wife's mysterious illness.* In a series, the concept is an idea that repeats each week or installment as a predictable formula, but plays out in unpredictable ways. *A doctor encounters a mysterious illness every week and must race to find a cure before the patient dies.* The concept for a genre series follows similar rules, but adds a "genre" twist, which, by its contemporary definition, is a supernatural, horror, sci-fi, fantasy, or mystery/detective element. *A doctor, who is also a werewolf, encounters a mysterious illness every week and must race to find a cure before the patient dies, while keeping his beastly nature a secret.*

Now for structure. Writing a series is not as simple as stretching a plotline out over successive installments (novel, comic book, episode). No matter what structure you follow, all stories must have a clear beginning, middle, and end. The same rules apply when writing a series, but with one important addition. The structure applies not only to each successive installment, but to the larger, overarching story as well. What would *The X-Files* have been like if Mulder hadn't been searching for his sister all those years? Would *Star Trek: Voyager* have been as compelling if the crew wasn't trying so desperately to get back to Earth? A series must have story goals in both the overarching story and each of its installments. But story goals have a very distinct focus in a genre series. The primary goal of the genre writer is to entertain, which means appealing to the masses. So, while literature can get away with more cerebral or internally driven story goals (i.e., to find themselves, to grow up, to learn to love), story goals in a genre series must be active, be externally driven, and carry important stakes (i.e., to get out alive, to save the village, to find the killer).

Finally, let's talk character development. It goes without saying that, for any series, the aim is to write compelling characters who are surprising and unique, and whom readers will want to see in action again and again. There is a near-endless list of genre traits—super-human abilities, psychic powers, alien species—to aid the writer in that effort. But it is important to point out that in most series, main characters don't change much, if at all. They become stronger or smarter, they add "weapons" (both actual and figurative) to their arsenal, they might entertain love . . . but they don't emotionally transform. If they did, they would cease to be the character audiences tune in to see or read each week. Special care should also be given to the supporting characters, which help define, drive, and aid the main character in their story goals. The longer format of a series allows characters to develop complex relationships that play out over time, which helps build an emotional bond with the audience and keeps them coming back for more. While *The Amazing Spider-Man* was a great superhero comic book series, comic readers didn't pool their lunch money and buy the latest issue to see Spidey sling webs and crawl up the side of buildings. They tuned in because they wanted to see if mild-mannered Peter Parker ended up with The Girl, or because they wanted to witness the moment when he discovered his best friend was also his deadliest enemy.

Heed these special rules for the concept, structure, and characters of your genre series, and not only will you be ahead of your peers, but you will also have a solid foundation on which to start writing.

EXERCISE

1. Establish the concept for your genre series. Is it a repeatable idea that the audience can watch play out in a surprising way through each episode or installment? What element categorizes it as a genre series? Keep the description succinct. You want just enough to create a distinct image in your mind.

2. What is the overarching story goal of your genre series? Remember, all story goals should be active and externally driven.

3. What are some ways your main character might accomplish that larger story goal? The answers generated here become seed ideas for the smaller story goals you need for the installments in your genre series.

4. Who are your main characters? How will you make them unique and compelling enough that readers will want to experience them again and again? Is there a genre element you might add to elevate your main character?

5. Develop an initial list of supporting characters, including formidable enemies. Find ways to make those relationships complex and compelling.

6. Have an ending in mind. We would all love to think that our favorite series would go on forever, but even the greatest of stories come to an end eventually. How will your genre series end? Will the hero win? Will she save the day but ultimately die? Will he succeed in accomplishing the larger story goal only to become a villain in the process?

7. How will the series be paced? What format are you considering? Comic books have different requirements than TV shows or

novels. Do the research. The format you choose will help determine where the story breaks will happen, and how to plot out each installment.

When you're done, you should have an engaging roadmap of your genre series. Good luck and happy writing!

JOE R. LANSDALE

A Writer Writes

JOE R. LANSDALE is the author of more than thirty novels and a large number of short stories. His work has received numerous awards and recognitions, including the Edgar, the British Fantasy Award, and nine Bram Stokers, one of those for Lifetime Achievement. He also received the Grandmaster of Horror Award and many others. Some of his works have been filmed.

This is supposed to be an article on writing exercises. So I may be a little in conflict with the subject. I dislike the idea of it. Writing exercises for exercise sake, I mean. Seems like a waste of energy.

Maybe it's how a person defines exercises. I was once told by a teacher in a class that writers should carry a note pad with them, and if they see a tree that is unusual, they should stop and try and describe it on their note pad.

I don't like doing things like that at all, which may be part of the reason I didn't graduate, went to work at hard manual labor, and then became a writer, passing the degree by altogether.

Let me repeat: This seems like a waste of energy and a false or forced exercise. Why write something that at that moment is of no interest to you? It may be fine for some people, but for me, not so much. I might make a note for a general story idea, but I don't waste my time doing exercises for exercise sake. I have to have a story, and if I'm going to do an exercise, if we must call it that, it has to be one that I think of as the real thing, not conscious practice, but instead, an exercise that builds a valuable and usable muscle. Achieving any measure of success in this field certainly leads to a lot of practice, but you should open up your stores of inspiration to do something worthwhile, not merely to noodle.

I started writing and selling in the seventies, and by the early eighties, I was full-time. Sometimes to get myself going on a project I was working on, I would do this: I would start by looking around my room to see if something might spur a sentence or two, and in turn activate a story. If an idea parachuted in, and it nearly always did, I started building on it. For me it was a way of getting started, and when I wrote this way, I had every intention of it turning into a story, not just an exercise.

Sometimes, in a morning, I would write an entire short story that way. Some of them were good, and some of them weren't. The best of them ended up being published. I wrote these before I dove into whatever it was I considered my major project. The major work could be a short story, a novel, a screenplay, whatever. Often times my warm-ups turned out better than the major project. If I didn't write it in one morning, I would do it over a series of mornings, but always stopping at an allotted time to work on the main project.

For a while I had two typewriters. (This was back in the Stone Age.) One on my desk that was electric and one on a slide-out shelf of my desk that was a manual. I kept the exercise, if we're going to call it that—and at this point it will be easier if we do—in the manual most of the time. If I started the exercise in the morning, then stopped to work on the main project, and if the main project lulled, or if I felt myself looking around the room, I turned to the manual and went back to work on the minor idea again. If nothing happened on either project, well, I continued to look around the room.

By using this method I ran a lot of words through the typewriters. Sometimes, at the end of a day, I looked at my "exercise" and determined that it didn't deserve to live, and I wadded it up and tossed it in the trashcan. But, often enough, I would realize I had something, and as I said before, it might turn into the major project, or at least replace the major project as soon as whatever was major at the time was finished.

I still do this a little. Have a major project and a not so major project going, but more often than not, now I concentrate on one piece and finish it before I start another. However, now and again I just can't help myself, and work on more than one thing in a day. I tend to do it more in reverse these days. I start with the main project, then switch to the goof-off project at the end of my short work days. I work about three hours a day, or three to five pages a day. If more comes, I don't fight it, but that's my certain goal each day, so I always feel like a hero. It's a rare day when I can't do three to five pages on something, and then, if I want, I can go to the playhouse and fiddle with another idea for a while.

What did this method do for me when I was starting out?

I ran a lot of words through the machine and became more facile and confident about my work, even if I tossed out a lot of it. But I never wrote to toss. I wrote to create the best material I could, something that could hopefully be published.

So for me, it wasn't wasted time, because it wasn't, strictly speaking, an exercise. I guess the pieces that didn't work out and that I threw away could be called exercises, but they were not that on purpose. I was trying hard on each and every piece I wrote.

In our family there was a story about a fellow who was little, who was called Shorty, and he got into a fight, and the guy he was fighting was huge and held Shorty by the head while the smaller man swung his arms savagely in the air, hitting no one. Someone said, "Shorty, what are you doing?"

"Fighting like hell," he said.

I felt that way when I wrote. I was fighting like hell. No matter how useless the work might turn out to be, every day I went in with the mission to fight that blank page and beat it. Those warm-ups that I wrote helped, and I was very serious when I wrote them, even if they were a way of getting started on the main project. I always thought of writing as fitting the axiom that Bruce Lee stated about practicing martial arts. He said, "Play seriously."

I always have.

EXERCISE

Try any of the exercises in this book that spark your imagination and take them seriously—apply them to either your main project or use them to start on or work on a minor project. Treat whatever you write as real writing, not just "an exercise."

CONTRIBUTOR WEBSITES/PAGES

Acevedo, Mario	marioacevedo.com
Anderson, James G.	stoneharp.com
Anthony, Piers	hipiers.com
Barnes, Steven	lifewrite.com
Bender, Aimee	flammableskirt.com
Benest, Glenn	glennbenest.com
Benulis, Sabrina	sabrinabenulis.com
Bernheimer, Kate	katebernheimer.com
Briggs, Peter	imdb.com/name/nm1486009
Brin, David	davidbrin.com
Burke, Kealan Patrick	kealanpatrickburke.com
Campbell, Ramsey	ramseycampbell.com
Carl, Lillian Stewart	lillianstewartcarl.com
Carlson, Eric Stener	ericstenercarlson.com
Carver, Jeffrey A.	starrigger.net
Clark, Simon	nailedbytheheart.com
Conradt, Christine	christineconradt.com
Cooper, Sara B.	imdb.com/name/nm0153384
DeGeorge, Edward	youtube.com/user/EdwardDeGeorge/videos
Densham, Pen	ridingthealligator.com

Dinsmore, Danika	danikadinsmore.com
Dower, Kim	kimfromla.com
Durham, David Anthony	davidanthonydurham.com
Edson, Eric	http://www.imdb.com/name/nm0249672/
Ellison, Harlan	harlanellison.com
Fredsti, Dana	danafredsti.com
Freeman, Brian James	brianjamesfreeman.com
Graham, Stacey	staceyigraham.com
Gresh, Lois	loisgresh.com
Gruber, Xaque	huffingtonpost.com/xaque-gruber
Hamilton, Sequoia	sequoiahamilton.wordpress.com/
Hardy, Janice	janicehardy.com
Howard, Chris	SaltwaterWitch.com
Johnson, Kij	kijjohnson.com
Jones, Lisa Renée	lisareneejones.com
Kent, Derek Taylor	ScarySchool.com
Ketchum, Jack	jackketchum.net
King, E. E.	elizabetheveking.com
Kress, Nancy	nancykress.blogspot.com
Klick, Todd	amazon.com/Todd-Klick/e/B0050OMZYA
Kozlowski, Jan	jankozlowski.com
Lake, Jay	jlake.com
Lansdale, Joe R.	joerlansdale.com
Laurence, Elliot	luminalmedia.com
Mazmanian, Lance	mazmanian.net
McAllister, Bruce	mcallistercoaching.com
McCoy, Karen	kbmccoy.com
Mcgowan, Douglas	nothingexceptional.com
McIntyre, Vonda N.	bookviewcafe.com/bookstore/bvc-author/vonda-n-mcintyre
Mewes, Wendy	wendymewes.com
Modesitt, Jr., L. E.	lemodesittjr.com
Morrell, Jessica Page	jessicamorrell.com
Morton, Lisa	lisamorton.com

Moss, Gabrielle · gabriellemoss.net

Nolan, William F. · williamfnolan.com

Nye, Jody Lynn · jodynye.com

Obstfeld, Raymond · raymondobstfeld.com

Pete, Derrick D. · derrickpete.com

Peterfreund, Diana · dianapeterfreund.com

Reaves, Michael · imdb.com/name/nm0714184/

Reed, Rainbow · wickedpoetry.jigsy.com

Royle, Nicholas · nicholasroyle.com

Rubenstein, Devorah Cutler · thescriptbroker.com

Rubenstein, Scott · imdb.com/name/nm0747936

Saus, Steven · stevesaus.com

Schreiber, Brad · bradschreiber.com

Scott, Melissa · mescott.livejournal.com

Scott, Michael Dillon · dillonscott.com

Scott, Sharon · storyhousestudios.com

Sebanc, Mark · stoneharp.com

Selbo, Jule · fullerton.academia.edu/JuleSelbo

Sevi, Mark · marksevi.com

Shirley, John · john-shirley.com

Skipp, John · facebook.com/john.skipp.7

Thompson, Ben · badassoftheweek.com

Valenzuela, Diego · facebook.com/TheDiegoValenzuela

Vaughn, Vanessa · thedirtyblondeburlesque.com

Wagner, Jeremy · jeremy-wagner.com

Wales, Vincent M. · vincentmwales.com

Wanless, James · voyagertarot.com

Winner, Brianna · winnertwins.com

Winner, Brittany · winnertwins.com

Zicree, Marc Scott · marczicree.com

ABOUT THE EDITOR

LAURIE LAMSON was co-editor of *Now Write! Screenwriting* with her aunt Sherry Ellis and completed *Now Write! Mysteries* after Ellis's untimely death in March 2011.

Lamson is a screenwriter with a filmmaking background who has written on assignment for several producers. She is delighted to share her passion for screenwriting as the teleconference host for International Screenwriters' Association. She offers coaching and editing to fellow writers of scripts and books—both fiction and nonfiction.

She is the author of a magic realism book for girls, *Witch Littles: Magic in the Garden*.

jazzymaemedia.com
laurielamson.com

DISCOVER THE ART AND CRAFT

OF WRITING WITH *NOW WRITE!*

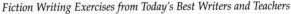

Now Write!
Fiction Writing Exercises from Today's Best Writers and Teachers

This treasure of personal writing exercises from some of today's most acclaimed names in fiction—including Steve Almond, Amy Bloom, Robert Olen Butler, Jill McCorkle, Alison Lurie, Jayne Anne Phillips, and Virgil Suarez—covers everything a fiction writer should know, from creating a believable scene to jump-starting a stalled story, and much more.

Now Write! Nonfiction
*Memoir, Journalism, and Creative Nonfiction Exercises
from Today's Best Writers and Teachers*

This essential handbook—featuring the personal writing exercises that Gay Talese, A. J. Jacobs, Reza Aslan, John Matteson, Lee Gutkind, Tilar Mazzeo, and other masters of nonfiction use to push through writers block, organize a story, fine-tune dialogue, and more—belongs on every nonfiction writer's bookshelf.

Now Write! Screenwriting
Screenwriting Exercises from Today's best Writers and Teachers

This volume—featuring never-before-published writing exercises from the acclaimed screenwriters of *Raging Bull, Ali, Terminator 2, Fame, Groundhog Day, Cape Fear*, Lost, True Blood, The Shield, and many other hit films and television shows—can help and inspire both new and experienced screenwriters.

Now Write! Mysteries
*Suspense, Crime, Thriller, and other Mystery Fiction Exercises
from Today's best Writers and Teachers*

The indispensible guide for writers of whodunits, techno-thrillers, cozies, and everything in between—featuring never-before-published personal writing exercises from John Lutz, Louise Penney, Hannah Ives, and more of today's bestselling and award-winning mystery writers.